The economics of
teacher supply

The economics of teacher supply

ANTONI ZABALZA
Lecturer in Economics,
London School of Economics and Political Science

PHILIP TURNBULL
Statistician, Department of the Environment

GARETH WILLIAMS
Professor of Educational Planning, University of Lancaster

CAMBRIDGE UNIVERSITY PRESS
CAMBRIDGE
LONDON · NEW YORK · MELBOURNE

CAMBRIDGE UNIVERSITY PRESS
Cambridge, New York, Melbourne, Madrid, Cape Town, Singapore,
São Paulo, Delhi, Dubai, Tokyo

Cambridge University Press
The Edinburgh Building, Cambridge CB2 8RU, UK

Published in the United States of America by Cambridge University Press, New York

www.cambridge.org
Information on this title: www.cambridge.org/9780521133920

First published 1979
This digitally printed version 2010

A catalogue record for this publication is available from the British Library

Library of Congress Cataloguing in Publication data
Zabalza, Antoni, 1946–
The economics of teacher supply.

Bibliography: p.
Includes index.
1. Teachers – Salaries, pensions, etc. 2. Teachers
– Supply and demand. I. Turnbull, Philip, joint author.
II. Williams, Gareth L., joint author. III. Title.

LB2842.2.Z3   331.1′26   78-967

ISBN 978-0-521-22078-1 Hardback
ISBN 978-0-521-13392-0 Paperback

Contents

Introduction

Teachers' pay is always in the news. But its implications have so far been the subject more of speculation than analysis. Speculation has revolved around a number of issues. First, and most crucial, how do salary levels affect the aggregate supply of teachers? In other words, is teaching a vocation so that salaries make no difference, or does pay matter? The next question concerns the effect of the age-profile of salaries. Some British teachers' unions have maintained that steeper profiles are essential for retaining older teachers in the profession. Are they right? Another issue has been the power of salary policy to redistribute teachers into slum areas. It has also been suggested that in Britain the salary structure is responsible for high rates of teacher turnover – too many teachers changing schools each year. And lying behind all these questions has been the general issue – how much difference do the administered salary scales make? Or does the system manage to adjust within this framework to the underlying pattern of shortage and surplus?

All these questions can be subjected to systematic analysis, and it seemed to Gareth Williams and ourselves that it was high time they were. We were lucky enough to persuade the Department of Education and Science to give us access to the complete tapes of the teachers' record for 1963–72, suitably anonymised. Though the three of us directed the study, we were extremely fortunate in finding Antoni Zabalza and Philip Turnbull to carry it out. They have proved an outstanding research team, combining great technical skill and inventiveness with a careful concern for the realities of the teachers' market. The study was undertaken in the Centre for Labour Economics at the London School of Economics.

We believe this book represents a real advance in the subject. It shows that salaries do make a difference. The supply response to a change in wages is, as one might expect, larger for men graduates than for women. Not only starting salaries, but the whole salary profile, affect the numbers entering teaching. The salaries paid at older ages have a relatively greater effect on the numbers who leave the profession than they do on the numbers who enter. The structure of pay also affects the rate of turnover between schools. There is more turnover when the difference in promotion prospects between schools widens. The direction in which teachers move is also affected by salary levels, teachers moving towards higher salaries and better promotion prospects.

The national salary scales do not uniquely determine what an individual teacher is paid. This depends also on what grade he is appointed to. Schools thus have scope to pay more for shortage subjects and skills. Do they use it? Though maths teachers are paid more than others of the same age and qualifications, the difference is small. But graduate teachers command a premium over nongraduates that exceeds the official 'graduate allowance'. And what about equal pay? The scales are identical for men and women. Yet men of a given age earn more than women. This is mainly due to differences in length of teaching experience. Holding that constant, men earn on average only $1\frac{1}{4}$ per cent more than single women otherwise similar, and 3 per cent more than married women.

Results of this type are obviously of interest to any serving teacher. They are also of interest to educational administrators of all kinds. But the study has a wider aim – to provide a prototype of how to study a public sector labour market. It provides an improved methodology that salary-setters can use to forecast the supply effects of any salary scale they determine. Though salary-setters can determine the scales, they are often not the final employing agencies. In such cases they also need to forecast the quality and other adjustments that the employing agencies are likely to make when using the administered salary scales.

The problem here differs between Britain and the United States. In England and Wales uniform salary scales apply throughout the country, while in the US each school board sets its own scales. Moreover, the extent of trade union activity is much less among American than English teachers. To explore the lessons that could be learnt from contrasting UK and US experience, a UK/US workshop was held at the University of Chicago in December 1976 sponsored by the Ford Foundation. At this workshop, the present study was subjected to much fruitful comment, and has been considerably revised as a result. In order to bring out some of the wider perspectives that emerged from the conference, Professor Mary Jean Bowman was asked to write an additional chapter. We hope the book will be found useful by teachers and all concerned with teachers' pay and recruitment policies, as well as by students of occupational choice in general, on both sides of the Atlantic.

M. Blaug
Research Unit in the Economics of Education
University of London Institute of Education

R. Layard
Centre for Labour Economics
London School of Economics

Foreword

This book reports the findings of an economic study of the labour market for school teachers in England and Wales, carried out at the Centre for Labour Economics, London School of Economics, from 1973 to 1975. The study was financed by the Social Science Research Council and was based mainly on computerised data files supplied by the Department of Education and Science. These data files consisted of the records of all full-time teachers in service in maintained schools from 1963 to 1972 inclusive. Most of the analytical work reported here is based on random samples taken from the original data files.

The research project began its career within the context of a long term persistent 'teacher shortage'. However, it soon became apparent that supply was quickly catching up with demand and in the late 1970s some teachers are having difficulty in obtaining jobs. It might be argued that supply problems are no longer worth studying. This would be a great mistake. Proper personnel management within such a huge enterprise as education is essential, whatever the demand and supply situation at any particular moment, and proper personnel management cannot take place without an understanding of how economic factors operate in the labour market.

Several problems of presentation were raised by the attempt to write for a diverse audience, especially with respect to the econometric and statistical techniques used in parts of the analysis. We have attempted to overcome this by delegating most of the mathematics to the end of the book in a section of technical appendices. Chapter 4, however, remains a rather difficult chapter for the lay reader, but as indicated at the beginning of that chapter, the non-technical reader will lose little by skipping most or all of it.

No study such as this can proceed without the help and support of men and women from all sections of the academic and education worlds. We have had discussions with people from educational organisations, including the Department of Education and Science, from various teachers' unions, and with academics of many disciplines. Our colleagues at the Centre for Labour Economics, Dr P Fallon and Mr M Stewart, deserve a special mention for the help they provided during frequent discussions of our work.

The National Union of Teachers, through Mr Maxwell, Head of the Salaries Department, were especially helpful in discussions and in providing valuable background material at an early stage of our project. The Department of Education and Science was especially helpful in arranging for material to be copied from their confidential data files in such a way that complete anonymity was preserved. Peter Wakeford, Manager of the LSE Computer Unit and Geoffrey Cooper, Senior Programmer at Queen Mary College have been more than generous in the time and effort they put into helping us.

Among the many academics with whom we held discussions, Professors Mary Jean Bowman and Arnold Anderson of the University of Chicago gave particularly valuable advice during their stay at the London School of Economics in 1975. Professor David Metcalf of the University of Kent and Stephen Nickell of the London School of Economics read several parts of the book and contributed important comments and suggestions. In addition, we also benefited from the reactions to this book by the participants to the UK/US conference on teacher markets held in Chicago; we would like to thank in particular Eric Hanushek, Boyan Jovanovic, Elisabeth Landes, Edward Lazear, Robert Michael and Sherwin Rosen.

Finally, no acknowledgement is complete without a thanks to those whose unenviable task it is to type, correct English and spelling, and generally produce a readable text from an illegible scrawl. Bettie Jory and Pam Mounsey of the Centre for Labour Economics have been unfailingly professional and cheerful in completing this task over the past three years.

London School of Economics A. Zabalza
P. Turnbull
G. Williams

1

Teacher supply in Britain

1.1 A panoramic view of the study

This book is about the economics of labour supply in a particular occupation. Its aim is to examine the extent to which teacher supply in England and Wales is influenced by economic variables. It should be made clear at the outset that there is no implication that economic factors are the only considerations which affect people's occupational choices. Teaching in particular is one of the groups of occupations in which it is widely believed that a strong sense of vocation is important, and surveys of secondary school pupils and university students often elicit responses indicating that intending teachers have a strong desire to work with children, or to do a job that they feel will be socially worth while. Our concern is not to deny that such factors are important, but to examine the complementary claim that changes in the economic circumstances of the profession also have an effect. We believe we have shown that this claim is valid.

Our research essentially shows a relationship between the number of people opting for a teaching career and the level of salaries. Higher salaries tend to attract a large number of people with a given basic qualification into the profession. Why should this be so?

If occupational decisions were influenced solely by vocational preferences, salaries would have little influence on teacher supply. Some people would be vocationally inclined to enter teaching and others would be inclined to enter other occupations. Within wide limits changes in salaries would make no difference to these choices.

The above explanation, however, ignores fundamental characteristics of human behaviour. Preferences are not absolute. Rather we find a range of intensities in people's inclination towards teaching. Individual A will be more inclined toward teaching than individual B, who in turn will be more favourably inclined than individual C. Once we accept the existence of such different degrees of interest in (or dislike of) teaching, it is easy to understand that vocational preference cannot be the only factor influencing occupational decisions. If his preferences for teaching are very high, individual A may enter teaching for very low pay.[1] However, individual B will, by definition, require a larger compensation in exchange for his services, and an even larger amount will be needed to attract C into teaching. In general, it is reasonable to expect that the less favourable the individual's view of teaching, the larger the pecuniary compensation will have to be in order to attract him, or her, into the profession.

Out of any group of potential teachers, a given teacher wage, relative to the wage paid in other occupations, will attract a certain proportion into the profession. The spectrum will range from that individual who would have taught at a very low relative wage to that individual who at the present relative wage is *just* willing to teach. If wages increase, all those who were willing to teach at the previous wage will also be willing to do so at the new wage. But additionally, other people will now feel that they are sufficiently rewarded by taking up teaching rather than another occupation. If wages decreased, we should expect the reverse. The person who previously was just willing to teach, together with those who now feel they are underpaid, will now decide *not* to enter teaching. Clearly, the higher the relative wage, the larger will be the proportion of qualified people attracted into teaching, and vice versa. This is precisely the relationship which we study and try to quantify in this book.[2]

In making occupational decisions, people are likely to consider earnings not in an absolute sense, but rather in relation to what they could get in alternative occupations. There is, however, another important respect in which the simple concept of earnings can be vague and misleading. When an individual is making up his mind about whether to enter an occupation, he may take into account the wage he is going to get immediately, or the wage he may expect in, say, ten years' time, or the wage he hopes to obtain by the time he is about to retire. Clearly all of them will affect occupational decisions to some extent, therefore it is likely that their relative importance will differ between different people. If the individual is not myopic, or irrational – and one of our basic assumptions is that he is neither – he will consider not only *current* earnings but also *expected* earnings in making his decisions. Unless his rate of discounting the future is extremely high or, in other terms, his desire for immediate gratification is inordinately great, he will not choose an occupation with, say £3,000 per year during all his working life, as opposed to another occupation in which, although the starting salary is only £2,000, he is certain to receive an increase of about £500 per year throughout his whole working life.[3] Clearly, for a large range of rates of discount, the *present value*[4] of earnings over the *whole* working life of the individual will be much larger in the latter than in the former occupation. In this book, we have attempted to consider earnings not only in terms of wages or salaries at one given moment in time, but also in terms of the expected lifetime profile of earnings that different occupations offer. As far as we have been able to ascertain, this is one of the first empirical labour market studies that has explicitly considered, albeit in a rudimentary manner, the slope of the earnings profile as a factor helping to explain occupational choices. We were therefore gratified to discover, as Chapters 5 and 6 show, that both for new entrants and leavers, the *separate* effect of career prospects and of salary levels are clearly identifiable. Perhaps the most notable finding is the different reaction of male and female teachers to these two elements of the earnings profile. In general, we have found that men are very sensitive to changes in career prospects, while women – although still taking this factor into account – are much more influenced by changes in immediate earnings.

Earnings and vocational preferences are two important variables in occupational decisions, but clearly not the only ones. The availability of jobs is also an important factor. If people find it difficult to obtain employment in a given occupation, they may opt for another, even though this is less preferred and less well paid. For most people there is a limit to the length of time they are able to wait for the right job to come along. We have found that job opportunities are indeed a relevant factor at least for some categories of teachers. In effect, graduate new entrants and female leavers appear to have been influenced by this variable. The harder it has been to find jobs outside teaching, the larger has been the inflow of graduate teachers (both male and female) and the lower has been the outflow of female teachers. Non-graduate new entrants and male leavers, on the other hand, do not seem to be significantly affected by the availability of jobs in other sectors of the economy.

So far, we have considered mainly the aggregate level of supply in the labour market for teachers. How is this overall supply distributed within the profession? In attempting to answer this question in Chapters 7 and 8, we follow the same fundamental approach as when analysing the level of teacher supply. The decision to move within different areas of the teaching profession, and the decision to choose teaching as opposed to other occupations, are both decisions made by individuals and are susceptible to analysis within the same framework. We have considered the occupational decision as an act of investment which takes into account not only the *present* but also the *expected future* returns. We have treated the decision to change school or region also as an act of investment. For a given set of nonpecuniary preferences, a teacher will only move his location within the market if he believes that his earnings prospects are significantly increased by doing so. We have found in Chapter 7 that this pecuniary explanation of the moving decision is relevant in terms of explaining the movements of teachers between different types of schools and between different regions, but the evidence also suggests that nonpecuniary elements are also a significant factor. In Chapter 8 this general framework is applied to study the effect on the allocation of the stock of teachers of the only two formal spatial wage differentials existing in this market – the 'London Allowance' and the 'Social Priority Allowance'.

We would like to have been able to analyse the demand for teachers in the same explicit manner as we have analysed supply. As discussed in Chapter 2, however, the concept of demand in the context of a market like teaching is much more elusive and difficult to handle than that of supply. Therefore, our analysis of demand had to be more indirect than we would have wished. The influence of demand has been inferred from what actually happens to the salaries of teachers with different characteristics.

The stock of teachers can be divided into many different categories. There are differences in qualification, length of teaching service, sex, school in which they teach, post they occupy, subject specialisation, and so forth. Some of these differences, such as graduate allowances, are taken into account in the salary structure. Other differences, however, are ignored in the formal salary structure. A primary school teacher of given qualifications and experience should get the same salary as a secondary school teacher. Likewise, graduates in mathematics are supposed to earn the same as similarly experienced graduates in any other subject.

From an economic point of view, this situation would be stable if the market value of teachers with different characteristics was exactly the same. However, if these characteristics are valued differently in the external market, the existence of a uniform salary structure is bound to create imbalances within the teaching profession. We can illustrate this point in terms of a concrete example. Let us suppose that mathematics graduates can obtain a higher salary in occupations outside teaching, than, say, modern language graduates. By paying a standard salary, the teaching profession will tend not to get as many mathematics graduates as required, and to recruit more language teachers than needed. If, however, teachers' wages were allowed to adjust freely, the satisfaction of the specific subject teacher requirements would create a wage differential between these two types of teachers with mathematics graduates earning more than language graduates.

In Chapter 9 we show salary differentials within the teaching profession, many of which lend support to the belief that market adjustments like these do take place within the limits allowed by the salary structure. For example, after standardising teachers' earnings for length of service, qualifications, sex, and sector (primary/secondary), we have found that mathematics graduates in 1971 earned on average 3.2 per cent more than other graduates, while modern languages graduates earned 1.6 per cent less. Among the other subjects, only chemists earned significantly more than the rest (2.2 per cent). Similarly, we found that among teachers with different qualifications, those with good honours degrees (1st and 2nd class honours) earned on average 9 per cent more than other graduates, who in turn earned on average 14 per cent more than non-graduates. These differentials represent considerably higher earnings than those due to the graduate allowances which would produce differentials of about 7 per cent and 6 per cent respectively on average salaries, and much lower differentials on higher salaries.

Something essentially similar may happen with respect to geographical area. If the wage rate is uniform for the whole country, but the areas to which supply can be allocated have different characteristics, we are bound to find imbalances that vary between areas. Following the same reasoning as before, and on the assumption that some internal adjustments are made, we should expect the appearance of differentials between such areas. Other things being equal, areas which enjoy abundant supply would not need to pay such high wages as those who have difficulties in attracting people into their schools.

Evidence pointing in this direction can be found in the case of Wales. This is a good example of a region which for many years has been relatively oversupplied with teachers. We found Welsh teachers to earn 1.7 per cent less than teachers in other regions.

The analysis in this book is largely positive. We do not indulge ourselves in disquisitions about how things in this market should work, rather we have attempted to discover how things actually do work. However, it is difficult to resist the temptation to attempt to draw some of the normative implications of many of our findings, and we attempt a cursory account of them in the final chapter. In essence we show that our findings about the earnings elasticities of different groups of teachers have some definite implications as to the shape of earnings profiles in the teaching profession.

1.2 The practical and theoretical rationale

Before entering further into details about the methodology and results of our study, we want to address ourselves to two fundamental questions. First, to what extent is such a study of the economics of teacher supply a relevant issue for practical planners? Second, to what extent does the theory developed in this study add to the present knowledge of labour economics? We have hinted above at one possible use of our results, but before proceeding it is useful to consider the current state of the planning of teacher training and supply.

In Britain this generally means manpower forecasting. The difficulty with this approach is that it usually ignores costs – both the costs of training the desired number of teachers and the salary costs of attracting the desired number and type of people to become teachers. Although this deficiency has long been generally recognised by academic labour market economists, very little attention has been devoted to the problem of determining the responsiveness of teacher supply to salaries and to external market conditions. The only published study so far attempted in this direction (Thomas, 1975) restricted its analysis to graduate new entrants, and worked with highly aggregated data. One of the objectives of this book is to fill this gap by estimating wage elasticities for different categories of teachers and for flows of both entrants and leavers. Its principal purpose is, however, to go beyond this and to demonstrate the validity and practicability of a methodology that would improve the planning of teacher supply and help to avoid both the problems of chronic shortage which were experienced in the quarter of a century after the end of the Second World War and the tendency to surplus that has begun to emerge in the mid 1970s.

It might be claimed that although knowledge of wage elasticities is important in a situation of manpower shortage – such as the one that has characterised this market in the past – it is not relevant if there is a tendency to oversupply of teachers. While in the past it was essential to know how to attract teachers into the profession, in the future it is likely that demand considerations will be uppermost in deciding how to allocate an excess supply of manpower. This is fallacious however. On the one hand, a better understanding of teacher demand, and therefore of teacher productivity, is needed in a situation of surplus as well as in a situation of shortage if a given supply of teachers is to be efficiently allocated. On the other hand, the existence of abundant labour does not imply that the response of supply to economic incentives is not relevant. On the contrary, in the context of a labour market such as teaching, in which salary scales are rigidly fixed, a knowledge of supply responses is needed if the structure of the teaching force is to conform to planned requirements and if equilibrium is to be achieved between supply and demand, thus eliminating the tendency to surplus.

As we have already shown, there is another way in which our results on wage elasticities can be useful for practical purposes. Differences in working time horizons and in alternative work opportunities can result in different wage elasticities among teachers. If this is so, the results may be useful not only to determine the adequate level of wages, but also to help in the design of an efficient salary structure. Far too often, salary structures in public sector markets are determined on the basis of principles of equity or custom, and have perverse effects under existing market conditions, with unintended results such as variations in quality, regional imbalances, and so on. Criteria to guide the design of these structures are therefore important, so that actual salaries paid to different groups of teachers do not have such unintended, and sometimes harmful, side effects.

Another aspect of teacher supply we examine is the job mobility of teachers between schools. Although from the point of view of aggregate supply, internal mobility of teachers is irrelevant, from an educational point of view the frequency with which a teacher changes his school may be vitally important. On pure economic grounds, it is difficult to establish what is the desirable level of mobility. On the one hand, some movement can promote the dissemination of new ideas and prevent staff common rooms from becoming too inward looking. On the other hand, if there is too much mobility, this means that pupils have little opportunity of developing strong relationships with particular teachers because of the rapid turnover that high rates of mobility imply. Our findings can provide the educational planner with instruments to help control the rate of internal mobility at the level that is deemed educationally desirable. Furthermore, by estimating the response of teachers to geographical differentials in earnings, we can arrive at some conclusions as to the role of area differentials in reallocating a given supply of manpower.

In general, we believe that the analysis of occupational supply carried out in this study will result in a better understanding of the workings of the labour market for teachers, and can help in the design of salary and teacher supply policies in primary and secondary education. This is the justification of the subject matter of this work from a practical point of view. We now turn to its justification from a theoretical point of view.

Human capital theory (Schultz, 1963 and Becker, 1964) views educational choice as an act of investment which is governed by an evaluation of future returns. This idea can readily be extended to the related issue of occupational choice. Usually different occupations require different levels of education, so that the choice of occupation can be associated with previous educational decisions. Even in the case in which a given level of education opens the possibility of entering several occupations, the final choice is likely to be influenced by the expected returns offered by each of them. These returns will be partly financial as reflected by earnings prospects, but may also be much less tangible and include such factors as anticipated job satisfaction and the social environment of the job.

Despite its apparent simplicity, it has been notoriously difficult to incorporate this idea into the analysis of occupational choice, the main reason being the inadequacy of empirical data on earnings. Given this difficulty, some models of occupational choice have from the outset formulated the problem as a one-period decision. All the work carried out in the US to investigate the factors determining the choice of a military career belongs to this class of models (cf. Fisher, 1969, Altman, 1969, and Altman and Barro, 1971). Other researchers have taken into account the effect of life-time earnings in their theoretical analysis, but have largely ignored it in their empirical work. An example of this type of study can be found in Weiss (1971). He develops a model which views the occupational choice of an individual as a two-step decision process. His empirical analysis, however, is only loosely connected with the model; he studies the factors that determine earnings in several occupational categories, but does not investigate the way in which lifetime earnings may affect occupational decisions.

Probably the most complete attempt to deal with this problem has been that of Freeman (1971). The bulk of his empirical analysis considers either starting or average salaries as the relevant variables of the occupational supply functions, and in this sense it is not substantially different from the studies on military manpower reported above. In his analysis of career decisions of PhD manpower, however, he explicitly takes into account lifetime earnings as the explanatory variable of occupational choices. For each of the specialities considered, Freeman estimates discounted lifetime earnings on the basis of geometric mean incomes for graduates in several previous classes. However, he is faced with serious problems to arrive at a similar measure for alternative occupations, and does not clearly specify the complex method of estimation he used. Although still consistent with theoretical expectations, his results are not as neat and convincing as those obtained with only starting or average salaries, and in subsequent work (Freeman, 1975a and 1975b) he has abandoned this line of analysis, to come back to the simpler specifications.

In our view, the analysis of occupational choice developed in the present study goes some way towards the solution of these persistent difficulties. The effect of lifetime earnings on occupational decisions is explicitly considered in a theoretical model from which we derive empirically testable hypotheses. The basic idea is to reduce the earnings profile to two dimensions: its level and the rate at which earnings increase with age. In this manner we achieve two important results. First, by measuring the profile with two variables rather than one (as is in fact done when only average, or starting salaries, or even present values, are used), we are able to disentangle two different supply responses: the response to salary levels, and the response to future earnings prospects. This procedure gives considerable insight into the behaviour of groups of individuals with different characteristics (e.g. men and women), and it also has direct implications for the design of salary structures. Secondly, our model suggests an empirically convenient way of taking into account lifetime earnings which relies only on starting salaries and average salaries. Given the inadequate data with which most occupational studies have to work, this procedure may prove a useful methodological advance in this area. In his recent survey of the empirical status of human capital theory, Blaug (1976) concludes that the hypothesis that individuals take a life-cycle view of career opportunities is yet to be properly tested. We hope that the results reported in this study are a significant contribution to the empirical work in this area.

Our second main area of analysis is internal labour mobility. Here our model opens an approach which, to our knowledge, has no direct precedent in the field of labour economics. Labour mobility has usually been viewed in economics as a response to spatial earnings differentials, and consequently most of the studies done on the subject have concentrated on geographical movements. To the seminal paper by Sjaastad (1962), many others have followed (e.g. Beals, Levy and Moses, 1967, Sahota, 1968, and Jack, 1970) all concerned with mobility of the labour force as a whole. Few economic studies have concentrated on mobility of labour within a particular occupation, and still fewer have incorporated into their analysis the influence of the institutional structure of the labour market at the occupational level.[5] The only studies that to some extent take into account the institutional structure of occupations are those belonging to the class of stochastic manpower models, but they are exclusively based on mechanistic relationships, and do not incorporate into the analysis any behavioural assumptions.[6]

The mobility analysis developed in Chapter 7 brings together in an integrated framework the effects of both the promotion and career structure of the teaching profession, and the wealth maximising behaviour of teachers. From this framework we derive a testable hypothesis concerning the determinants of the level and pattern of internal mobility of labour. The model is relevant to the analysis of inter-school teacher mobility, but its applicability is more general. We believe that extensions of this approach could prove very useful to the study of labour mobility within professions which, like teaching, have a well specified career structure.

1.3 Methodology and data

Both theoretical and empirical analyses are used. The theoretical analysis developed is based on the human capital framework, and is built upon assumptions about individual behaviour within a specific economic and institutional environment. Both the choice of occupation and the choice of workplace within an occupation are viewed as acts of investment which are guided by their expected return.

In the design of the theoretical models particular emphasis has been placed on the empirical applicability of their conclusions. Our main object-ive in building these models was to understand the workings of the labour market for teachers in England and Wales; therefore, they are closely suited to the characteristics of the problem at hand, and the concepts they use have clearly defined empirical counterparts. This does not mean to imply that their use is restricted to the analysis of this particular labour market. On the contrary, the model has a high level of generality, and, suitably extended or modified, can be applied to the study of many other labour markets.

The data against which the predictions of these models have been tested come from three main sources. Data on alternative earnings and unemploy-ment come from published statistics by the Department of Employment. Data on qualified manpower and some of the data on teachers come from statistics published by the Department of Education and Science. The major part of the data on teachers come from three random samples based on the computerised individual teacher records which the Department of Education and Science made available to us specially for this study. The '1 per cent sample' includes about 3,500 teachers in maintained primary and secondary schools in England and Wales. The '5 per cent graduate sample' includes approximately the same number of graduate teachers also in maintained primary and secondary schools in England and Wales. Finally, the 'SED[7] clustered sample' contains *all* teachers in social priority schools plus a 1 per cent sample of primary school teachers clustered within schools (for comparison with social priority teachers). Details of the basic data made available, suitably anonymised, to the Centre for Labour Economics, London School of Economics can be found in the data appendix of this book, together with explanations of the sampling method and details of the samples. These samples provide information on individual teacher characteristics (e.g. age, length of teaching service, type of school, region, qualifications, post held and salary) and from them we are able to obtain aggregate data on flows in and out of the teaching profession, on internal mobility, on promotions and on average salaries. The time span covered by the data is 1963–71 for the '5 per cent graduate sample', and 1963–72 for the '1 per cent sample'.

1.4 The structure of the book

The remaining chapters are organised as follows. Chapter 2 is still introductory in character. Its objective is to provide a comprehensive picture of the teachers' labour market, taking into account all the elements involved and the way in which they have interacted over the period under study. It therefore deals, in very aggregated terms, with both demand and supply, and with the process of wage determination. This exercise gives a feel for the main magnitudes involved, and provides a frame of reference for the more specific analysis to be carried out in subsequent chapters. Chapter 3 provides a different sort of introduction. It describes each of the various negotiations which have fixed teachers' salary scales during the period under review, including some discussion of the main issues at the time. The chapter also describes the complicated salary structure of the teaching profession in England and Wales and its evolution. This basic background information on the institutional structure within which market forces operate, is an essential prerequisite for a proper understanding of the workings of a labour market such as this.

The following three chapters include the basic analysis of the flows that constitute teacher supply. Chapter 4 sets up the theoretical framework by outlining the model of occupational choice, from which equations specifying the determinants of the flows of both new entrants and leavers are derived. The properties of the model and of the estimating equations are then explored in detail. Chapter 5 applies the theoretical framework to the flow of new entrants into teaching. Both graduate and non-graduate new entrants are examined, and differences between graduates of different subject specialisations are also investigated. Chapter 6 applies a similar analysis to the flow of leavers from the teaching profession.

While the previous three chapters analyse the determinants of the flows which comprise the supply of teachers, Chapters 7 and 8 are concerned with the distribution of teachers between different types of school and between different geographical areas. In chapter 7 a theoretical model explaining the main determinants of the level and pattern of inter-school mobility is expounded, and the hypotheses derived from this model are then empirically tested. Chapter 8 considers the operation of the London allowance and the social priority allowance and their effectiveness in attracting teachers.

Our data did not permit an analysis of the demand for teachers equivalent in rigour to our examination of teacher supply. However, we were able to examine some aspects of this demand by considering the factors that determine the actual earnings of individual teachers by means of an earnings function approach. In Chapter 9 the earnings of individual teachers were related to their age, sex, qualifications and other characteristics.

Finally, as previously mentioned, in Chapter 10 we bring some of our main findings together to consider some policy implications. In particular, we consider the estimation of a salary profile that would be optimal in relation to particular policy objectives under given constraints.

2
An overview of the labour market for teachers

During the 1960s the labour market for teachers exhibited two main characteristics: an overall manpower shortage and a deterioration of relative salaries. This situation has changed dramatically in the present decade. Shortages have been rapidly eliminated and, for the first time since before the second world war, unemployment of teachers has begun to appear. The purpose of this chapter is to provide an introductory overview of the different elements that enter into this market, and of their evolution over time, in order to set the analysis developed in further chapters within a more general perspective. Additionally, we show that the proper consideration of the trends to which demand and supply have been subjected could have led to the anticipation of the problems of oversupply during the late 1970s. In practical terms it may be claimed that it was two major Committees of Enquiry that failed to carry out an appropriate analysis of the implications of their recommendations. The James Committee (James, 1972) failed to make any overt quantitative analysis of the supply of and demand for teachers and the Houghton Committee (Houghton, 1974) failed to consider how the salary changes it recommended on equity grounds would affect the supply of teachers.

2.1 The supply of teachers

For any given year, we define supply as the total number of people serving as a teacher. This total is formed of two main groups. Those who *enter* the profession during that year, and those who, having entered before, *remain* in the profession during that year.

The first group, which may be called the flow of *entrants* into school-teaching, can be disaggregated into new entrants, re-entrants and transfers from other educational sectors. The flow of new entrants consists of people coming from colleges of education and people coming from universities. The former have normally undergone a three-year course to qualify as teachers;[1] the latter have taken a three-year course that has qualified them in one of the specialist subjects taught in universities plus, in the majority of cases, a one-year training course specific to teaching. We will refer to the first category as *non-graduate new entrants*, and the second as *graduate new entrants*.

Re-entrants are teachers who come back to the profession after having left it earlier in their careers. Many of them are married women who have left teaching temporarily in order to have children. Transfers into school-teaching consist of qualified teachers who enter the maintained primary and secondary sector from some other sector of education.

Table 2.1 presents the evolution of these flows from 1960 to 1973. Except for 1961 and 1963, the total flow of entrants increased every year, although by the end of the period these increases had almost stopped. The reduction in 1963 was a result of the increase in the length of the teachers' training course in colleges of education from two to three years from 1960, which meant that the number of non-graduate new entrants to teaching in 1963 was severely reduced. Non-graduate new entrants comprise the largest category of entrants. Throughout the period being considered their number was always greater than or about equal to the other two components combined.

TABLE 2.1   *Entrants to maintained primary and secondary schools*

Year	Non-graduate	Graduate	Re-entrants	All entrants
1960	12,662	4,276	8,707	25,645
1961	12,994	4,142	7,183	24,319
1962	15,033	4,578	7,813	27,424
1963	6,454	4,452	9,333	20,239
1964	15,812	4,656	8,354	28,813
1965	16,023	4,498	9,996	30,517
1966	17,728	4,353	11,323	33,404
1967	19,737	5,283	10,318	35,338
1968	21,544	5,643	11,321	38,508
1969	26,520	6,066	10,500	43,086
1970	26,678	7,154	12,758	46,590
1971	28,181	8,801	14,197	51,179
1972	28,118	10,433	13,671	52,222
1973	26,975	11,897	13,960	52,832

Source: DES (annual – a).
Notes:
1. Flows of qualified full-time teachers.
2. The flow of re-entrants includes transfers into the profession.
3. For the years 1960 and 1961, the proportion between entrants and re-entrants has been estimated; also for these years transfers into the profession are not included in re-entrants.
4. Due to the computerisation of the data system, there is a break in continuity between the first three years and the rest.

Although lower in absolute terms, the number of graduate new entrants increased at a faster rate than that of non-graduates (180 per cent compared with 110 per cent). The non-graduate increase follows closely the increase in the output of colleges of education, but that of graduates varies con-

siderably in relation to the growth of the total number of university graduates. From 1960 to 1966 the number of graduate new entrants remained
practically unchanged while the output of universities increased by 44 per
cent. Thereafter, however, the increase in the number of new graduate
teachers was substantial. Between 1966 and 1973 it grew much faster than the
number of graduates produced by the universities and polytechnics com-
bined. The flow of re-entrants also showed a rising trend, but it fluctuated
considerably. The growth in the number of re-entrants is to some extent
explained by the increase in the number of teachers, but as a proportion of
this total number, it oscillated around the 4 per cent level.

The aggregation of these various flows produces the total supply of
entrants into teaching. Table 2.2 presents the figures for the number of

TABLE 2.2   *Teachers 'staying' in maintained primary and secondary schools*

Year	Teachers at the beginning of the year	Teachers who left during the year	Teachers remaining in the profession at the end of the year
1960	255,212	18,112	237,100
1961	261,215	19,032	242,183
1962	266,502	21,949	244,553
1963	273,155	22,904	250,251
1964	270,490	25,331	245,159
1965	233,972	27,501	246,471
1966	276,988	27,249	249,739
1967	283,344	29,402	253,942
1968	289,281	30,516	258,765
1969	297,273	31,417	265,856
1970	312,122	31,152	280,970
1971	328,174	32,503	295,671
1972	346,536	33,326	313,210
1973	365,432	34,722	330,710

Source: DES (annual – a).
Notes:
1. Flows of qualified full-time teachers.
2. The flow of leavers includes quits, retirements, deaths and those transferring to
   other sectors of the educational system.
3. For the years 1960 and 1961 the flow of leavers also includes transfers into the
   profession.
4. Due to the computerisation of the data system, there is a break in continuity
   between the first three years and the rest. The figures given for the year 1973
   are provisional.
5. There is a slight discrepancy between this table and Table 2.1 in that Teachers
   at the beginning of year $t + 1$ should equal Teachers at the beginning of year
   t *minus* leavers during year t *plus* entrants during year t. This discrepancy
   derives from the published *Statistics of Education* in which there is insufficient
   information to account for it.

teachers who remained in the profession for any given year. This figure is obtained by subtracting the number of leavers from the number of teachers who were in the profession at the beginning of the year. In absolute terms the flow of leavers increased consistently during the period under study; however, as a proportion of the number of teachers at the beginning of the year, it generally increased up to the year 1968 and decreased steadily thereafter.

The aggregation for any given year of the total number of *entrants* and the number of *stayers* gives us the total supply of teachers for that given year.[2] Although this flow (which is presented later in Table 2.3) increased consistently over the span of time considered here, its trend can be divided into two distinct periods. Up to the mid 1960s its rate of increase was moderate; from 1960 to 1966 supply increased at an average annual rate of 1.3 per cent. From then until the end of the period, however, the rate of increase was considerably larger, averaging an annual rate of 5 per cent.

One factor that clearly influences the flow of new teachers is the rate at which the educational system produces qualified manpower. In particular, the number of non-graduate new entrants is largely determined by the output from colleges of education. However, the evolution of overall supply does not correspond at all closely to the expansion of the higher education system. The flows of leavers and re-entrants are independent of the number of graduates produced and the flow of new graduate teachers departs substantially from the trend in output from universities and polytechnics. Even non-graduate new teachers do not follow exactly the trends in output from colleges of education.

What other factors influence these flows? This is the question to which a large part of this book is addressed. The issue is basically one of occupational choice. Why do some qualified people choose teaching instead of an alternative occupation? Why do some people, having originally decided to teach, leave the profession?

It is hypothesised that, for a given set of preferences at any moment in time, people will choose from among the courses of action open to them, that for which the expected net benefits (pecuniary and non-pecuniary) are greatest. Among the non-pecuniary benefits are usually included such intangibles as working conditions and job security; among the pecuniary benefits the most important element is earnings. Given the difficulties of measurement, the first group of benefits is rarely considered explicitly, leaving earnings as the main economic variable that attempts to account for these choices. *Other things being equal*, an increase of teachers' earnings relative to those in other occupations will make the net benefits of teaching greater than those of alternative occupations, and will result in both more people entering and fewer people leaving the profession.

We have therefore singled out two variables which we believe are relevant in explaining the supply of teachers: the level of relative earnings, and the output of qualified people from colleges of education and universities.

This hypothesis, crude as it is, incorporates the basic elements of what economists understand by the concept 'supply function of labour'; it expresses, for a given rate of output of graduates, a positive relationship between the number of teachers in the profession during a certain period of time, and the level of earnings in teaching relative to that in other occupations. We shall see in subsequent chapters that other variables such as employment opportunities and expected earnings may also influence occupational choice.

For many practical purposes we are less interested in total supply than in investigating the determinants of the particular flows that comprise total supply. In subsequent chapters, therefore, we concentrate in particular on the flows of graduate and non-graduate entrants, and on the rate of leavers from the profession. We also analyse the responses to salary changes of different categories of teachers according to their sex or their level of training, and examine the way in which this overall supply is geographically distributed and the causes which determine the movements of teachers inside the profession.

2.2 The demand for teachers

The demand for labour services is a 'derived demand'. Labour is not demanded for its own sake, but rather because it contributes to the production of some final good. Firms demand labour as a consequence of consumers' demands for their final goods. The particular relationship between the final demand for goods or services and the derived demand for labour is determined by the way in which labour is used in the production of the final good, and by the degree of competition to which the enterprise employing the labour is exposed. In a competitive situation, the demand for labour by a firm will reflect the value of the marginal contribution of labour to the production of the final good.

In the labour market for teachers there are several reasons why such an analysis is inadequate. The public sector is a near monopolistic supplier of education and a near monopsonistic buyer of teachers' services. This however is not the main difficulty in analysing the economic demand for teachers. A more crucial problem arises out of the special character of the final good with which we are dealing – education. Whereas, in principle at least, it is straightforward to determine the value of the marginal product of labour in, say, the steel industry, it is very difficult to derive such a measure for education and some commentators would claim that it is intrinsically impossible. First it is not at all clear what the output of education is and there is no agreement on how to measure it. Secondly, the way in which teachers' services combine with other inputs in the production of education is not well understood.

This book is accordingly mainly concerned with the analysis of teacher supply. It is necessary, however, to advance some general remarks about the nature of the demand for teachers in England and Wales. There has been considerable discussion in Britain and in the United States about the determinants of, and the most appropriate conceptual approach to the demand for the services of teachers.[3] One fact that must be taken into account is that in the present institutional framework the provision of education, together with its price, are strongly influenced by the value judgements of policy makers.

As far as the demand for labour is concerned, these value judgements are usually revealed in terms of a desired number of teachers for a given school population – a desired pupil–teacher ratio. If this desired level represents the preferences of the public authorities as to the allocation of a certain overall amount of the resources at their disposition, there is little else that the economist can say about the determinants of demand. The allocation of resources will have already been made on the basis of political considerations, and the number of teachers demanded will then constitute a datum of the problem rather than something subject to economic analysis. In practice things do not work as neatly as this. There is sometimes very little relation between the proportion of resources devoted to the hiring of teachers and the stated policy as to the desired teacher–pupil ratio. In such cases, the datum of the problem rather than being the number of desired teachers would be the number of teachers who, given the amount of money the public authorities are willing to spend on teachers, could be hired at the present wage rates. We can single out three independent variables in the analysis of the demand for teachers: first, the number of pupils to be educated and the desired pupil–teacher ratio; second, the amount of money the public authorities are willing to spend on teachers' salaries; and third, the average level of salaries per teacher. One of the main problems in planning teacher supply in Britain is that decisions about these three interdependent constituents of demand are usually taken in isolation from each other.

It is useful to examine the relationship between these three constituents with the help of a simple diagrammatic example. In Figure 2.1 we plot average wages (W) on the vertical axis and number of teachers per unit of time on the horizontal axis (S). SS is a linear representation of the supply relationship discussed in the previous section, drawn for a given level of output from the educational system (i.e. we hold constant along this schedule the number of graduates per year from both colleges of education and universities), and for a given level of alternative earnings. The vertical line D shows the relationship between wages and the 'demand' for teachers based on a given desired pupil–teacher ratio. It assumes that the public authorities will spend whatever is necessary to obtain the required number of teachers. If it is believed that a certain number of teachers per year is needed in order to fulfil a given staffing objective (S_1), this will be so quite independently of the level of wages. Conversely, the curves BB

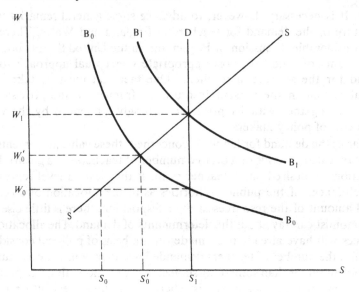

Figure 2.1   *Two views of demand in the labour market for teachers.*

represent the demand relationship as seen from the point of view of a given financial budget constraint. Each of them shows all possible combinations between wages and supply of teachers which will exhaust a given budget which the authorities are willing to devote to teachers' salaries. Along each of them the result of multiplying average wages by the number of teachers is always equal to a particular teacher salary bill. Thus each of the BB curves represents different ways of spending a fixed budget for teacher salaries. High salaries and fewer teachers or lower salaries and more teachers. Naturally, if this constraint is raised (i.e. if the government is prepared to spend more on teachers) the whole curve will shift to the right (from B_0B_0, say, to B_1B_1).

Let us imagine that the policy maker decides upon S_1 teachers as the supply necessary to meet desired staffing requirements. Let us suppose also, however, that he fixes a budget for teachers' salaries corresponding to the curve B_0B_0 and an average wage W_0. Inspection of the diagram shows that in this case the average salary will call forth a supply of teachers equal to S_0 which does not even use up all the available budget for salaries. If salaries rose to W_0' the salary bill would be used up and the supply of teachers would increase to S_0' but this would still not meet the estimated need for teachers. Only by raising salaries to W_1, and by providing a corresponding amount of resources to meet these salaries, can the desired staffing ratio at S_1 be met.

Figure 2.2 expresses what appears to have been the situation in England and Wales during the major part of the period from 1960 to 1973. For a

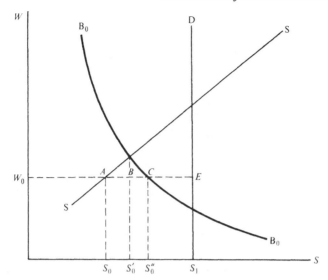

Figure 2.2   *Three concepts of shortage in the labour market for teachers.*

given desired number of teachers (S_1), the budget allocated (that corresponding to the curve $B_0 B_0$) has been too small to cover the wage bill even on the assumption that all required teachers would have entered the profession at the current level of the average wage (W_0). During this period there were jobs available for any sufficiently qualified person, so we may assume that the curve BB intersects the supply function above the point A. We thus have three concepts of shortage. One, measured by the distance AE, which is based on the preferences of the government as expressed by its staffing goals and the salary it is willing to offer; a second, measured by the distance AC, which is based on the preference of local authorities and central government as revealed by their allocation of financial resources in relation to fixed average salaries; and, a third, measured by the distance AB, which is based on the difference between the number who would be willing to be employed within the financial constraint if wages were flexible and the number who are actually willing to come forward at the fixed wage offered.[4] In all cases it is true that when speaking of shortages we are making a judgement that ultimately rests upon the value presuppositions incorporated in government educational policy (Bowman, 1963).

We can readily redraw the diagram to illustrate the corresponding three types of teacher surplus that are appearing in the second half of the 1970s. This is done in Figure 2.3. Here we have a situation in which at the going wage rate W_0, S_0 qualified people would like to become teachers. The educational planner would like to employ S_1 in order to meet his desired pupil–teacher ratio. However, the Government and educational authorities

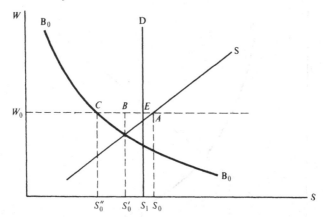

Figure 2.3   *Three concepts of surplus in the labour market for teachers.*

are willing only to allocate sufficient financial resources to employ S_0'' at the fixed wage rate. Finally S_0' people could be employed as teachers with the given budget constraint if wages were flexible. We thus have CA as a measure of what are often called 'unemployed teachers', i.e. the difference between the number of people who would like to be teachers at the going wage rate and the number who can actually get jobs. EA is a measure of the surplus of potential teachers at the going wage rate over and above what the Government would like to employ if it felt it had the resources. Finally, BA measures the difference between the number who could be employed out of the given budget if wages were flexible and the number who would be forthcoming at the artificially high fixed rate.

For the shortage situation that has characterised our period of analysis we would like to have data about the point C in Figure 2.2. The only available information, however, relates to point E: the desired number of teachers needed to meet a given staffing ratio. We have estimated the desired number of teachers by applying the pupil–teacher ratios used as targets in the seventh and ninth reports of the National Advisory Council on the Training and Supply of Teachers to the actual number of pupils (NACTST, 1962 and 1965). The results of this calculation give us a desired stock of teachers for each year, which is shown in column 1 of Table 2.3. In column 2 we present the supply figures obtained from the aggregation of the flows of entrants and stayers (i.e. the stock of teachers at the end of the year) and in column 3 the resulting gap between the number of teachers theoretically needed and the number actually serving.

The deceleration of the birth rate in England and Wales explains the relatively moderate increase in the demand for teachers. To maintain the same staffing standards during the whole period under review, the total number of teachers would have needed to increase by less than 25 per cent. In fact the total supply of teachers increased by 46 per cent and as a result, the shortage of teachers diminished substantially, especially during the last four years of the period.

2.3 The quota system

So far we have considered both demand and supply as overall aggregates. However, given that England and Wales have a national educational system, it is pertinent that we should also consider the geographical distribution of these two flows.

The stated aim of the Government during the period under review was to achieve an even distribution of staffing standards across all geographical areas.[5] In particular, this objective has often been formulated as an equalisation of the pupil–teacher ratios between local authorities as the immediate employers of teachers. In other words, demand should be evenly distributed over the whole country.

On the supply side, because of the fact that working conditions differ between areas, the supply of teachers differs also. In general supply tends to be proportionally larger in areas with good working conditions than in those

TABLE 2.3 *Demand, supply and implied shortage*

Year	Demand	Supply	Implied shortage
1960	328,404	261,215	67,189
1961	332,071	266,502	65,569
1962	335,002	273,155	61,847
1963	332,686	270,490	62,196
1964	338,776	273,972	65,804
1965	340,998	276,988	64,010
1966	344,539	283,344	61,195
1967	350,976	289,281	61,695
1968	360,955	297,273	63,682
1969	370,483	312,122	58,361
1970	380,324	328,174	52,150
1971	390,665	346,536	44,129
1972	400,851	365,432	35,419
1973	409,127	383,542*	25,585

Source: DES (annual – a).
Notes:
1. The pupil–teacher ratios used to estimate the demand series for the years 1960 and 1961 are 27:1 for primary and 16:1 for secondary (*Seventh Report* of the NACTST). For the period 1962–73 they are 26.3:1 for primary, 16.3:1 for secondary (first five years) and 10.6:1 for sixth form (*Ninth Report* of the NACTST).
2. * = provisional.

with bad working conditions. The relative cost of living of the area, the social background of its pupils, and the teaching facilities it offers, are some of the items which vary between areas.

This resulted in a situation in which, while some local authorities did not have any difficulty in recruiting teachers even in the years of general shortage, others tended to be chronically understaffed. The shortage defined earlier thus has a very different impact in different areas. To avoid this the Government introduced in the 1950s what was known as the *quota* system. The general aim of this system was to redistribute the supply of teachers in a more equitable manner by setting a suggested limit to the number of teachers that could be hired by those local authorities whose pupil–teacher ratios were lower than the national average. In this manner it was hoped that the teachers who could not find jobs in these favoured areas would look for positions in less attractive local authorities, and would thereby help in redistributing the overall supply. In general, the evidence seems to indicate that this voluntary policy achieved its objectives since the spread of the pupil–teacher ratios across local authorities narrowed considerably.[6]

One implicit assumption on which the quota system was based, was that teachers really will look for a job in other areas when they are unable to obtain one in their chosen location. If this condition is not fulfilled then inevitably this system would lead to the loss of some supply, since some teachers unable to find a job in their preferred area would opt for an occupation other than teaching. In the period under review, in which the overall situation was one of shortage, this loss of manpower might be expected to have operated against the overall staffing objectives. The fact that the quota system succeeded in equalising pupil–teacher ratios suggests that at least some of those teachers who were not able to find jobs in their preferred area did in fact attempt to work in other locations.

Whether this was the way in which the quota system operated is an empirical question which we did not study. We did, however, investigate a more fundamental question as far as the redistribution of supply is concerned. That is, whether teachers are responsive to spatial earnings differentials in choosing their location of work. It is important to study this issue, because the more sensitive teachers are to spatial earnings differentials the lower the actual salary difference needs to be in order to achieve a given redistribution of labour. In these circumstances, salary policies may be a more efficient instrument than the quota system inasmuch as while achieving the same results they will in principle avoid the potential waste of supply associated with a quota system.

2.4 Wages

The level of wages or salaries paid to teachers is the result of a complex process of negotiation between representatives of the government, local authorities and teachers' unions. In these negotiations the different participants decide not only upon the level of wages but also upon matters such as the scale structure, age increments, and special allowances. Chapter 3 outlines these negotiations during the period since the second world war.

To a large extent, therefore, teachers' salary levels are 'administered'. They do not result from the individual bidding of demanders and suppliers but are uniformly laid down for all teachers of a particular grade with a particular level of qualification and experience. This does not mean, however, that the state of the market exerts no influence in its determination. Such influences can appear in two ways. First, in the determination of the overall level of the salary structure they can affect the bargain struck in the wage negotiations; and secondly, they can influence the translation of this structure into the actual earnings of individual teachers. The first of these influences is considered in the following chapter and the second is analysed in Chapter 9. It is reasonable to assume that some relation must exist between the overall level of wages and the number of teachers both demanded and supplied. Evidently, in the salary negotiations those negotiators who represent the bodies paying teachers' services will aim to keep salaries at the minimum level compatible with various educational and social objectives, whereas those representing teachers will tend to push them as high as they can. However, within these general strategies, the actual situation of the market may change the relative bargaining power of either side.

In Table 2.4 we present average teachers' salaries throughout the period we are considering and their value relative to the average salaries of other white collar workers. During the first few years of the 1960s, teachers' salaries rose slightly more than alternative salaries; in 1965 relative average salaries were about 4.5 per cent higher than in 1960. During the second half, however, the upward trend changed drastically into a fairly sharp decline to 1971; in that year relative salaries were 10 per cent lower than in 1960 for men and 15 per cent for women.

2.5 An evaluation

The tendencies to which demand and supply in the labour market for teachers have been subjected are clearly shown in Table 2.3 and in the corresponding Figure 2.4. Despite the fact that demand has been estimated using the ideal pupil–teacher ratios put forward by the educational authorities, and that supply has only taken into account full-time qualified teachers, it is obvious from Figure 2.4 that the shortage in this market was being rapidly eliminated during the period under study. Assuming that the average rates of increase of demand and supply had persisted, the market would have been very near to its equilibrium point (i.e. to the point where demand equals supply) by 1980. This is a crude evaluation which ignores many relevant aspects,[7] but it is sufficient to suggest the main features of the problem.

TABLE 2.4   *Average wages in the teaching profession*

Year	Male		Female		Total	
	Absolute	Relative	Absolute	Relative	Absolute	Relative
1960	1,077	1.03	923	1.81	993	1.22
1961	1,164	1.07	1,004	1.87	1,073	1.26
1962	1,251	1.09	1,085	1.90	1,152	1.28
1963	1,330	1.10	1,154	1.91	1,226	1.29
1964	1,340	1.05	1,156	1.82	1,233	1.23
1965	1,510	1.09	1,304	1.89	1,392	1.28
1966	1,520	1.05	1,296	1.81	1,392	1.22
1967	1,575	1.04	1,332	1.78	1,435	1.21
1968	1,626	1.00	1,374	1.73	1,480	1.17
1969	1,743	1.00	1,451	1.69	1,572	1.15
1970	1,873	0.95	1,564	1.58	1,691	1.09
1971	2,083	0.94	1,728	1.57	1,873	1.08
1972	2,317	0.96	1,893	1.55	2,066	1.08

Source: DES (annual – a), Department of Employment (monthly), and 1 per cent sample.

Notes:

1. Absolute average salaries are as of 1 April of every year and therefore refer to the salary paid *from* that date until 31 March of the following year. Relative average salaries are obtained by dividing absolute salaries by non-manual average earnings at the middle of that period (October of each year).
2. Absolute salaries for the years 1960 to 1962 are estimated. The figure reported in *Statistics of Education* for 1967, on the other hand, is not representative of the average salary paid from 1 April 1967 to 31 March 1968 due to a wage freeze. We therefore adjust this year by taking the arithmetic average of the figures reported for 1967 and 1968.

By that time the desired pupil–teacher ratios would have been reached and the system would then have started generating a 'surplus'; that is, at the going relative wage more teachers would be forthcoming than the number that would need to be hired to achieve the 'desired' pupil–teacher ratios. The implications of this for the educational planner are quite evident. The knowledge of these tendencies, and of the way in which they interact between each other, should have made educational authorities aware of the potential tension to which the market was moving and should have prompted the necessary measures to avoid these tensions without the need for painful adjustments such as those that we experienced in the mid 1970s.

As we have said, our discussion suggests that if the trends of the 1960s had persisted, the system would have reached a saturation point by 1980. However, things did not remain the same. The stringent overall economic situation of 1975 and 1976 led to substantial cuts in educational expenditure, which, in turn, reinforced the deceleration of the demand

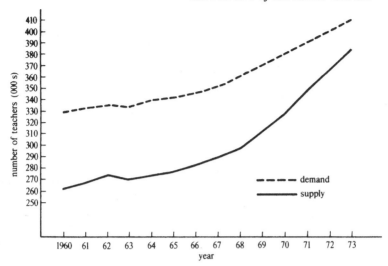

Figure 2.4   *Demand and supply in the teachers' market.*

for teachers. Another important change which occurred in this market was the substantial increase in relative salaries following the Houghton Report in 1974. Although not analysed, it is very likely that the implications of this increase were a further reduction in demand, due to additional labour costs, and an overall increase in supply due to the more favourable pay conditions. Given these circumstances, it is not surprising that by the mid 1970s, for the first time since the war, the supply of teachers was larger than actual demand. What would have occurred a few years later was brought forward by the public expenditure cuts. There is an important difference between the two situations; whereas the eventual outcome would have implied a fulfilment of the desired staffing standards in terms of educational criteria, the actual outcome stopped short of that target. There is also, however, an unpleasant similarity; in both cases, the resulting situation was one of disequilibrium in the sense of lack of jobs for many potential teachers.

3

Salaries and wage negotiations

The previous chapter has outlined a simple economic framework for the teachers' labour market which relates the supply of teachers to relative salaries. Reference is made in that chapter and subsequently throughout the book to some of the institutional arrangements by which salary levels have been determined. Before proceeding to a more detailed empirical analysis of teacher supply, the present chapter considers the actual wage negotiations and settlements during the period under review.

The chapter describes the debates and issues which were dominant at each round of negotiations from 1956 to 1974 and the salary levels and scales which emerged from them. We begin with a short background section which describes the development and current status of the Burnham Committee within which teachers' salaries are negotiated.

3.1 The Burnham primary and secondary committee

This salary negotiating body is one of four set up by the 1944 Education Act,[1] although forerunners of these committees had existed since 1920 under the same name (after Lord Burnham, their first Chairman). Table 3.1 shows the composition of the primary and secondary committee during our period. These Burnham Committees for negotiating salaries in the maintained educational sector are unusual within British industrial relations, in having their agreements backed by force of law.[2]

3.2 An account of salary settlements from 1956 to 1974

In this section we examine in detail each round of salary negotiations from 1956 to 1974 and bring out the main themes and debates dominant at the time. The actual salary scales agreed, or at least the basic scale, are set out in Table 3.2.

The 1956 and 1959 Reports. The 1956 report greatly increased the numbers of deputy heads and posts of responsibility in the schools; it also established heads of department posts and second master/mistress posts. All these changes were in line with then current thinking on enhanced career struc-

TABLE 3.1   *The composition of the Burnham Primary and Secondary Committee*

Organisations represented on the Panel	Number of seats		
	1944–62	1962–65	1965–74
Teachers' Panel			
National Union of Teachers (NUT)	16	16	16
Joint Four Associations (see note 2)	6	6	6
Association of Teachers in Technical Institutions (ATTI)	4	4	2
National Association of Head Teachers (NAHT)	·	1	1
National Association of Schoolmasters (NAS)	·	2	3
Total	26	29	28
Authorities' Panel			
County Councils Association (CCA)	9	9	9
Association of Municipal Corporations (AMC)	6	6	6
Association of Education Committees (AEC)	6	6	6
London County Council (now replaced by Inner London Education Authority)	3	3	3
Welsh Joint Education Committee	2	2	2
Department of Education and Science	·	·	2
Total	26	26	28

Source: Education (1972).
Notes:
1 · = not applicable
2 Consists of: The Association of Assistant Masters, Association of Assistant Mistresses, Association of Headmasters and Association of Headmistresses.

tures, by Government, Management Panel and the Joint Four secondary teachers' associations. The majority of these higher paid posts went to secondary schools, a change in the age weighting of pupils aged 13 to 15 benefiting Modern schools as well as Grammar schools. Thus, in relative terms, primary school teachers suffered and this, together with a generally held belief within the profession that teachers were not sharing in the general growth of earnings experienced by other workers during the 1950s, led to increasing dissatisfaction within the National Union of Teachers (NUT).

After some months of delay and an interim 5 per cent rise from February 1959, a new agreement was reached to run from 1 October 1959. This report involved few changes from the 1956 report, but for the first time it was accepted that a two year interval between negotiations was appropriate rather than the previous norm of three years.

The 1956 report had also contained a provision relating to equal pay for women teachers, to be paid in six equal instalments from 1 April 1956, the final instalment being paid on 1 April 1961. This concession had

TABLE 3.2 *Details of the basic salary scale, 1961–70, and salary scale 1, 1971–75*

Burnham Report	Operative date	Basic		Number of increments	Size of increment	Allowances		
		Minimum	Maximum			Graduate	Good Honours graduate	London
1961	1 January 1962	£570	£1,170	16	£30–60	£100	£200	£45 and £60
1963	1 April 1963	£630	£1,250	15	£30–60	£100	£200	£45 and £60
1965	1 April 1965	£730	£1,400	14	£30–60	£100	£220	£70
1967	1 July 1967	£800	£1,500	14	£30–60	£100	£220	£70
1969	1 April 1969	£860	£1,600	14	£30–60	£105	£230	£85
(1970 interim increase)	1 April 1970	£980	£1,720	14	£30–60	£105	£230	£85
		Scale 1						
1971	1 April 1971	£1,055	£2,090	15	£76–99	2 increments	4 increments	£118
1972	1 April 1972	£1,179	£2,279	15	£78–109	2 increments	4 increments	£118
1973	1 April 1973	£1,306	£2,406	15	£78–109	2 increments	4 increments	£118
1974	1 April 1974	£1,449	£2,553	15	£78–111	2 increments	4 increments	£351, £267 and £141
(Post-Houghton)*	24 May 1974	£1,677	£3,069	13	£102–114	2 increments	4 increments	£351, £267 and £141
1975	1 April 1975	£2,253	£3,744	13	£93–123	2 increments	4 increments	£351, £267 and £141

Source: DES (annual – b).

Notes:

The School of Exceptional Difficulty allowance was introduced on 1 April 1968 and changed to the current Social Priority Allowance from 1 June 1974 (see text of this section and Chapter 8).

* Threshold cost of living payments negotiated under the 1974 report and amounting to some £230 p.a. were payable on top of these salary scales.

been partly induced by a similar agreement covering the civil service made in 1955.

The 1961 Report. Amid threats of strikes a provisional agreement was reached, but upon presentation to the NUT conference for ratification, it was rejected as inadequate and plans were made for strike action in support of a higher settlement.

In the meantime, a pay freeze was announced. It meant that no increase could be paid at all until 1 January 1962 and that the increase would in any case have to be less than that already rejected by the NUT. Faced with this situation, and an unexpectedly small majority supporting strike action in an NUT referendum, the Executive accepted the lower offer. The bitterness felt by many NUT members, and particularly men teachers, at this 'betrayal' caused a number of defections to the rival National Association of Schoolmasters (NAS). One of the attractions of the NAS was its commitment to militant tactics, exemplified in 1961 by its successful strike action to gain admittance to the Burnham Committee.

The 1963 Report. The Teachers' Panel was reorganized in 1962; prior to the beginning of negotiations the National Association of Schoolmasters was given two seats and the National Association of Head Teachers, one. Immediately that year, the NAS created a minor storm of protest by publishing details of the current negotiations, this being against the agreed rules of the Teachers' Panel. In part this action was a response to the constraints imposed upon them by procedural rules which prevented their views from being heard after their long awaited success at getting into Burnham in the first place. Also their long-term aim was a complete, independent review of the whole question of teachers' salaries and the Burnham machinery.

After the relative failures of 1959 and 1961, the Teachers' Panel was now more than ever committed to a substantial increase on the basic scale; an agreement was eventually reached in February 1963 putting the whole of the proposed increase on the basic scale. The Management Panel had reluctantly agreed to this because increases for higher paid teachers had been quite substantial in previous reports. However, the Minister for Education, Sir Edward Boyle, had not been consulted by the Management Panel on this final offer, and he rejected the agreement on the grounds not that the total sum was too much, but that the distribution of this sum was wrong. All the teachers' unions, the Management Panel and other bodies connected with education condemned the Minister's action, feeling that he had exceeded his statutory duties in interfering with the internal distribution of a salary award. Nevertheless, despite protests, lobbies and well-organized NUT publicity campaigns, the Minister imposed salary scales by Act of Parliament from 1 April 1963 until 31 March 1965. Subsequently, further legislation was prepared to permanently alter the Burnham system so that such a situation could not happen again.

The 1965 Report. The Remuneration of Teachers Act 1965 prepared by the outgoing Conservative government was passed unchanged by the incoming Labour government. It gave two seats on the Burnham Management Panel to the Department of Education and Science, who were now to be given prior consultation and effective control on all offers made by the Panel. In the event of a breakdown in negotiations provision was made for arbitration; the one major concession to the teachers involved the backdating of awards whenever the negotiations dragged on beyond the expiry date of a previous agreement.

During the 1964 negotiations, the NAS took industrial action in support of their salary policy of special increments after periods of continuous teaching service, as on previous occasions they also wanted to see a complete review of the teachers' salary structure and the Burnham machinery. Their salary policy was, however, not included in the official teachers' claim and could not therefore be formally considered by the Management Panel.

After a breakdown in negotiations, the teachers' claim went to arbitration, and the resulting decision (DES, 1965) introduced two important new elements into the salary system. A £50 per annum 'merit' addition to salaries was now payable for the possessors of certain qualifications, the principle being the same as that of the graduate addition or allowance. The qualifications included were one year specialist diploma courses for serving teachers and the diploma awarded for the one year graduate training course. The second important change involved placing head teachers on separate salary scales, independent of the basic scale, and involving no additions for qualification. This change had been advocated by the Management Panel, but was opposed in principle by the NUT, who saw any departure from the basic scale principle as divisive and retrogressive. The basic scale principle regarded all qualified teachers, whether head teachers or not, as professional practitioners with little difference in status between them. The opposing argument that modern education required an approach based on career structures as in industry and other professions won the day, and separate scales for heads were introduced.

The 1967 Report. Once again, as in 1963, the NAS published details of the negotiations while they were still in progress, though by this time they took no active part in the deliberations of the Teachers' Panel. Nevertheless, for the first time the NAS was outflanked in militancy by a campaign of sanctions launched by the NUT. The aims of the campaign were: (1) a much improved basic scale; (2) abolition of the primary/secondary differential; (3) abolition of school meals duties; (4) elimination of unqualified teachers from the schools.

The sanctions themselves centred around the last two of these issues with NUT members refusing to supervise school dinners or collect dinner money and refusing to work alongside unqualified teachers. The inadequacies of Burnham were again demonstrated here in that these issues, not directly relating to salaries, could not be discussed in Burnham salary negotiations but only directly with the DES.

A wage freeze introduced in 1966 meant that not only had the implementation of a new award to be delayed until 1 July, but also the government's incomes policy implied that a much smaller salary award could be expected. Consequently the NUT executive discreetly switched the emphasis of their sanctions campaign towards the other items, with a certain amount of success. After long direct negotiations with the DES over these items, concessions were made on the last two, enabling the NUT to accept a pay award of much less than they had demanded.

The 1969 Report. An offer within the government's incomes policy was reluctantly accepted by the NUT majority on the Teachers' Panel, partly because it contained a provision reducing the differential between primary and secondary schools, promised by the working party set up after the 1967/68 campaign. The agreement was rejected by the minority NAS and ATTI members of the panel. Nevertheless, it was implemented, but soon afterwards many other groups of workers obtained salary rises above the incomes policy norm. At the Easter conference of the NUT, a resolution was passed committing the union to negotiate a flat rate interim pay rise from 1 April 1970, even though the 1969 agreement had been intended to run for two years.

The 1970 interim increase. Soon after the 1969 award, the NUT and the NAS were cooperating for the first time in their history in the planning of widespread strike action. The joint aim of the action was a £135 flat rate increase upon the salary of every teacher. Only £50 was initially offered by the Management Panel and soon the first ever large scale national teachers' strikes were under way. The dispute dragged on until March 1970 when a £120 offer was conceded by the Management Panel and accepted by the teachers.

The 1971 Report. Once again agreement could not be reached, but this time it was not governmental limitations on the maximum pay offer, but an insistence by the Management Panel on a restructuring of salaries. The proposal was not only for separate scales for heads, which existed already, but also for deputy heads and a further five separate scales for assistant teachers, instead of the graded post system. The actual average pay increase proposed of $9\frac{1}{2}$ per cent was not much below what the teachers would have been prepared to accept, but the NUT refused to sanction any move away from the basic scale principle, and arbitration was resorted to. The resulting recommendations (DES, 1971a) involved a slightly higher version of the management offer, with a guaranteed minimum increase of 10 per cent for all teachers. This was the most substantial pay award for teachers for many years.

The 1972 Report. Arbitration was once again called upon after deadlock was reached between the teachers' claim for a £250 *flat rate increase* and the management offer of a smaller *percentage* increase all round. It was unofficially agreed by both parties that no tinkering with the new system should take place until there had been time to assess its effects. Once again the teachers were not satisfied with the resulting arbitration report (DES, 1972a) which involved a compromise between the flat rate and the percentage increase, and an overall award considerably less than the teachers had sought.

The 1973 Report. Governmental incomes policy once again restricted the negotiations to the distribution of a fixed sum determined by the government. In the light of this situation, the Management Panel accepted with only slight modifications the teachers' claim for a flat rate increase of £135. The actual amount offered was £127 with certain higher paid teachers getting up to £150. The Pay Board's refusal to sanction any significant rise in the London allowance, which was due for revision, created a certain amount of agitation in the London area. The Management Panel offered a £5 per annum increase which was rejected by the Teachers' Panel and the allowance remained unchanged.

The 1974 Report. The government's statutory incomes policy did not leave much room for negotiation and a settlement was quickly reached in March for a £143 flat rate increase (averaging 8 per cent) plus a provision for cost of living payments (threshold payments) tied to the retail prices index.

Prior to the 1974 settlement, the outstanding issue of the London allowance was referred to the Pay Board. The Pay Board was the government agency through which its pay policy was implemented and its terms of reference on this issue were to look at the whole question of the 'London Weighting' for all workers covered by national pay agreements but particularly for the public sector. Their report, published in July, recommended a two-tier allowance at £400 for Inner London (4 miles radius of Charing Cross) and £200 for Outer London. Translated into the flat rate allowance for teachers, this would have meant £250 compared with the teachers' claim for £350.

After long negotiation, an agreement was finally reached in September for a three-tier allowance, backdated to 1 April. The highest level of £351 covered the Inner London Education Authority, and several of the outer London boroughs with the most difficult staffing problems. The remainder of the area within which teachers originally received the flat rate London allowance received £267, and a new outer metropolitan 'fringe' area was created within which teachers received £141. This extension of the area covered by the allowance had been insisted upon by the local authority representatives on the Management Panel, who felt that a large single step at the boundary of Greater London would have created staffing difficulties in the so-called 'fringe area'.

Soon after the 1974 settlement, a Labour government took office and one of their first actions was to provide extra finance for a new, more extensive, Educational Priority allowance to replace the old School of Exceptional Difficulty allowance.

This new social priority allowance was to be paid from 1 June 1974, but the final designation of schools was not made till February 1975. The allowance covers about 10 per cent of the teaching force but is concentrated in urban areas and includes over 50 per cent of teachers in some Local Educational Authorities (see Chapter 8).

The Houghton Report. By the time of the 1974 settlement, it had been widely recognised that teachers' salaries had fallen behind those of workers in comparable occupations. In fact, part of the 1974 settlement had been a promise from the Conservative government that the teachers' case would be referred to the Pay Board as a special case (i.e. to obtain a salary increase above the normally permitted limit of the pay policy). Even though the Pay Board was abolished by the new Labour government in 1974, the feeling that the teachers had a good case was so strong that they set up a Committee of Inquiry into teachers' pay, under the Chairmanship of Lord Houghton. This committee was given a wide brief to make recommendations on the pay and career structure of all non-university teachers. The Houghton Committee was set up in June 1974, reported in December 1974, and the resulting pay increases were backdated to May 1974.

The committee's main recommendations as far as primary and secondary teachers were concerned were: an average 29 per cent salary increase (to be followed by an additional cost of living increase on 1 April 1975); a reduction in the number of salary scales from five to four (by merging the original scales 2 and 3); and a substantial change in the points system to favour primary and small secondary schools (see Section 3.4). The recommended salary increase was deliberately made smaller on the lower salary levels in order to increase differentials and improve career prospects.

Following the Houghton Report, the Burnham Committee agreed to implement the package almost without change, despite attempts by the Teachers' Panel to get the relatively low increases in starting salaries (16 per cent) improved.

The 1975 Report. It had been understood all along that an additional 'cost of living' increase would be negotiated on top of 'Houghton', but the Teachers' and Management Panels could not agree on a figure and the issue was referred to arbitration. Initially, the teachers had put in a claim for 22 per cent, but after a large 26 per cent pay award to Civil Servants the teachers raised their claim to this level. The management panel could only offer 16 per cent, but the resulting arbitration award was 22 per cent. With the agreement of the Management Panel this was distributed more than proportionally to those on the lowest salary levels (34 per cent on starting salaries) thus off-setting to a large extent the widening of differentials resulting from the Houghton award.

3.3 Summary of the negotiations and their effects

This brief account of teachers' salary negotiations from 1956 to 1976 reveals that there were three main recurrent themes. First, was the obvious one of the teachers' organisations seeking the largest obtainable overall increase while the representatives of employers sought to limit overall expenditure. The relative strength of these two forces depended partly on the overall economic situation at the time. The second theme was the debate about differentials within the profession. Here the main disagreements were within the profession, where the NUT very broadly can be considered as having, during that period at any rate, represented the interests of teachers in primary schools and those low down in career hierarchies. (A majority of its members are women.) This union aimed, wherever possible, to obtain flat rate pay increases for all teachers rather than all round percentage increases. It was normally opposed to any widening of differentials within the profession. Its main opponent was the National Association of Schoolmasters, representing career teachers, mainly men. The policy of this union was to widen differentials in favour of career experience and seniority. Much of the economic analysis of subsequent chapters of this book is concerned with the implications for teacher supply of changes in the overall level of teachers' salaries and changes in wage differentials within the profession. The third theme was the debate about special allowances in London and in schools of exceptional difficulty. The teachers tended to argue the case on equity grounds. However, there was a strong underlying case in terms of efficiency, as is shown in Chapter 8.

As we have said above, the question of salary differentials within the profession has been a continuing concern of the Burnham Committee. The 1963 provisional agreement was rejected by the government on the grounds that it would reduce differentials. However, if the imposed salary scales of 1963 increased differentials, then the 1965 award must have reversed this increase. Table 3.3 shows that the lower quartile of the salary distribution increased by more than the upper quartile between 1963 and 1966.[3]

TABLE 3.3 *Salary increases and dispersion, 1961–73. Full-time qualified teachers in maintained primary and secondary schools*

Salary	31 March 1961	31 March 1963	1 April 1966	1 April 1968	1 April 1969	1 April 1970	31 March 1973
Average (£)	948	1,134	1,402	1,493	1,581	1,695	2,066
Index (1961 = 100)	100	120	148	157	167	179	218
Approximate median (£)	940	1,120	1,450	1,510	1,630	1,660	2,000
Index (1961 = 100)	100	119	154	161	173	177	213
Approximate lower quartile (£)	710	850	1,070	1,130	1,150	1,270	1,530
Index (1961 = 100)	100	120	151	159	169	179	215
Approximate upper quartile (£)	1,130	1,400	1,700	1,800	1,900	2,000	2,500
Index (1961 = 100)	100	124	150	159	168	177	221

Award notes (positioned between columns):
- Salary award from 1 January 1962 (between 31 March 1961 and 31 March 1963)
- 2 salary awards 1 April 1963 and 1 April 1965 (between 31 March 1963 and 1 April 1966)
- Salary award 1 July 1967 (between 1 April 1966 and 1 April 1968)
- Salary award 1 April 1969 (between 1 April 1968 and 1 April 1969)
- Interim Increase 1 April 1970 (between 1 April 1969 and 1 April 1970)
- 2 salary awards 1 April 1971 and 1 April 1972 (between 1 April 1970 and 31 March 1973)

Source: DES (annual – a).

The 1969 salary award, with its large increase in the number of above basic scale posts in primary schools, also increased differentials, but this was offset by the 1970 flat rate salary award. The indices for the upper and lower quartile at the salary distribution again do not show any widening between 1969 and 1970.[4]

A considerable widening did, however, occur between 1970 and 1973 due to the introduction of the new salary structure in the 1971 salary award. Between 1970 and 1973, the lower quartile index rose by only 36 points compared to a 44 point increase in the upper quartile index. After the last available salary figures in Table 3.3 (31 March 1973) there were two flat rate salary increases plus the flat rate threshold agreement. Differentials were therefore reduced once more, but the 1974 Houghton award incorporated a large increase in differentials. Thus, at the time or writing, we are probably back in the 1973 position as far as differentials within the teaching profession are concerned.

In retrospect, it appears that the period 1961 to 1975 was a period of internal salary stability. There were large increases in salary differentials during the 1950s and increases in 1971 and 1974, but there was very little overall change.

3.4 The salary and career structure of the teaching profession

Perhaps as a consequence of their statutory authority each Burnham report is a very complex document, setting out in detail how all teachers in maintained primary, secondary and special schools should be paid. It specifies exactly the value of most types of allowances and even sets fairly narrow limits to the number and type of allowances to be allowed within each size category of school. The local authority is left a small amount of discretion to pursue its own policy within these limits, but this discretion has been progressively reduced over the years, and no teacher can be paid a salary or an allowance different from that specified in the Burnham reports. Disagreements about the interpretation of any particular clause in the reports are referred to a sub-committee of Burnham which is continuously in session for this very purpose.

Major changes were made in the principles of teachers' pay by the 1971 Report and for this reason the two systems have been described separately. In describing the 'old' system, which was in operation throughout most of the period reported in this book, we have used the 1969 Report as a base and, to give an indication of the relative importance of the various components, values determined by the 1969 Report are reported.

3.4.1 *The pre-1971 salary structure as exemplified by the 1969 Report*

All full-time and part-time[5] qualified teachers in maintained primary and secondary and special schools, except heads,[6] had their salary determined by a system of basic scale plus allowances of various kinds until April 1971. The following formula adequately represents this system where each of the elements making up the total are explained in detail below:

$$Salary = Basic + A(Posts) + A(Qual) + A(Other)$$

Basic For many teachers this was all they received, and can be looked upon as the minimum allowable under Burnham. The basic salary scale had 15 incremental points ranging from £860 to £1,600 with increments increasing in value from £30 at the minimum to £60 at the maximum. On 1 April each year, every teacher who had been in service for the full year moved up the scale one whole increment, unless of course he was already at the maximum of the scale. Thus a teacher's position on the scale is determined by his length of teaching experience known as 'service for salary'.[7] This is the basic principle, but unfortunately things are not quite so simple. Each of the yearly increments were divided up into twelfths to take into account completed months of service, as well as years. Suppose a new teacher had completed 7 months' service by 1 April in his first teaching year, he would then be awarded $\frac{7}{12}$ of the first increment, and on the subsequent 1 April, he would move up to incremental point $1\frac{7}{12}$, and so on.

An example of the calculations involved will perhaps serve to explain this system: suppose we call the 15 yearly incremental points *Burnham (I)*, $I = 0, 14$. On 1 April, a particular teacher's 'service for salary' stands at x years y months, then his new basic salary is calculated by the following formula:

$$Basic = Burnham\ (x) + y/12\ [Burnham\ (x + 1) - Burnham\ (x)]$$

If x is greater than, or equal to, 14, he would be on the maximum of the basic scale, i.e. *Burnham* (14).

A(Posts) Posts of special responsibility and heads of department posts, which were held by nearly 40 per cent of teachers, mostly in secondary and the larger primary schools. The actual titles of these posts and the values of the allowances associated with them were:

(i)	Scale post 1	£132
(ii)	Scale post 2 or departmment head grade A	£222
(iii)	Scale post 3 or department head grade B	£334
(iv)	Department head grade C	£472
(v)	Department head grade D	£664
(vi)	Department head grade E	£742

Deputy heads had a fixed allowance depending on the Burnham group of the school (15 groups) ranging from £132 for the smallest schools to £1,225 for the largest schools. The post of second master or second mistress which was allowed in schools of group 7 and above was not fixed, and was left to the discretion of the Local Education Authority (LEA), but to quote the 1969 Report, 'The teacher so designated shall receive an additional payment, the amount of which shall be determined by the Authority and appropriately related to the deputy head teacher allowance for the school.'

A(Qual)   These are the qualification allowances consisting of: the good honours graduate allowance (£230) for holders of first or second class honours degrees; the graduate allowance (£105) for other graduates and certain graduate equivalent qualifications recognised by the DES; and the so-called 'merit' addition (£50) payable for certain specified qualifications other than degrees. The most important of these later qualifications was the diploma obtained by graduates who successfully undertake a one-year teacher training course. Various specialised one-year supplementary courses for serving teachers were also recognised for this addition.

A(Other)   Other allowances not included under the previous two headings include the London allowance (£85), the school of exceptional difficulty allowance (£75), and the special school allowance (£137) payable to all teachers in special schools (schools for the blind, deaf, handicapped, maladjusted, etc.).

Safeguarding allowances were also paid to teachers who lost their post due to reorganisation or closure of a school, thus ensuring that their salary did not drop. The same was true for deputy heads and heads, if, for any reason, the school entered a lower Burnham group than that previously applicable.

Head teachers   Heads were the only teachers not tied to the basic scale; they were on separate scales, one for each Burnham group. The only allowances payable above these salary scales were those under the last category. Thus the formula in this case becomes:

$$Salary = Salhead + A(Other)$$

The salary scales '*Salhead*' are specified in the report for each of the Burnham groups 2 to 14 with, in each case, 5 incremental points. For example, in group 2, the scale ranged from £1,875 to £2,035 and in group 14, from £4,265 to £4,583. The newly promoted head started at the minimum of these five points unless his previous salary had been higher, in which case he started at the next highest increment (though the maximum could not be exceeded).

The Burnham group and unit totals   Two issues need further explanation: the determination of the Burnham group of a school, frequently mentioned above, and the determination of the number and distribution of posts of responsibility and head of department posts within each school. Both of these are related to a points system determined by the number and ages of pupils in the school and known as the 'unit total'. This system is still in operation under the post-1971 structure, but with some alterations which are described in the next section. In 1969, the unit total was calculated as follows:

For each pupil under 13 years	score 1½ units[8]
For each pupil between 13 and 15	score 2 units
For each pupil between 15 and 16	score 4 units
For each pupil between 16 and 17	score 6 units
For each pupil aged over 17	score 10 units

The 'unit total' for a particular school then becomes either the sum of these units, or an average taken over the previous three years, whichever is the higher. This unit total is then used to determine the Burnham group (0–14) and a 'score' (0–78) for the school. The Burnham group determines the appropriate salary scale for the head teacher and the appropriate allowance of the deputy head. Under the pre-1971 system, the 'score' determined the number of scale posts allocated to the school: a scale 1 post counted one point, a scale 2 post counted two points, and a scale 3 post counted three points against this 'score'.

The number and grade of head of department posts, on the other hand, was almost entirely left to local authority discretion, though guide lines were laid down in the Burnham reports specifying only grade A (the lowest) in group 5 schools (mostly large primary), up to grade B for group 6 schools, rising progressively to grade E for group 10 and above. This allowances system is summarised in Figure 3.1.

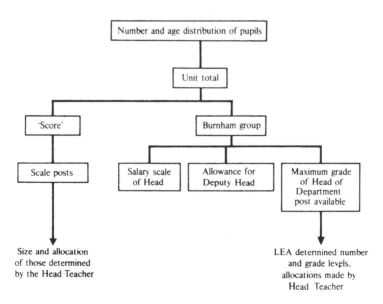

Figure 3.1   *The pre-1971 Burnham allowance system.*

3.4.2 *The post-1971 salary structure*

The 1971 Report introduced a degree of rationalisation into the complex 'score' system described in the previous section. The unit total and Burnham group system remained as before, but a new increased score[9] was allocated to each of 27 ranges within which the unit total could fall. *All* posts in the school except head, deputy head and second master/mistress were now allocated from this score as had previously been the case for scale posts only.

Posts in a school were no longer rewarded by specific allowances. Instead, the teacher was placed on one of five overlapping salary scales, Scale 1 corresponding to the previous basic scale. A point score was attached to these higher salary scales as follows:

Salary scale 2 (equivalent to old scale 1 post)	score 1 point
Salary scale 3 (equivalent to old scale 2 post, or head of department, grade A)	score 2 points
Salary scale 4 (equivalent to old scale 3 post, or head of department, grade B or C)	score 3 points
Salary scale 5 (equivalent to head of department, grade D or E)	score 4 points

The sum of these points would be equal to, or slightly less (if there are vacant posts in the school)[10] than, the allocated 'score' for that particular school. Deputy head teachers and second masters/mistresses were also now paid on separate salary scales, one for each of the Burnham groups.

The allowances classified in the previous section under *A(Other)* remained as additions to these salary scales, but the qualifications allowances were now consolidated into the scales, with 4 increments for the good honours graduate, 2 increments for the graduate and 1 increment corresponding to the previous 'merit' addition. Scales 1, 2 and 3 had an extension at the maximum for good honours graduates, but otherwise, the maximum was the same for all qualified teachers.

Complex rules exist for promotion from one scale to another, based on the simple idea of: 'Add two increments to your existing salary at the incremental rate of the scale you are now on, and then move across to the new incremental scale to be paid at the next highest $\frac{1}{12}$ of an increment on this new scale.' This promotion system unfortunately means that it is now impossible to calculate from a teacher's 'service for salary' his exact position on the incremental scale,[11] this now depends on the time of his promotion. Indeed, the 'service for salary' concept is now almost redundant.

3.4.3 *Subsequent changes to the 1971 salary structure*

The 1974 Burnham agreement contained a provision to move away from the complexity of twelfths of increments (as described on page 137) towards halves of increments, and ultimately to whole increments. It was also decided to change the standard incremental date from 1 April to 1 September, to correspond with the school year. From 1 September 1974, every teachers' salary was rounded up to the next highest half incremental point on their respective salary scales.

The Houghton salary award, implemented in February 1975, made three further amendments to the 1971 system, some of them backdated to 1974.

(i) Halves, as well as twelfths, of increments were abolished; this provision was backdated to 1 September 1974.

(ii) Salary scales 2 and 3 were merged into a new scale 2, and scales 4 and 5 were renamed 3 and 4 respectively. The points system described on page 401 remained essentially the same:

For each teacher on salary scale 2, score 1 point;
For each teacher on salary scale 3, score 2 points; and
For each teacher on salary scale 4, score 3 points.

Because there were now fewer scales, and hence fewer points, the points score ranges were correspondingly reduced. The changeover to salary scales was backdated to 24 May 1974, but the new points score ranges were only introduced from 1 March 1975.

(iii) The age weighting of pupils used to determine the unit total and, hence, the above points score ranges and Burnham group of the school (see page 39) were altered from 1 March 1975. The new weightings shown below are more favourable to primary schools and secondary schools with larger proportions of younger pupils than those used previously.

For each pupil under 14 years	score 2 units
For each pupil between 14 and 15	score 3 units
For each pupil between 15 and 16	score 4 units
For each pupil between 16 and 17	score 6 units
For each pupil over 17	score 8 units

4

A model of occupational choice

The purpose of the next three chapters is to consider in more detail the factors that determine the supply of teachers. We begin by setting up an abstract model of occupational choice which will help in organising our discussion. Then, in Chapters 5 and 6, we apply the model to the empirical data on entrants and leavers respectively.

The classical economic model of occupational choice (Adam Smith, 1776) predicts that individuals will make their choices in terms of comparative total net advantages; this prediction, because of its generality, is difficult to test empirically. The need for more formal and readily testable models led subsequent economists to single out relative wages as, *ceteris paribus*, the main economic explanatory variable of the occupational decision. This narrowing down of the hypothesis, although good for some purposes, has proved to be excessive in most cases. By holding constant other relevant factors, not only has the explanatory power of the model decreased, but the net influence of wages has been obscured. The objective of the model presented in this chapter is to identify explicitly some of these factors while still keeping the model susceptible to empirical testing. Additionally, we attempt to consider explicitly the effect of lifetime earnings on occupational decisions.

While the present chapter is an essential step in the development of the basic model being developed in this book, it is largely theoretical in nature and the non-specialist reader will lose little by jumping straight to the empirical results in Chapters 5 and 6. The non-specialist reader may also like to be assured that, although it is convenient to express the process of occupational choice in terms of formal algebraic logic, we are not claiming that any individual actually goes through formal processes in deciding whether to become a teacher. What we do claim – and as we shall show later, empirical evidence lends some support to our claim – is that if we wish to formalise the intuitive occupational choice of those who become teachers in the period under review, the model presented here is a valid way of doing so. In order to aid readers who may wish to follow the main intuitive threads of the argument, each important step is summarised verbally, and this is italicised.

In summary, the chapter develops a model in which the supply of new teachers and the proportion of leavers depend partly on the starting salary that is offered, partly on the (discounted) earnings that are expected throughout a whole teaching career as compared with prospective earnings in other possible occupations, and partly on the probability of obtaining jobs in the desired occupation. Different individuals will respond to these three factors in different ways, depending on their preferences and in particular on the way they themselves discount the prospect of higher income in the future, and on their expected working time horizon. If for example a prospective entrant to teaching does not expect to be a teacher after five years, he or she will not be interested in the likely earnings of teachers with more than five years' experience and will consequently be unaffected by changes at the top end of the scale in deciding whether or not to become a teacher. These considerations suggest reasons why the supply of female teachers may respond differently from males to wage changes. They also suggest why, due to the different range of alternative job opportunities, the elasticities of graduate and non-graduate teachers may differ.

4.1 The entry decision with flat earnings profiles

4.1.1 *The individual decision*

The occupational choice decision is analysed by means of comparison of the pecuniary returns that might be anticipated from different courses of action. These returns are considered to be uncertain due to the probabilistic nature of the labour market. We introduce this uncertainty in a very simple manner: each course of action is identified by a single outcome to which a given probability is attached.[1] Further, we assume that only two alternatives are considered, these being exhaustive of all the available possibilities.

Given his training, the individual has the possibility of entering two different occupations: A and B. In the present context, the reader can think of A as teaching, and of B as any other alternative occupation. Non-pecuniary preferences are assumed to be equal as far as each occupation is concerned. The individual has knowledge of the wage paid in each occupation: W_a and W_b. He also knows that the specific situation of the market may pose difficulties in obtaining a job; he measures this difficulty by a subjective probability per period of finding a job in each occupation: p_a and p_b. Finally, the working time horizon of the individual (T) is assumed to be finite.

Given his subjective probabilities concerning the ease with which jobs can be found in the two occupations, the individual can estimate the expected time he will be looking for a job. If he chooses A, he can expect to spend a period $t_a = 1/p_a$ searching for a job in this occupation; similarly, if he chooses B, the expected time until he starts working will be $t_b = 1/p_b$. We select the unit period of time in such a way that jobs can only be started at the beginning of a given period, and we assume for convenience that t_a and t_b are integers. We also assume that t_a and t_b are less than T.[2]

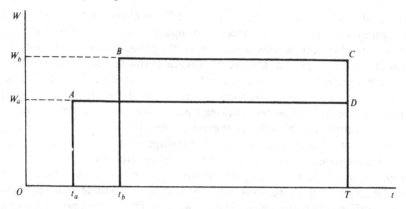

Figure 4.1   *Flat earnings profiles.*

Defined in this way, the alternatives faced by the individual can be represented by Figure 4.1, where the vertical axis measures money and the horizontal axis, time. In the figure, where t_a and W_a have been assumed to be less than t_b and W_b, the total return out of alternative A is measured by the area $t_a ADT$ and that of alternative B by the area $t_b BCT$.

The individual, however, makes his decision at the beginning of the first period ($t = 0$). He therefore evaluates the two alternative returns in terms of the present value of the corresponding benefits. If we assume that the subjective rate of discount of the individual is r, the expected returns of the two alternatives, ER_a and ER_b, discounted to $t = 0$, can be expressed as follows.

$$ER_a = \sum_{t=t_a}^{T} \rho^t W_a = W_a \sum_{t=t_a}^{T} \rho^t$$

$$ER_b = \sum_{t=t_b}^{T} \rho^t W_b = W_b \sum_{t=t_b}^{T} \rho^t$$

where ρ is the discounting factor, and equals $1/(1 + r)$.

The summation terms in the above two expressions can be easily reduced to a single element.

$$ER_a = \left[\frac{(1 + r)^{T-t_a+1} - 1}{r(1 + r)^T}\right] W_a$$

$$ER_b = \left[\frac{(1 + r)^{T-t_b+1} - 1}{r(1 + r)^T}\right] W_b$$

The individual will select one or the other alternative depending on which of them offers the higher discounted expected return. In particular, he will choose, A, if

$$ER_a > ER_b$$

or

$$\frac{W_a}{W_b} > c \qquad (4.1)$$

where

$$c = \frac{(1 + r)^{T-t_b+1} - 1}{(1 + r)^{T-t_a+1} - 1} \qquad (4.2)$$

(4.1) and (4.2) constitute a formal expression of the relative reservation wage of the individual for occupation A. Whenever the relative wage W_a/W_b is greater than some factor c, he will offer his services to occupation A, instead of B. Within the present framework, and despite the absence of non-pecuniary preferences for A, W_a does not need to be greater than W_b for the individual to select occupation A. In effect, if, for instance, t_a is less than t_b, then c is less than unity, and W_a/W_b can be greater than c, even if W_a is less than W_b. *In other words, when the probability of finding jobs differs between the two occupations, it may pay to choose the lower paid one if the chances of getting jobs in this occupation are larger than the possibilities in the other one.*

As is clear from (4.2), for a given set of tastes concerning non-pecuniary characteristics of the two occupations the relative reservation wage depends on three factors: the subjective rate of discount, the working time horizon, and the relative probabilities of finding a job. The direction of the change of c, when any of these factors change, will give us the sign of the partial effect of these variables on the reservation wage.

Assuming that t_a is less than t_b, we have that $\partial c/\partial r < 0$.[3] *That is, the higher the subjective rate of discount, the lower need be the relative wage for the individual to select the occupation in which it is easier to find employment. When the future is heavily discounted, the salaries lost during the period of unemployment become relatively more important than the subsequent wage differential. On the other hand, a low rate of discount will tend to make higher wages a more attractive feature than quick employment in the evaluation of alternative occupations.*

The influence of the working time horizon can also be analysed in terms of the present framework. It can be shown that $\partial c/\partial T > 0$, which implies that *the longer an individual expects to work, the more important the wage differential becomes, and the higher will be the relative wage required to enter the occupation with more job opportunities. In other words, the advantage of quick employment versus higher salary diminishes in importance the longer the working time horizon.*

This result indicates that people with different characteristics, as far as working time horizon is concerned, will respond differently to changes in the relative wage. Young women, for instance, could be identified as a group of individuals with, on average, a shorter working time horizon than men. The present analysis suggests that, even on strictly economic grounds, we cannot expect women to behave like men in their occupational choice behaviour. In their evaluation of different occupations, women will tend to consider rapidity of employment as a more valuable characteristic than level of wages. The relative wage needed to attract them to occupations in which employment is guaranteed will be much lower than when job opportunities are scarce; similarly, men will in general require a higher relative wage than women to be recruited into occupations characterised by abundant job opportunities.

The two factors so far studied depend on the characteristics of the individual in question. The probability attached to the outcome of finding a job in each of the two occupations, however, depends on something external to him. We will assume that he arrives at these probabilities on the basis of previous experiences of himself or of other workers, and that the results of those experiences are determined by the situation of the market in each occupation. For a given discount rate and working time horizon, the way in which the expected searching period will affect the relative reservation wage can be expressed as follows: $\partial c / \partial t_a > 0$, and $\partial c / \partial t_b < 0$. *The more difficult it is to find employment in occupation B, the lower will be the relative wage required for the individual to enter occupation A. Similarly, a decrease in job opportunities in occupation A will, ceteris paribus, call for a higher reservation wage if the individual is to select this alternative. The state of the market will, therefore, influence the occupational decision. At the margin, for a given relative wage, employment difficulties in one occupation will tend to make it easier to recruit labour in the other.*

4.1.2 *The aggregate supply function*

We have so far derived an expression for the relative reservation wage of a given individual. *It is now necessary to examine the implications of this result for the market as a whole. In the derivation of expressions (4.1) and (4.2) the absence of non-pecuniary preferences has been explicitly assumed. When we consider a plurality of individuals it is reasonable to modify this assumption; while some people will be indifferent between the two occupations, others will, ceteris paribus, tend to prefer one to the other. The plausibility of this assumption can be clearly seen by considering the consequences for a market of ignoring it. Suppose that all individuals belonging to a given group – with the same characteristics concerning rate of discount, probabilities of employment and working time horizon – have the same non-pecuniary preferences as far as the two occupations are concerned. Then it will follow that they will all have the same relative reservation wage as well. If the relative market wage is above the unique reservation level, then all individuals will choose to work in A, while if it is below that level, all will choose to work in B.*

Clearly, the real world does not correspond to these facts. It is not difficult to find people with similar observable characteristics whose asking wage to enter a given occupation is different. Those who prefer this occupation to other occupations will be willing to enter at lower relative wages than those who are either indifferent or who positively dislike it.

In formal terms we can incorporate this idea by assuming that the reservation wage of the ith individual is equal to the element c as defined in (4.2), corrected by a factor Z_i measuring his preferences for occupation A relative to occupation B in terms of the relative wage W_a/W_b, and that, for a given group of people, individual preferences are distributed according to some probability function. The particular way in which the element c is corrected by the factor Z will depend on the probability distribution of the variable Z. If Z is normally distributed, with mean 0 and standard deviation σ, the correction will be $c' = c + Z$, where c' is a variable normally distributed, with mean c and standard deviation σ. If Z is long-normally distributed (log Z having mean 0 and standard deviation σ) the correction will be $c' = cZ$, where c' is also log-normally distributed, (log c' will have mean log c and standard deviation σ.)

Imagine for simplicity that Z is normally distributed, then the probability distribution of the variable c' is that depicted in Figure 4.2, where the horizontal axis measures the value of the reservation wage c' and the vertical axis the proportion of individuals with a given reservation wage. It follows that, out of the total possible number of potential workers, the proportion selecting occupation A will be given by those whose reservation wage is less than, or equal to, the market relative wage; that is, $P(c' \leqq W_a/W_b)$ shown in the figure by the shaded area.

It is clear that *among those selecting occupation A there will be some people who would have entered the occupation even if the relative market wage had been*

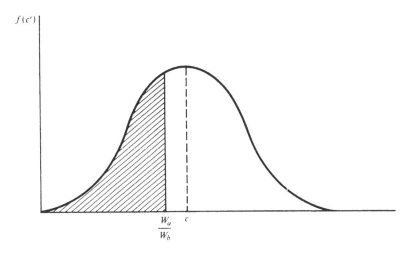

Figure 4.2 *Distribution of reservation wages.*

much lower than that shown in the figure; these are people who have a clear preference for occupation A relative to B, and are said to be receiving rents, since small changes in the relative wage are not likely to affect their occupational choice. Others, however, will be very sensitive to changes in the market since their relative reservation wage, taking account of their preference for occupation A, will be very close to the relative market wage; these may be called 'marginal teachers'. Clearly, a lower relative market wage will discourage some of these people from entering teaching while a higher relative market wage will induce some other potentially marginal teachers to enter who otherwise would have opted for occupation B. It is also clear from Figure 4.2 that even those who, on balance actively prefer occupation B and who therefore have a very high relative reservation wage, could be attracted to teaching if a sufficiently high relative wage were offered to them.*

Within this model, the variation in occupational preferences is precisely the reason for an upward sloping shape of the supply curve. This can be seen more directly by constructing another diagram where the shaded area of the previous figure (the proportion of people selecting occupation A, N_a/N) is plotted against the relative market wage (W_a/W_b). This is done in Figure 4.3, which depicts a conventional occupational supply curve.[4] Higher relative wages will result in a higher proportion of people selecting occupation A; the flatter the curve is, the stronger the effect. The curve will be bounded at the level $N_a/N = 1$, thus indicating the maximum number of people that could possibly be attracted into occupation A.

So far, we have considered the effects on relative supply of changing

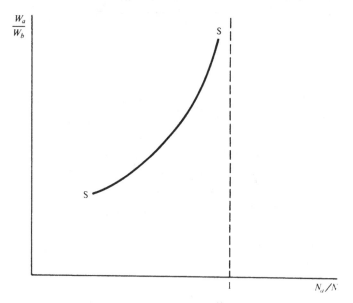

Figure 4.3   *Occupational supply curve.*

relative market wages for a given probability distribution of the reservation wage c'. This means that in drawing the curve SS, we are holding constant all the factors that determine the probability distribution depicted in Figure 4.2. However, changes in that probability distribution, even for a constant relative market wage, will also result in changes in the proportion of people selecting occupation A.

Changes in the probability distribution of the reservation wage can occur for two reasons: (a) due to changes in the variables that determine the factor c; and (b) due to changes in the variation of individual preferences concerning occupation A relative to B. In what follows, we will restrict ourselves to the first type of changes, thus assuming that the variation of individual preferences remains constant. That is, we want to consider the effects on relative supply of shifting the mean of the distribution keeping its shape constant. This is done in Figure 4.4. In panel 1 we show the effect of decreasing the mean of the variable c', from c_0 to c_1; for a given relative market wage $(W_a/W_b)_0$, the shift to the left of the distribution will increase the probability that the variable c' is less than, or equal to, the relative wage. In panel 2 we show this effect with reference to the occupational supply curve; the decrease in c will mean a shift to the right of the supply curve from S_0S_0 to S_1S_1; for a given relative wage $(W_a/W_b)_0$, the proportion of people entering occupation A will increase from $(N_a/N)_0$ to $(N_a/N)_1$.

In formal terms the relationship between relative supply, relative wages, and the mean of the distribution can easily be established by defining a new variable $(c' - c)$, with density function f' and cumulative function F'. It is then possible to express the proportion of people selecting occupation A in terms of W_a/W_b and c as follows:

$$P(c' \leqq W_a/W_b) = F'(W_a/W_b - c)$$

Since the function F' is by definition an increasing function, the proportion of people selecting occupation A will increase when the relative wage increases, and when c, the mean of the variable c', decreases, which is precisely the result discussed above in diagrammatic terms. We can then specify a labour supply function to occupation A and the signs of its partial derivatives (shown below, equation 4.3) as follows

$$N_a/N = S(W_a/W_b, c) \qquad (4.3)$$
$$+ \qquad -$$

If the underlying distribution of Z is log-normal, we obtain a similar result to (4.3), only that instead of c, the second variable of the function will be log c. Since changes in any of the elements that form c will change log c in the same direction, we have that for both cases the relative supply function, and the signs of its corresponding derivatives, can be expressed as

$$N_a/N = S(W_a/W_b, t_a, t_b, r, T) \qquad (4.4)$$
$$+ \quad - + + -$$

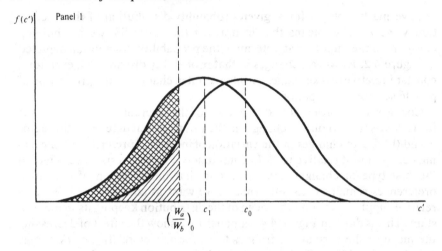

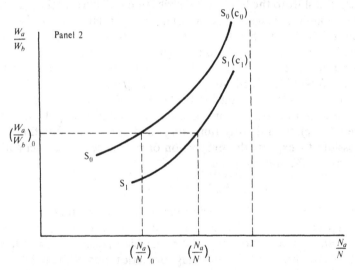

Figure 4.4   *Effect of a shift in the distribution of reservation wages.*

That is, relative supply will depend not only on relative wages but also on the probabilities of obtaining a job in each occupation, on the rate of discount, and on the working time horizon. Changes in any of the last four variables will result in shifts of the supply curve drawn in Figure 4.3. If we assume that $t_a < t_b$, a decrease in job opportunities in occupation A (higher t_a) will shift the supply curve to the left, a decrease in job opportunities in occupation B (higher t_b) to the right, an increase in the subjective rate of discount to the right, and finally an increase in the working time horizon to the left.

It is interesting to introduce the concept of elasticity of supply in terms of this framework,[5] we use the term 'wage elasticity' to refer to the percentage change in the supply of teachers as indicated by the shaded area of Figure 4.2 which results from a one per cent increase in the relative wages of teachers. The question that we want to consider is whether our model can make any predictions as to the size of the wage elasticity of different groups of teachers or potential teachers. Imagine that we can identify two groups of potential entrants to occupation A with different probability distributions; that of group 1 having the same variance (spread) as that of group 2, but a larger mean (i.e. $c_1 > c_2$). Assume further that the relative wage paid to both groups is the same. The question is: will a one per cent increase in relative wages have the same effect on the relative supply of both groups? *In diagrammatic terms, the problem is depicted in Figure 4.5. For an initial level of relative wages w_0, the relative supply of the two groups is given by the respective shaded areas. Assume that a one per cent increase in relative wages raises w from w_0 to w_1. We want to evaluate whether the relative increase in supply for group 1 (area BCDE/area ABC) is equal, larger or smaller than that for group 2 (area B'C'D'E'/area A'B'C'). From the way the figure has been drawn, it is clear that the two percentage increases are not equal; in fact, it is quite*

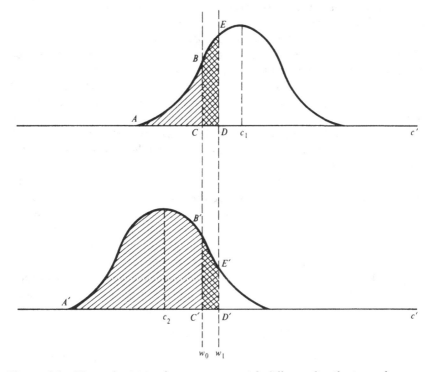

Figure 4.5 *Wage elasticities for two groups with different distributions of reservation wages.*

safe to venture that the wage elasticity of group 1 will be larger than that of group 2. In fact, it is possible to ascertain that if the reservation wages are log-normally distributed, the wage elasticity of the group whose distribution has a larger mean will always be larger than that of the group with a lower mean distribution.

The proof of the above statement follows from a previous result obtained by Fisher (1970). Following Fisher, we know that for any log-normal distribution the supply elasticity is always decreasing as we move to higher levels of wages (i.e. as we move to the right of the distribution). Since the two distributions considered in our problem only differ in their location, it follows that comparing elasticities in two distributions at one given level of wages is equivalent to comparing elasticities in one distribution at two different levels of wages. In our case, relative to their respective distributions, the wage is further to the left in group 1 than in group 2; therefore, the wage elasticity of the first group has to be larger than that of the second group.

We are interested in this question because sometimes it is possible to identify groups of people with different reservation wage distributions. Concerning the labour market for teachers, two such groups would be male and female new entrants. There are at least two plausible explanations of a lower mean for the distribution of the female reservation wage. First, the shorter working time horizon of women (on average) than that of men; this would make the factor c of females lower than that of males, thus shifting their distribution to the left. Second, a stronger preference for teaching relative to other occupations on the part of females; this would be incorporated by assuming that their distribution of preferences (Z) has a negative mean in the case of a normal distribution, or a mean between 0 and 1 in the case of a log-normal distribution; in both cases the female distribution of reservation wages would also be to the left of that for males. Under these circumstances then, *our model predicts that the wage elasticity of males should be larger than the wage elasticity of females.*

This result is derived under the assumption that the relative wage is the same for both groups. If this is not the case, then the final conclusion depends on the type of distribution being assumed, as well as on the way in which the relative wage differs. In the case of teaching, due to the lower sex differential in this occupation as compared with alternative occupations, female relative wages are on average larger than male relative wages. Under the assumption that the reservation wage is log-normally distributed, this difference clearly reinforces the above conclusion.[6]

4.2 The entry decision with increasing earnings profiles

The model developed in Section 4.1 gives rise to a supply function in which, once account has been taken of non-wage variables, the differential in earnings profiles is represented by a single measure: the relative wage W_a / W_b. This provides the *theoretical basis for considering only one wage variable in empirically estimated supply equations:* either *the relative average wage,* or *the relative starting wage. Such a procedure, although commonly used,*[7] *is unsatisfactory. First, the shape of a lifetime earnings profile is difficult to represent by a single measure. Second, the interpretation of results concerning the elasticities with respect to starting and average wages is problematic. Usually, changes in salary profiles involve different variations in starting levels and averages. Thus, the conclusions reached as far as the effect of this change on supply is concerned may be quite different, depending on whether we consider the response of supply to starting salaries or to average salaries. In this section, we develop a more comprehensive measure of the earnings supply,* on the basis of the theoretical model considered in Section 4.1. To keep things simple, we will first describe the model under the assumption that $t_a = t_b = 0$; then we will consider the implications of assuming $t_a \neq t_b \neq 0$.

4.2.1 *The individual decision*

Above we have assumed that the level of salaries paid in each of the two occupations (W_a and W_b) were constant over all the working time horizon. Now we modify this assumption and suppose instead that salaries (in each occupation) grow over time at a constant rate. In particular, let us assume that

$$W_{at} = W_{a0}(1 + \alpha t)$$

$$W_{bt} = W_{b0}(1 + \beta t)$$

where W_{a0} and W_{b0} are the respective starting wages, and α and β the respective proportional slopes of the earnings profiles.[8] A possible configuration of these profiles is shown in Figure 4.6.

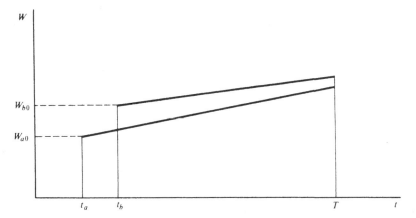

Figure 4.6 *Increasing earnings profiles.*

Assuming first that $t_a = t_b = 0$, the discounted returns from choosing occupation A are now

$$R_a = \sum_{t=0}^{T} \rho^t W_{at} = \sum_{t=0}^{T} \rho^t W_{a0}(1 + \alpha t) = W_{a0}\sum_{t=0}^{T} \rho^t + \alpha W_{a0}\sum_{t=0}^{T} t\rho^t$$

where ρ is the discounting factor, and equals $1/(1 + r)$.

Solving the summation terms, we have

$$R_a = W_{a0}\left[\frac{(1 + r)^{T+1} - 1}{r(1 + r)^T}\right] + \alpha W_{a0}\left[\frac{(1 + r)^{T+1} - r(T + 1) - 1}{r^2(1 + r)^T}\right]$$

Similarly,

$$R_b = W_{b0}\left[\frac{(1 + r)^{T+1} - 1}{r(1 + r)^T}\right] + \beta W_{b0}\left[\frac{(1 + r)^{T+1} - r(T + 1) - 1}{r^2(1 + r)^T}\right]$$

Therefore, the individual will select occupation A, if

$$R_a > R_b$$

or

$$\frac{W_{a0}}{W_{b0}} > c_S \tag{4.5}$$

where

$$c_S = \frac{m + \beta n}{m + \alpha n} \tag{4.6}$$

$$m = r\left[(1 + r)^{T+1} - 1\right], \text{ and } n = \left[(1 + r)^{T+1} - r(T + 1) - 1\right]$$

(4.5) and (4.6) constitute the new relative reservation wage of the individual for occupation A; it is now expressed in terms of the relative starting salary, and it includes explicitly the relative difference in career prospects between the two occupations (β/α). Given that the factor n is larger than zero, increases in β/α will increase the value of the relative starting wage needed for the individual to choose occupation A. If we consider the two variables separately, we see that increases in α will lower the value of the reservation starting wage, while increases in β will raise it.

The relaxation of the assumption $t_a = t_b = 0$ does not change things substantially. If we assume $t_a \neq t_b \neq 0$, the new expected return expressions will be

$$ER_a = W_{a0}\left[\frac{(1 + r)^{T-t_a+1} - 1}{r(1 + r)^T}\right] + \alpha W_{a0}\left[\frac{(1 + r)^{T-t_a+1} - r(T - t_a + 1) - 1}{r^2(1 + r)^T}\right]$$

$$ER_b = W_{b0}\left[\frac{(1 + r)^{T-t_b+1} - 1}{r(1 + r)^T}\right] + \beta W_{b0}\left[\frac{(1 + r)^{T-t_b+1} - r(T - t_b + 1) - 1}{r^2(1 + r)^T}\right]$$

and the new reservation wage will be

$$\frac{W_{a0}}{W_{b0}} > c_{SS} \tag{4.7}$$

where

$$c_{SS} = \frac{m_b + \beta n_b}{m_a + \alpha n_a} \tag{4.8}$$

$$m_i = r[(1 + r)^{T-t_i+1} - 1] \quad (i = a, b)$$

$$n_i = [(1 + r)^{T-t_i+1} - r(T - t_i + 1) - 1] \quad (i = a, b)$$

Here again, *the higher the slope of the earnings profile offered by a given occupation as compared with that offered by other alternative occupations, the lower the starting relative wage needs to be in order to attract people. Two other unambiguous results – identical to those of the simple model – can be obtained from the new reservation wage: a decrease in job opportunities in occupation B will lower the reservation wage for occupation A, and vice versa. Finally, the effects of the working time horizon and of the rate of discount depend on the relative magnitude of* β *and* α. Still maintaining the assumption that t_a is lower than t_b, if β is larger than α, increases in T will raise the reservation wage and increases in r will lower it. However, if β is lower than α, the result is ambiguous; increases in both T and r will first raise the reservation wage and, after reaching a maximum, will lower it.[9] *Table 4.1 summarises these qualitative results.*

4.2.2 *The aggregate supply function*

The aggregation of the individual results obtained above can be done in this case following the same procedure as in Section 4.1.2. By assuming that non-pecuniary preferences towards occupation A relative to occupa-

TABLE 4.1 *Qualitative effects of changes in the variables that determine the reservation wage*

	$\beta > \alpha$	$\beta < \alpha$
$\partial c_{SS}/\partial(\alpha/\beta)$	−	−
$\partial c_{SS}/\partial\alpha$	−	−
$\partial c_{SS}/\partial\beta$	+	+
$\partial c_{SS}/\partial t_a$	+	+
$\partial c_{SS}/\partial t_b$	−	−
$\partial c_{SS}/\partial T$	+	+ 0 −
$\partial c_{SS}/\partial r$	−	+ 0 −

tion B are distributed according to some probability function, we can generate a distribution of the reservation wage for occupation A. The only difference in the present case is that the mean of the distribution, c_{SS} [or log (c_{SS}) if the underlying distribution of preferences is log-normal], will also depend on the variables α and β, in addition to employment opportunities, working time horizon and rate of discount.

An increase in α, which for a given starting level is equivalent to an increase in the steepness of the earnings profile of occupation A, will ceteris paribus shift the mean of the distribution to the left, thus increasing the proportion of people choosing this occupation. Similarly, a decrease in β, equivalent to a decrease in the steepness of the earnings profile of occupation B, will also shift the mean of the distribution to the left and increase the level of relative supply to occupation A. The effect of the other variables will have a similar effect on relative supply as before, with the exception of the rate of discount and the working time horizon whose influence will now depend on the relationship between α and β, as is indicated in Table 4.1.

The agregate supply functions resulting from the model and their derivatives can then be specified as follows:

$$N_a/N = S(W_{a0}/W_{b0},\ \alpha/\beta,\ t_a,\ t_b,\ r,\ T) \qquad (4.9)$$
$$\qquad\qquad +\qquad +\quad -\quad +\quad ?\ ?$$

Expression (4.9), then, gives us the relative supply function for occupation A. It states, consistently with other approaches, that the relative wage is an important variable in the selection of a given occupation. It indicates, furthermore, two other results. First, it shows that the measurement of expected earnings by means of a single variable may lead to some mis-specification; in themselves, neither relative average salaries nor relative starting salaries can provide a comprehensive description of the profile of earnings offered by the two occupations; our model suggests that a more satisfactory specification would include, together with the relative starting wage, some measure of the relative difference in career prospects offered by each alternative. Second, it implies that other variables such as job opportunities, working time horizon and subjective rate of discount, may be relevant in determining occupational choices.

These results are by no means new; it is common knowledge that other factors besides the relative wage will affect the behaviour of people in their occupational decisions. Their treatment, however, has not always been satisfactory, since most of the time these other factors have indiscriminately been relegated into the error term of empirical regressions. What the above framework has tried to do is to identify explicitly the nature of some of these other factors and to examine what influence they exert on supply decisions. If the reasoning behind expression (4.9) is correct, the consideration of the suggested additional variables should not only improve our understanding of occupational choices, but also help to clarify the role that relative wages play in such choices.

4.3 The leaving decision

The above discussion has been carried out in terms of the entry decision; but the same framework, with only slight modifications, can be used to analyse the leaving decision. In general people leave jobs for alternatives which have non-pecuniary characteristics better suited to their preferences, and/or which offer a higher remuneration. Two basic circumstances, either alone or in combination, are sufficient to justify the presence of movements between jobs: imperfect information and changing market conditions.[10] The first implies that in most cases decisions concerning the selection of jobs will have to be made not knowing for certain all the characteristics of the selected employment, nor those of possible alternatives; as this knowledge becomes available, the initial decisions will be modified. In addition, even if information was perfect, and workers could select the best possible job, given their constraints, a change in market conditions might render already made choices inadequate; in these circumstances, job movements would also be observed.

The decision to leave is interpreted as a wealth maximising response of the individual to modifications in relative wages and job opportunities. In this sense, it can be studied in similar terms to the entry decision. The individual moves because, given his tastes, the new set of constraints, as he views it, has altered the return calculations that made him choose teaching in the first place. If at any point in his career, the present value of his remuneration in an alternative occupation (account being taken of his probability of employment) is larger than that in his present occupation, he will leave his present job.

Following a formal reasoning similar to that of section 4.2, we would end up specifying the following leavers function for occupation A.

$$L_a/S_a = L(W_{a0}/W_{b0}, \alpha/\beta, t_b, r, T) \qquad (4.10)$$
$$\;-\qquad\quad-\quad-\;?\;?$$

where L_a is the number of people with a specified level of experience leaving occupation A, and S_a is the total number of people with that level of experience working in occupation A.[11]

4.4 The workings of the model

The measurement of the earnings profile by means of two variables, rather than by a single measure, introduces the possibility of being much more specific when analysing the effects of wage changes on occupational decisions. In this section we illustrate this point by means of a simulation of the model, which gives us a better understanding of its workings, and permits us to identify the elasticities that are being measured by our entry and leaving equations.

As is obvious from the above argument, the wage elasticities will depend on the distribution of the reservation wage for each category being considered. In

Section 4.1.3 we derived some qualitative results for new entrants by assuming certain differences between the distributions of men and women. The problem is more complicated for leavers because in addition to sex differences, it is plausible to imagine that the distributions also differ between groups of people with different periods of service. However, despite these difficulties it would be interesting to study the effects of changes in the profile on supply responses. We approach the problem in simpler terms; instead of looking at the effect of profile changes on overall elasticities, we investigate the effect of profile changes on the discounted return of individuals with different periods of service. Although this is one step short from analysing group elasticities of supply, it at least gives us an idea of the properties of the model.

We want to evaluate for otherwise identical individuals with different periods of service, what is the percentage effect on their discounted return resulting from a certain percentage change of some of the parameters of the earnings profile. We will concentrate our analysis on occupation A, the assumption being that all variables related to occupation B remain constant.

Assume that in occupation A, the initial annual salary is £1,283 and that it increases at a constant rate of £88 per year.[12] The discounted return for an individual with S years of service, with a rate of discount of 10 per cent and with a working time horizon of 40 years, is shown in Figure 4.7.[13] For people at the point of entry, the discounted return will equal about £22,500. This return will increase for individuals with a longer service, reaching a maximum for those

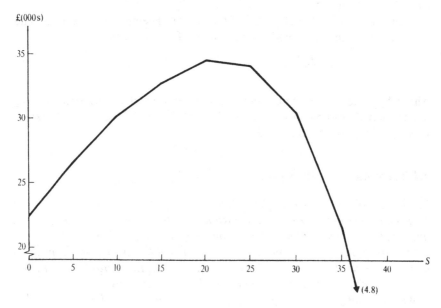

Figure 4.7   *The discounted return for different periods of service* ($r = 10\%$).

with 20 years in the occupation. Finally, for those individuals about to retire, the return will be £4,803 which is precisely the undiscounted annual salary that they will get in their last year. Higher interest rates would lower all returns (pull the graph downwards), and shift the maximum point to the right.[14]

We are interested in the effects on the discounted return of two different types of changes in the earnings profile, which relate to the elasticities directly estimable from the functions (4.9) and (4.10). The first is the effect of a, say, 50 per cent increase in the starting point of the profile holding constant the proportional slope, and the second is the effect of a 50 per cent increase in the proportional slope holding constant the starting point. These are equivalent to increasing W_{a0} by 50 per cent while holding constant α, and to increasing α by 50 per cent while holding constant W_{a0}. The two effects will correspond therefore to the two elasticities directly measured from functions (4.9) and (4.10). *Figure 4.8 shows schematically what these two changes imply as far as the shape of the profile is concerned. The first change involves a proportional increase of the whole profile, and corresponds to the sort of changes most frequently made in the real world (i.e. keeping constant the relative differentials between different scales in a given occupation). The second, on the other hand, involves only an increase in the slope, holding the starting level the same.*

Figure 4.9 shows the percentage effect of this type of change on individuals with different periods of service. The effect of a proportional increase in the whole profile is, as expected, the same irrespective of the years of service and equal to 50 per cent. The effect of an increase in the slope, on the other hand, is low for individuals with a short period of service and increases with experience.[15] *The difference between the two effects is therefore progressively smaller, the shorter the remaining working life of the individual. In this sense, and notwithstanding the reservations pointed out at the beginning of this section, we should expect two facts in our empirical regressions: first,*

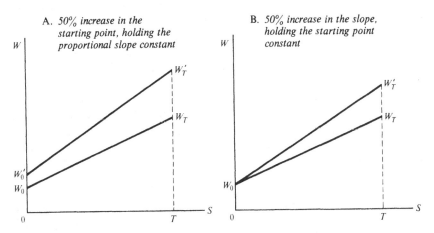

Figure 4.8   *Change in earnings profile.*

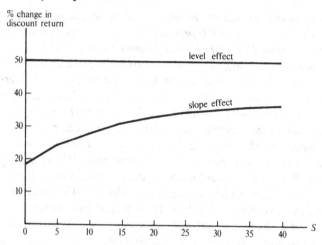

Figure 4.9   *Effect on discounted return for different periods of service* ($r = 10\%$).

the elasticity with respect to W_{a0} should be greater than the elasticity with respect to α for both new entrants and leavers; second, the difference between these two elasticities should be larger for new entrants than for leavers.

4.5 Specification of the entry and leaving equations

From an operational point of view, the variables that enter in the argument of functions (4.9) and (4.10) deserve further clarification. The subjective rate of discount (r) and the working time horizon (T), reflect personal characteristics of the individual making the occupational decision; the effect of these variables can then be best examined by standardising the supply response in accordance to differences in individuals with respect to these variables. In particular, *the separation of men from women in the measurement of wage elasticities seems to be a natural first approximation* in order to control for the effect of these two factors. Despite the fact that t_a and t_b also originate in personal assessments, it is plausible to assume that their level will be largely determined by circumstances outside the individual in question. In general, the subjective evaluation of the difficulties in obtaining jobs in a given occupation will be determined by the actual situation of the market, and its effect is likely to be quite uniform over all individuals. In this sense, it is sensible to introduce a proxy for this market situation – such as the rate of unemployment – as a variable entering in the above function.

We then specify the relative supply[16] to occupation A as a function depending on relative starting salaries (W_{a0}/W_{b0}), relative slopes of the earnings profile (α/β), and – assuming that there are no difficulties whatsoever in obtaining a job in occupation A – on the rate of unemployment (U).

The logarithmic specification used in the empirical analysis can be written as follows:[17,18]

$$\log (RS_a) = \eta_0 + \eta_1 \log \left[\frac{W_{a0}}{W_{b0}}\right] + \eta_2 \log \left[\frac{\alpha}{\beta}\right] + \eta_3 \log(U) \quad (4.11)$$

where RS_a stands for relative supply to occupation A, and the ηs (except η_0) are the different supply elasticities with respect to the corresponding variable. As mentioned above, η_1 and η_2 are direct measures of the effect on supply of changes in the profile such as those described in Section 4.4. In effect, η_1 is the elasticity of supply with respect to (W_{a0}/W_{b0}) holding constant (α/β) (and, of course, any other variable in the equation). That is, η_1 measures the effect on supply when the initial level of the profile is increased holding constant the proportional slope; such change corresponds precisely to a movement of the profile similar to that depicted in panel A of Figure 4.8. η_2, on the other hand, is the elasticity of supply with respect to (α/β) holding constant (W_{a0}/W_{b0}). That is, η_2 measures the effect on supply when the slope of the profile is increased, keeping the starting point constant, such as is shown in panel B of Figure 4.8.

In equation (4.11) the variables α and β are not directly observable, but they can be easily expressed in terms of available data on salaries. Given that the profile is assumed to be linear, the absolute slope can always be defined by two points of this profile. In Figure 4.10 we express this point diagrammatically for occupation A. The wage level at time $\bar{t}$ is $\overline{W}_a$; then the absolute slope of the profile A, $W_{a0}\alpha$, can be expressed as

$$W_{a0}\alpha = \frac{\overline{W}_a - W_{a0}}{\bar{t}}$$

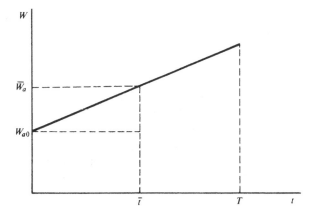

Figure 4.10.

from where it follows that the proportional slope is

$$\alpha = \frac{1}{t}\left(\frac{\overline{W}_a - W_{a0}}{W_{a0}}\right)$$

Similarly, for occupation B

$$\beta = \frac{1}{t}\left(\frac{\overline{W}_b - W_{b0}}{W_{b0}}\right)$$

Then substituting these two expressions in (4.11) we have

$$\log(RS_a) = \eta_0 + \eta_1 \log\left(\frac{W_{a0}}{W_{b0}}\right) + \eta_2 \log\left(\frac{(\overline{W}_a - W_{a0})/W_{a0}}{(\overline{W}_b - W_{b0})/W_{b0}}\right) + \eta_3 \log(U)$$

$$(4.12)$$

which is expressed in terms of directly observable variables.

In (4.12), because the time period at which $\overline{W}$ is defined is the same for both occupations, t cancels out. This is not strictly necessary; even if the time period chosen for each occupation was different, say $\overline{t}^a$ and $\overline{t}^b$, the constant fraction $\overline{t}^a/\overline{t}^b$, would be incorporated in the intercept, leaving the equation as it is, only with a different intercept. In such an event, however, we will require that both $\overline{t}^a$ and $\overline{t}^b$ be constant over the period over which (4.12) is estimated. That is, the $\overline{W}$s must always be measured at the same age level in the profile.

4.6 Implications of the model for the subjective rate of discount

Equation (4.11) will allow us to estimate the elasticity of supply with respect to the earnings profile and with respect to the rate of unemployment. Within the context of our model, these estimates have definite implications for the subjective rate of discount used by teachers.

For instance, if people use a high rate of discount, they will tend to respond strongly to changes in the probability of being unemployed in an alternative occupation – i.e. η_3 will be large. Due to their high discount rate, present earnings will matter much more for them than future earnings and they will therefore prefer to enter teaching (with immediate employment) than to face the risk of having to wait for a period before they start earning income. A similar line of reasoning can be applied to the earnings profile. People who respond strongly to the expectation of future earnings must use a lower discount rate than people who respond weakly to such expectations. A low η_2 is indicative of a weak response to increase in the slope of the earnings profile for a given starting point and would therefore imply a high discount rate. On the other hand a large η_2 would imply a lower discount rate.

In Appendix 4A we discuss how the elasticities shown by equation (4.11) can be used in order to obtain estimates of the subjective rate of discount used by teachers. We will in fact have two types of estimates – the one implied by the slope elasticity and the one implied by the unemployment elasticity – which do not necessarily have to be the same. The first will give us a measure of the rate of discount used by people who are earning income and who are responding to a redistribution of this income over time. The second will indicate the rate of discount used by people who are faced with the possibility of no income at all (being unemployed).

The rate of discount implied by the slope elasticity is

$$r = \alpha \left(\frac{\eta_1 - \eta_2}{\eta_2} \right) \tag{4.13}$$

which consistently with our previous discussion shows that, for a given level elasticity, the higher the slope elasticity is the lower will be the implied rate of discount ($\partial r/\partial \eta_2 < 0$). The rate of discount implied by the unemployment elasticity, on the other hand, can be approximated by

$$r = \left(\frac{\eta_3}{\eta_1} \right) 2 \, (\log U)^2 \tag{4.14}$$

which, also as expected, is higher the higher the unemployment elasticity ($\partial r/\partial \eta_3 > 0$).

5

New entrants

The aim of this chapter is to test the previous theoretical analysis against actual data on new teachers in England and Wales. In essence the hypothesis is that the proportion of school leavers and graduates choosing to become or to train as teachers depends on relative starting salaries, longer term salary prospects and relative job opportunities, and that the response is affected by the degree to which people value longer term prospects as opposed to immediate earnings. In particular we have predicted a more marked response by men than by women.

In the first section we analyse the flow of graduate new entrants to teaching. After a statistical description of the main trends, we present a summary of the results of the regression analysis, with empirical estimates of the supply elasticities with respect to wages and unemployment. Then we investigate the existence of possible differences in the supply response between graduates of different subject specialisms. In the second section we consider the flow of non-graduate new entrants, presenting a statistical overview of the proportion and quality of school leavers entering Colleges of Education and the proportion of newly trained teachers who in fact enter the profession. Finally the results for graduate and non graduate entrants to teaching are compared.

5.1 Graduate new entrants

5.1.1 *Preliminary analysis*

The number of university graduates entering teaching increased from 4,300 to nearly 12,000 between 1960 and 1973. This represented about 25 per cent of all graduates in 1960 and 28 per cent in 1973. Much of this increase was due to the increasing proportion of female graduates. There were, however, substantial year to year fluctuations and it is these that provide the main basis for our analysis. During the period under review some new graduates entered teaching directly ('untrained' graduates) and others ('trained' graduates) took a one-year postgraduate certificate of teacher training. For the proportion of untrained graduates entering teaching, the relevant denominator is the output of graduates one year before; while the base for the proportion of trained graduates is the output of university graduates two years before.[1] In our analysis we therefore adopt as a denominator a weighted average of the university output during those two years. Trends in these proportions are shown in Figure 5.1.

Our main hypothesis is that relative salaries and unemployment are two important variables in the determination of relative supply to a given occupation. Figure 5.2 shows trends in relative average salaries of teachers and unemployment rates among new graduates. Unemployment rates for newly trained teachers during this period were effectively zero, so it is legitimate to treat the trend in unemployment as indicative of relative changes in unemployment among teachers and other graduates.

It is difficult to discover the precise connection between these variables by simple inspection of the graphs; however, there are some general features which deserve to be considered. The more or less stable proportion of graduates entering teaching from 1960 to 1964 appears to be associated with the stable level of relative salaries up to 1963; the sharp decline in supply of the years 1965 and 1966, and the partial recovery in 1967 and 1968, show some relation to the fluctuating behaviour of salaries in the period 1964 to 1966. After 1968 supply decreases for one year and thereafter increases monotonically; this is in contradiction to the persistent deterioration of relative salaries up to 1970. However, it can probably be explained if we take into account the increases in unemployment among new graduates.

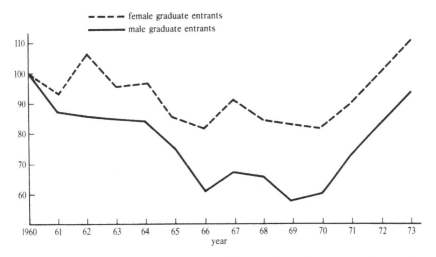

Figure 5.1 *Evolution of the proportion of university graduates entering teaching* (1960 = 100).

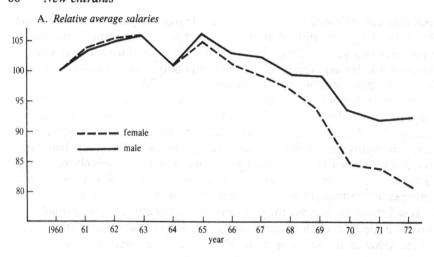

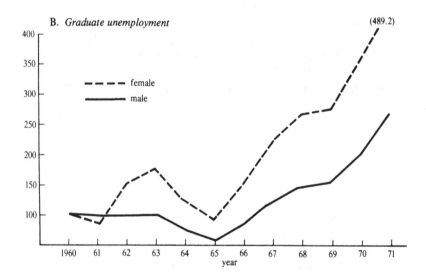

Figure 5.2 *Evolution of graduate relative salaries and graduate unemployment*
(1960 = 100).
Note: The 'unemployment' figures for graduates refer to the numbers not in
employment at the end of the year in which they graduate and as published
in UGC (annual). Although they are not strictly speaking unemployment
statistics, they do give a reasonable indication of the difficulty graduates
face in obtaining employment.

Graduates seem to have accepted a teaching post even with a low relative salary simply because alternative employment prospects were getting worse at the time.

5.1.2 *Operational specification of the model and data problems*

The regularities revealed by the data are consistent with our theoretical expectations, and suggest the existence of a relationship between relative supply, earnings and employment opportunities. We turn now to the econometric estimation of this relationship. The first part of this section discusses the data on which the estimation is based and this is followed by a description of the operational specification based on the theoretical model developed in Chapter 4.

The data used to estimate the model consist of a time series (years 1963–71) of graduates entering teaching from five different subject groups totalling 45 observations. The dependent variable (RS_{it} for relative supply) is defined as the proportion of university graduates of a particular subject group entering the teaching profession in a particular year.[2]

The data were obtained from a series of 5 per cent random samples of the graduate teacher population – one for each year of the period 1963–71 (see Appendix 5A). The five subject groups were classified in such a manner that all teachers would be included in the list. The criteria followed was twofold: first to obtain a reasonable number of observations for each of the divisions, and second to group subjects according to the similarity of their characteristics. The main subjects included in Group 1 were mathematics, physics, chemistry, and engineering; in Group 2, biology, geology, and biochemistry; in Group 3, French, German, and Spanish; in Group 4, English, history, and classics; and in Group 5, geography, education, and social sciences.

The number of university graduates was obtained from UGC, *First Employment of University Graduates* (UGC, 1972), following the same classification as the one used in the selection of the five subject groups. These data refer to student who qualified for first degrees in each of the corresponding subjects during the period 1 October to 30 September of each of the corresponding years.

We had the opportunity of obtaining data on salaries from different sources, and we defined three different measures of relative wages, all of which were later on used in the regression analysis. As far as data on teachers' salaries are concerned, we used the five per cent sample to obtain teaching average salaries (*TAW*), and DES, *Scales of Salaries for Teachers in Primary and Secondary Schools* (DES, annual –b), to obtain teaching starting salaries (*TSW*). As shown in Chapter 9, earnings differentials between subject groups are very small once age and other factors have been allowed for. We have therefore used the same average teacher salary for all subject groups.

For alternative salaries we used four main sources: the surveys on earnings of the Scientific and Professional Institutes;[3] the periodic information provided by the Department of Employment in its Gazette (DE, monthly); the *New Earnings Survey* (DE, annual); and, finally, a time series on starting salaries for graduates taken from the *Annual Reports* of the Leeds University Careers and Appointments Service.

The first source, although incomplete, is potentially interesting since it allows us to obtain, in conjunction with the *New Earnings Survey*, a subject specific measure of alternative average salaries (henceforth *AAW1*). The second measure for alternative average wages (*AAW2*) is the average annual earnings of non-manual workers. Finally, the series of alternative starting wages (*ASW*) were obtained from the *Annual Reports of the Leeds University Careers and Appointments Service*. The earnings of science graduates were considered as the alternative starting salaries for subject groups 1 and 2, and those of social sciences and arts for subject groups 3, 4 and 5.

Although we are aware of the different nature of these measures for alternative salaries, we thought it adequate to use them all in the regression analysis, so that the reader could have a comprehensive picture of the results obtained. The three different measures of relative salaries were defined as follows,[4]

Relative average wages

$$RAW1_{it} = TAW_{t-1}/AAW1_{it-1}$$
$$RAW2_t = TAW_{t-1}/AAW2_{t-1}$$

Relative starting wages

$$RSW_t = TSW_{t-1}/ASW_{t-1}$$

If an age-earnings profile is assumed to be linear, its slope can always be defined by identifying in addition to the starting salary one other point of the profile. As far as teaching is concerned this presents no problems, since we have at our disposal age specific salaries. For alternative occupations, however, our only data are starting and average salaries. This means that the second point of the alternative earnings profile will have to be the average salary. Therefore, in order to make the two slopes comparable, it was considered desirable to use average salaries as the second point of the teaching profile also. One problem still remains with this procedure. As discussed, in Ch. 4, we are interested in measuring the slope at the same age always. This constancy is likely to hold for the alternative measure, since over the nine-year period considered the age structure of the working population can be safely assumed constant. In teaching, on the other hand, these nine years have been a period of rapid expansion, which has tended to make the teaching population somewhat younger. To overcome this problem, we standardised for the changes in the teaching age structure by selecting for 1963 the age bracket in which the average wage falls, and by using that age bracket to determine the salary for all subsequent years. Let us denote this wage by *TBAW* (teaching bracket average wage), the teaching slope by *TS*, the alternative slope by *AS*,[5] and the relative slope differential by *K*; then we have,

$$K_t = \frac{TS_t}{AS_t} = \frac{(TBAW_{t-1} - TSW_{t-1})/TSW_{t-1}}{(AAW2_{t-1} - ASW_{t-1})/ASW_{t-1}}$$

The unemployment variable (U_{it}) is the proportion of graduates of the 'ith' group subject seeking permanent employment on 31 December of the year of graduation, as shown by the UGC *First Employment of University Graduates*. We should have liked to have used figures of unemployment amongst all graduates as an alternative variable, but these figures do not exist.

The three variants of the basic equation used in the regression analysis are,[6]

$$\log (RS_{it}) = a_0 + \text{subject dummies} + a_1 \log (RAW1_{it}) + a_2 \log (U_{it}) \quad (5.1)$$
$$\log (RS_{it}) = b_0 + \text{subject dummies} + b_1 \log (RAW2_t) + b_2 \log (U_{it}) \quad (5.2)$$
$$\log (RS_{it}) = c_0 + \text{subject dummies} + c_1 \log (RSW_t) + c_2 \log (K_t)$$
$$+ c_3 \log (U_{it}) \quad (5.3)$$

5.1.3 *Summary of the regression results*

The method by which we arrived at the final estimated specification of equations (5.1) (5.2) and (5.3) was as follows. In a first stage, we specified the equations with dummy variables for subject of study, both for the intercept and for the wage variables,[7] and we ran this specification by means of a stepwise regression method which would select variables according to their level of significance.

Once the set of dummies was selected, we obtained the lag structure of the wage and unemployment variables. It is plausible to expect that the effect of changes in the main economic variables (earnings and unemployment) will be subjected to several sorts of time lags. To start with, during most of the period we are analysing, the flow of graduate new entrants consisted of both those who entered directly from university and those who followed a one-year training course. The first group presumably makes its decision when entering the profession; the second makes two decisions: one when entering the training course, and another when actually taking up teaching. It would be reasonable to expect the effect of wages and unemployment to be distributed over time, if only on account of this institutional feature. However, other circumstances like availability of information and speed of response are likely to reinforce the delayed response of supply to changes in the relevant explanatory variables.

To estimate the lag structure, we followed the method proposed by Almon (1965) which assumes that the shape of the lag weights can be approximated by a polynomial. To select the final structure, we first tried unrestricted quadratic polynomials for both wage and unemployment variables. Then, according to the statistical significance of each coefficient, we imposed restrictions that resulted in the reduction of the number of lags considered, in the requirement that some weights be equal to zero, or even in the change of the degree of the polynomial. For relative wages and for the relative slope differential the resulting lag structures were linear, including two lags, and with the third lag constrained to be equal to zero; they were also common for male and female teachers. If we express the relative wage structure by RWL, and the relative slope structure by KL, we have that $RWL = 0.67RW_t + 0.33RW_{t-1}$, and $KL = 0.67K_t + 0.33K_{t-1}$. For the unemployment variable, the lag structures which best fitted the data were quadratic with both ends of the lag constrained to be equal to zero; for men the resulting structure was $UL = 0.5U_{t-3} + 0.5U_{t-4}$, whereas for women it included only the third lag of the variable; i.e. $UL = U_{t-3}$.

On the whole, these results are consistent with prior expectations about the workings of this market. This is especially so in the case of wages. Current wages should have the largest influence since they affect both untrained and trained entrants; one-period lagged wages on the other hand affect only trained entrants, and it is therefore reasonable that they should have a smaller weight than current wages in the lag structure. In the case of unemployment the results are more complex and cannot be so easily interpreted. It is clear, however, that they indicate a longer delay of response than in the case of wages.

Equations (5.1) to (5.3) were estimated by Ordinary Least Squares, and also b₁ Weighted least Squares methods to take into account the possibility of heteroscedastic errors. Equation (5.3) was run with the two slope coefficients unconstrained, and the validity of the restriction was tested by means of an F-test. The restrictions imposed by the lag structures were also tested by means of F-Test.[8]

The final results from the estimation of equations (5.1) to (5.3) were fairly encouraging for our hypotheses.[9] The coefficients on the dummy variables standardising for the different proportions of each subject group entering teaching were very much in accordance with what we would have expected. We considered Group 3 (modern languages) as a base, and in general we found that for males the only significant positive difference was that of Group 4 (classics); Group 1 (mathematics, chemistry, and physics) was not significantly different from the base group; and Groups 2 and 5 ('other sciences' and 'miscellaneous') were significantly negative. For women, on the other hand, Group 1 was, together with Group 4, higher than the intercept of the other three group subjects, thus confirming that female science graduates are, in relative terms, much more inclined to enter teaching than their male counterparts.

Table 5.1 summarises the earnings and unemployment elasticities found with each of the 3 equations employed. In the case of equation (5.1), the table shows that for male graduates a 10 per cent increase in teachers' average salaries relative to earnings in other subject specific white collar occupations will result in a 24 per cent increase in the proportion of male graduates entering teaching. For female graduates the corresponding response is much less – a 10 per cent increase in relative average salaries will result in only 3 per cent more new teachers. Although both these figures may be considered broadly of the right order and statistically significant, they should be treated with a great deal of care, due to the difficulties involved in the construction of the subject specific salary for alternative occupations.

The earnings elasticities of the second equation (5.2) are probably a little more reliable since they are based on a measure of alternative salaries which, although not subject specific, is a better reflection of both the

TABLE 5.1 *Summary of elasticities for graduate new entrants*

Elasticity with respect to	*Male*	*Female*
Equation (5.1)		
RAW1	2.4	0.3
	(4.5)	(2.4)
U	0.4	−0.0*
	(3.1)	(0.6)
Equation (5.2)		
RAW2	3.9	1.8
	(3.6)	(3.1)
U	0.4	0.2
	(3.2)	(2.1)
Equation (5.3)		
RSW	3.4	2.8
	(3.6)	(3.4)
K	1.6	0.4
	(2.4)	(1.9)
U	0.3	0.2
	(2.8)	(2.2)

Notes:
1. All elasticities are 'long-run' elasticities. The lag structure of each variable is specified in the text.
2. Figures in parentheses are absolute values of the *t*-statistic. Coefficients with one asterisk are *not* significantly different from zero at the 5 per cent level (one-tail test).

general evolution and level of earnings open to graduates outside the teaching profession. The elasticity estimates obtained with this new measure of relative salaries were somewhat larger than those given by the first specification (a 39 per cent increase in male supply and an 18 per cent increase in female supply from a 10 per cent increase in wages) and they were again significantly different from zero.

Results obtained with the two-variable measure of the earnings profiles (equation 5.3) were consistent with theoretical expectations; both the level and the slope variables took the right sign and were statistically significant, thus suggesting that relative differentials in earnings profiles may have a significant influence on occupational decisions. This was so both for males and females, although the latter showed a higher sensitivity with respect to the starting point and a lower sensitivity with respect to the slope. This is not surprising. Given their shorter working time horizon, it is natural that women would react less than men to changes in relative differences of career prospects. In effect, while men and women appear to react similarly to the level of the profile (around a 30 per cent increase in supply for a 10 per cent increase in the starting relative wage), men are about four times more sensitive than women to changes in the relative slope of the profile.

The estimated effect of alternative job opportunities on the supply of new entrants also corroborated our prior expectations.[10] We can safely conclude that the more difficult it is for university graduates to find alternative employment the larger will be the proportion choosing a teaching career, and that this effect will again be stronger for male than for female new entrants.

On the whole the present empirical evidence supports the hypotheses discussed in the previous chapter. Both men and women graduate new entrants respond to changes in relative wages and unemployment. Furthermore, the introduction of a more comprehensive measure of the earnings profile shows that prospective earnings are also a relevant factor. The expectation that men would have larger elasticities than women is borne out by the statistical analysis. By disentangling the supply response to earnings profiles we have also been able to arrive at a particularly interesting finding: women, albeit to a lesser extent than men, do also take into account career considerations in their occupational decisions; however, while men are relatively sensitive to changes in career prospects, women will place much more weight on changes in immediate earnings.

5.1.4 *Subject differences in response*

We examined differences in wage elasticity between subject groups by running the equations separately for each group.[11] In order to obtain a reasonable number of observations, we reduced the five groups to two: the first, Group A, includes Group 1 (mathematics, chemistry, and physics) and Group 2 (other sciences), and is called 'sciences'; the second, Group B, includes Group 3 (modern languages), Group 4 (classics) and Group 5 (miscellaneous), and is called 'arts'. Although substantially aggregated, these two basic divisions are of interest since they comprise two groups of people who, because of the different alternative opportunities they face in the general .labour market, should be expected to behave distinctively in their occupational decisions.

First we consider male graduate entrants. Table 5.2 summarises the results obtained. From inspection of the estimated elasticities, two general conclusions can be drawn about male graduate entrants to teaching. First, 'science' graduates appear to be very responsive to employment opportunities, while insensitive to wage changes. Second, 'arts' graduates are very responsive to wage changes, and insensitive to employment opportunities. All wage elasticities, except the one with respect to the slope, are significantly lower for 'science' graduates than for 'arts' graduates. Also, except for equation (5.1), all unemployment elasticities are larger for 'science' than for 'arts' graduates. This clear pattern implies that wage changes will be more likely to influence 'arts' graduates than 'science' graduates; employment opportunities, on the other hand, will influence the latter more than the former. Another interesting result concerns the slope of the profile; although 'science' graduates react less than 'arts' graduates to the wage levels, their responsiveness towards career prospects is similar.

The results for female graduate new entrants summarised in Table 5.3 are strikingly different but also follow a very well defined pattern. 'Science' graduates are the most responsive group both to salaries and to unemploy-

TABLE 5.2 *Subject differences in elasticities. Male graduate entrants*

Equations and variables	Group A('sciences') ($n = 18$)		Group B ('arts') ($n = 27$)	
Equation (5.1)				
RAW1	– 2.5**	(1.0)	5.9	(3.3)
U	0.6	(3.0)	0.3**	(1.3)
Equation (5.2)				
RAW2	1.6**	(1.0)	5.0	(3.1)
U	0.7	(3.6)	0.3*	(1.5)
Equation (5.3)				
RSW	0.4**	(0.2)	3.9	(2.7)
K	1.1**	(1.2)	1.6*	(1.3)
U	0.6	(3.4)	0.2**	(0.9)

Note:
Figures in parentheses are absolute values of the *t*-statistic. Coefficients with one asterisk are *not* significant at the 5 per cent level, and with two at the 10 per cent level (one-tail test).

TABLE 5.3 *Subject differences in elasticities. Female graduate entrants*

Equations and variables	Group A ('sciences') (n = 18)		Group B ('arts') (n = 27)	
Equation (5.1)				
RAW1	3.4	(2.4)	1.2**	(1.2)
U	0.5	(3.1)	−0.0**	(0.0)
Equation (5.2)				
RAW2	2.7	(2.9)	1.0**	(1.1)
U	0.5	(3.5)	−0.0**	(0.0)
Equation (5.3)				
RSW	2.7*	(1.6)	2.3*	(1.6)
K	1.1	(2.8)	0.2**	(0.5)
U	0.6	(3.6)	0.1**	(0.6)

Note: As for Table 5.2.

ment. This is a somewhat surprising result, but by no means unreasonable. Many female students in arts subjects already feel a vocational commitment to teaching and are strongly committed to it, irrespective of the level of wages and alternative job opportunities. As for men, the 'slope elasticity' is significantly greater for 'science' than for 'arts' graduates. Relative to other graduates, therefore, 'science' graduates, both male and female, appear to take career prospects very much into consideration in their occupational choices.

5.2 Non-graduate new entrants

5.2.1 *Preliminary analysis*

To a large extent, the rapid increase of teacher supply during the 1960s was made possible by the expansion of the Colleges of Education, and the concomitant rise in the flow of non-graduate new entrants. Although this rate of expansion was less than that of graduate entrants, the *number* of teachers involved was much larger.

In order to evaluate this expansion properly, we need to estimate the proportion of school leavers entering Colleges of Education and then to examine the 'quality' of this flow. The first and third columns of Table 5.4 show the number of male and female entrants to Colleges of Education as a percentage of qualified school leavers [12] (that is 'school leavers' with 5 or more 'O' levels or at least 1 'A' level). As can be seen in 1973, about 10 per cent of male qualified school leavers and 28 per cent of female qualified school leavers opted for Colleges of Education. Both percentages are only slightly higher than those in 1963, but over the period they underwent first a substantial increase – until 1967 and 1968 – and then a decline.[13] When we focus our attention on only those students with 2

TABLE 5.4 *Percentages of qualified school leavers entering Colleges of Education,
1963–73*

Year	Male		Female	
	All entrants	Entrants with 2 or more A levels	All entrants	Entrants with 2 or more A levels
	(1)	(2)	(1)	(2)
1963	8.8	6.7	25.0	27.9
1964	9.4	6.9	27.1	27.6
1965	9.7	6.6	29.5	27.8
1966	11.1	7.1	33.2	29.3
1967	11.6	7.3	35.6	29.5
1968	12.2	7.7	36.4	30.3
1969	11.5	7.4	33.8	28.9
1970	10.9	7.2	32.1	27.3
1971	11.6	7.6	32.1	26.5
1972	11.1	7.5	29.9	27.0
1973	9.5	6.8	27.7	24.9

Source: DES (annual – a).
Notes:
1. As a percentage of school leavers with 5 or more 'O' levels or at least 1 'A' level. Some entrants (generally older) are admitted 'exceptionally' and do not possess this level of qualification.
2. As a percentage of school leavers with 2 or more 'A' levels.

or more 'A' levels – that is, those who, in principle, could opt for a university education – the results are somewhat different. In the case of males, although the general pattern of the time evolution is the same as with the overall flow, the rates of change are much lower. The percentage at the end of the period is about the same as at the beginning and the maximum is reached in 1968 at a level only 12 per cent higher than at the beginning. In the case of females, not only are the rates of change lower, but also the general trend was down, not up, reaching in 1973 a level 10 per cent lower than in 1963. This second flow of entrants suggests that although there has been an expansion in the overall proportion of school leavers attracted into teaching, the quality of this intake has not increased.

Another way of considering the quality change is to compare directly the qualifications of entrants into Colleges of Education with the qualifications of school leavers. To this end we have constructed two indices of quality: Index 1 – The proportion of the 'qualified' with only one 'A' level; Index 2 – The proportion of the 'qualified' with 2 or more 'A' levels. (In this context 'qualified' means having 5 or more 'O' levels or at least 1 'A' level.)

These quality indices were constructed for College of Education entrants and all school leavers respectively and are presented in Tables 5.5 and 5.6. Index 1 gives us a rough idea of how well Colleges of Education have done compared with other forms of training below university level or with direct recruitment into other non-manual occupations, and Index 2 as compared with universities.

Among all male new entrants to Colleges of Education in 1973, 30 per cent held 1 'A' level, while among the comparable base of qualified school leavers, only 18 per cent had that qualification. For female new entrants, the percentage with 1 'A' level was almost 29 per cent, while the corresponding percentage among school leavers was 21 per cent. These larger percentages among entrants to Colleges of Education are not surprising. Over time, however, the quality of the Colleges of Education intake has not increased at the same rate as that of qualified school leavers in general. For males, the index in 1973 for school leavers was 35 per cent higher than in 1963, while for entrants to Colleges of Education it was only 14 per cent higher. For females, the difference is even greater; at the end of the period the index for school leavers was 47 per cent higher than at the beginning, while for college entrants only 8 per cent.

Has this relative loss been compensated by a relative gain in more qualified students? When we look at Index 2 showing the percentage of students with 2 or more 'A' levels, the answer appears to be, no. The general pattern is the same: the average quality of qualified school leavers as a whole increased more than the quality of the students entering teacher training.

TABLE 5.5   *Quality index 1, for qualified school leavers and entrants to Colleges of Education, 1963–73 (percentages)*

Year	Male		Female	
	School leavers (1)	Entrants to Colleges of Education (2)	School leavers (1)	Entrants to Colleges of Education (2)
1963	13.1	26.5	14.3	26.5
1964	13.7	26.9	14.7	26.4
1965	14.5	28.2	16.8	27.6
1966	15.5	28.4	17.5	27.8
1967	15.9	27.5	18.6	28.0
1968	16.5	27.8	19.6	28.1
1969	17.7	29.7	20.2	28.4
1970	17.9	28.9	19.4	28.3
1971	18.2	28.5	19.4	27.9
1972	17.8	29.8	20.9	29.1
1973	17.8	30.2	21.0	28.6

Source: DES (annual – a).
Notes:
1. The number of *school leavers with 1 'A' level* as a percentage of the number of school leavers with 5 or more 'O' levels or at least 1 'A' level.
2. The number of *entrants to Colleges of Education with 1 'A' level* as a percentage of the number of entrants to Colleges of Education with 5 or more 'O' levels or at least 1 'A' level.

TABLE 5.6   *Quality index 2, for qualified school leavers and entrants to Colleges of Education, 1963–73 (percentages)*

Year	Male School leavers (1)	Entrants to Colleges of Education (2)	Female School leavers (1)	Entrants to Colleges of Education (2)
1963	50.8	44.0	33.3	40.6
1964	51.8	43.0	35.2	40.3
1965	55.8	42.7	39.4	41.6
1966	56.4	40.5	40.1	41.3
1967	58.5	42.4	42.3	40.8
1968	58.5	42.1	42.8	41.1
1969	56.4	40.8	43.8	41.7
1970	56.7	41.3	44.9	42.0
1971	57.8	42.2	47.1	42.7
1972	55.8	42.2	44.8	43.6
1973	54.5	42.7	45.0	43.6

Source: DES (annual – a).
Notes:
1. The number of *school leavers with 2 or more 'A' levels* as a percentage of the number of school leavers with 5 or more 'O' levels or at least 1 'A' level.
2. The number of *entrants to Colleges of Education with 2 or more 'A' levels* as a percentage of the number of entrants to Colleges of Education with 5 or more 'O' levels or at least 1 'A' level.

Although the percentage of qualified male school leavers with 2 or more 'A' levels increased by only 8 per cent during the period, the percentage of College of Education entrants with those qualifications actually decreased. For women, the substantial increase of the index for school leavers (35 per cent) contrasts with a very small increase for College of Education entrants (7 per cent).

We then have a situation in which, while the educational sector produced a more qualified labour force year by year, the academic quality as measured by GCE results of the flow attracted to Colleges of Education remained, on the whole, remarkably constant. This is so not only for those students who could have opted for a university degree but also for those whose most likely alternative to Colleges of Education is entering the labour force directly. In the light of this evidence we must then conclude that although in absolute terms the academic quality of students training for teachers remained stable, in relative terms it decreased.

5.2.2 *Operational specification of the model*

Before attempting to specify the supply curve we must consider the possibility that the data we are observing may to some extent reflect demand rather than supply conditions. In the graduate entry exercise we assumed that this problem was not present, because of the generally acknowledged excess demand for graduates during the period under study. In the case of school leavers, however, it is important to be specific about whether the number of entrants to Colleges of Education was determined by the willingness of school leavers to take up a teaching career, or whether it was determined by the number of places made available. Our working hypothesis will be that the expansion of Colleges of Education was the effect, rather than the cause, of the increased number of qualified people willing to train as a teacher and, therefore, that the data on entrants and on wages belong to a supply curve. We recognise that this is a strong assumption and in the light of what we know about the history of the Colleges of Education in the mid 1960s, it is difficult to substantiate from documentary evidence. However it can be argued that government decisions to increase the number of training places were made in the belief that there were adequate qualified students to fill them.

A better approach would be to look at data on *applicants* rather than on *entrants* to Colleges of Education. There is, however, a problem with this data; only a part of the total number of applicants are genuine, the rest being an insurance policy made only to cover the possibility of non-acceptance at universities. Given this difficulty, we decided to confine our analysis to entrants and treat this data as a proxy for applicants. Another problem is that applicants differ in their qualifications. To assert that the number of *entrants* and their educational composition reflect the number of *applicants* and their educational composition amounts to making the further assumption that the proportion of applicants of each qualification level accepted by Colleges of Education remained constant.

The timing of the occupational decisions taken by non-graduate potential teachers is different from that of graduate new entrants. Essentially there are two periods during which the non-graduate entrant chooses among different career possibilities. First, when finishing school and deciding whether or not to apply to a College of Education; and second, three years later, when finishing his basic training and deciding whether or not to enter the teaching profession. We would expect the second decision to be much less sensitive than the first to economic circumstances and other explanatory variables since by then the individual has committed himself to quite a considerable extent, by having undergone three years of fairly specific training.

In essence the method followed to arrive at earnings and unemployment elasticities for non-graduate new teachers can be summarised as follows.[14] We specified a supply equation stating that the proportion of qualified school leavers undergoing teacher training is a function of relative earnings and job opportunities, and that these variables exert an influence both at the point of entry into Colleges of Education and at the end of College courses. To find out the lag structure with which these variables affect supply at these two points, we first run partial equations for both the proportion of qualified school leavers entering Colleges of Education and the proportion of trained teachers actually entering the profession; we then incorporated these lags into the final supply equation explaining the proportion of school leavers entering teaching.

5.2.3 *Summary of the regression results*

The preliminary estimates at the two points of entry were extremely weak, especially as far as female non-graduate new entrants are concerned. For this category of teacher we found that neither earnings nor job opportunities affected the proportion of school leavers entering Colleges of Education, let alone the proportion of those female trained teachers entering the profession. For men, on the other hand, although the preliminary estimates of the structural equation were statistically not very reliable, those of the final supply function indicated that although unemployment was not a relevant variable, earnings did exert some significant influence in the decision to enter the profession.

We summarise in Table 5.7 the final estimated wage elasticities with their respective confidence intervals. The male elasticities incorporate the effect of wages at both points of entry while those of females are based on the effect of wages at the point of entry to Colleges of Education only. It should be noted that the time period over which the non-

TABLE 5.7   *Summary of wage and earnings profile elasticities for non-graduate new entrants*

Elasticity with respect to	Male	Female
Equation (5.2)		
RAW	1.6	−0.1*
	(2.0)	(0.2)
Equation (5.3)		
RSW	4.2	−0.1*
	(5.0)	(0.2)
K	1.2	0.2*
	(5.1)	(0.7)

Notes:
1. All elasticities are 'long-run' elasticities. The lag structures for males include four values of the corresponding variable (t, $t - 1$, $t - 5$ and $t - 6$), and their weights are indicated in footnote 15. Those of females only include one value of the corresponding variable ($t - 4$).
2. Figures in parentheses are absolute values of the t-statistic. Coefficients with one asterisk are *not* significant at the 5 per cent level (one-tail test).

graduate elasticities apply is different from that of the graduate category, and therefore they are not exactly comparable.[15] However, in general the results conform to our expectations. In terms of their short-run impact (change in supply over the first year) graduate elasticities are always larger than non-graduate elasticities. For instance, the short-run elasticity with respect to starting wages is 2.3 for male graduate new entrants, and only 1.0 for male non-graduate new entrants. On the whole, male non-graduate new entrants are also sensitive to wage changes. For female non-graduates, on the other hand, we have not been able to find any significant influence of earnings. These results should be treated with some care, given the simplicity of the present exercise; however, they lend support to the framework for the analysis of occupational choice proposed in Chapter 4.

5.3. Estimation of the subjective rate of discount

As discussed in Chapter 4, our elasticity estimates have definite implications about the subjective rates of discount used by potential teachers. In this section we evaluate expressions (4.13) and (4.14) derived in Chapter 4 with the entry elasticities estimated above.

Table 5.8 shows the estimated rates of discount for graduate teachers and for non-graduate males. Given the insignificant results obtained for non-graduate females, we have not attempted to calculate the rates of discount for this category of teacher. The first column shows the rates implied by the slope elasticity; they have been calculated using expression (4.13) and the parameter α has been fixed at its mean value.[16] The figures obtained are very reasonable, both in terms of their magnitude and in terms of their relative ordering. Graduate males appear to have the lowest discount rate, as we would have expected from their relatively high response to expectations and increased earnings in later life. Female graduates, on the other hand, seem to use a fairly high discount rate (33%). This is again a plausible finding if we take into account the relatively short time that, on average, they remain in the profession. In other words, future earnings will be heavily discounted when making any occupational decision because in many cases there will be little expectation of ever obtaining them. For the same reason current earnings will figure prominently in their calculations and will

TABLE 5.8   *Estimated subjective rates of discount*

	Implied by the slope elasticity	Implied by the unemployment elasticity
Graduate males	8%	183%
Graduate females	33%	176%
Non-graduate males	15%	–

elicit a much stronger response from women in terms of occupational choice.

The second column of Table 5.8 shows the rates of discount implied by our estimated unemployment elasticities, which have been calculated with expression (4.14).[17] Since we could not estimate any significant response of non-graduate males to the rate of unemployment, it is not possible to evaluate their discount rate. The first thing to notice about the rates for graduate teachers is their much larger size than those implied by the slope elasticity. There are several factors that could explain this finding. One explanation could be that our estimates of the unemployment elasticity are excessively large, from which we ought to conclude that not too much weight can be placed on these figures (or for that matter, on the unemployment elasticities themselves). A second explanation could be the assumptions made about the way in which our theoretical variable t_b (expected duration of unemployment) is related to our empirical proxy U (rate of unemployment). Finally, a third explanation would justify the above rates of discount with reference to the particular situation in which they are likely to be used. If people are faced with the possibility of no income (being unemployed) they will use a very high rate of discount. On the other hand, if they are expecting some income in every period, the relative value of present income will be less. This would explain the difference between the rates implied by the unemployment elasticity on the one hand and the slope elasticity on the other.

More difficult to justify is the reversal in order between males and females as compared with the discount rates obtained with the slope elasticities. In principle we would have expected that the shorter working horizon of women would also affect their decisions concerning the choice 'employment/ unemployment', and would make them respond quite strongly to changes in the probability of being unemployed. The rates shown above indicate, on the other hand, that as far as unemployment is concerned, males and females discount the future in very similar terms. A possible reason for this similarity might be that, while women take into account their shorter working horizon, men take into account other factors such as career prospects which in the end make them as responsive as women to the possibility of being unemployed. The fact that noticeable unemployment spells can have detrimental effects on career prospects, may be the reason for the strong response to unemployment found for men and therefore for the implied high discount rates.[18]

6

Leavers

During the period covered by our empirical analysis the problem of 'wastage' was considered to be one of the main teacher supply problems.

Experience in the 1950s and 1960s showed how critically teacher supply planning is at the mercy of changes, which may occur quickly, in the rate at which teachers leave the profession. Future wastage rates, which may be powerfully influenced by demographic or economic factors, cannot be predicted with confidence but will have immediate effects. Wastage is and will remain an element of major uncertainty [DES, 1973].

The aim of this chapter is to help to reduce this uncertainty. The basic hypothesis we examine is that relative earnings and unemployment rates have a predictable influence on leaving rates.

6.1 Preliminary analysis

There are three broad definitions of leavers that might be used. First there is 'total leavers' which would comprise all teachers who were in service in maintained primary and secondary schools on 1 April one year and who were not on 31 March the following year.[1] This includes, however, a large and relatively easily predictable number who simply retire from work. There is some uncertainty because various superannuation provisions make it possible for some men to retire before the age of 65, and some men and women remain in the profession beyond the official retirement age. Such leavers are obviously of some importance as a planning instrument in a situation of surplus supply of teachers, such as is being experienced in the mid 1970s. They are not, however, readily susceptible to economic analysis and were not as important in the period under review. We have, therefore, concentrated on leavers below the age of 60 in the analysis of this chapter.

This group then forms our second definition of leavers. Included in this definition, as in the previous one, are teachers who transfer to other branches of grant-aided education outside the maintained primary and secondary sector (including further education and Colleges of Education, but excluding universities). Clearly this definition is of relevance to those planning teacher supply in primary and secondary schools, and this definition which we have called the 'gross leaving rate' was examined in some of the analyses reported below.

The final definition we have called the 'net leaving rate', and this refers to those teachers who voluntarily cease their employment in maintained primary or secondary schools and who do not transfer to other branches of grant-aided education. This is the definition on which most of the subsequent analysis is based.

Figure 6.1 compares the changes over time between the 'gross rate of leavers' and the 'net rate of leavers'. There is an evident difference between men and women: while the rate of female transfers remains practically constant throughout the period, the rate of male transfers shows much more variation and a much higher level. Panel A also suggests the marked decrease of the male gross rate of leavers during the last four years of the period is to a large extent due to the decline of transfers to other educational sectors, rather than to a fall of the number of teachers leaving the profession. In

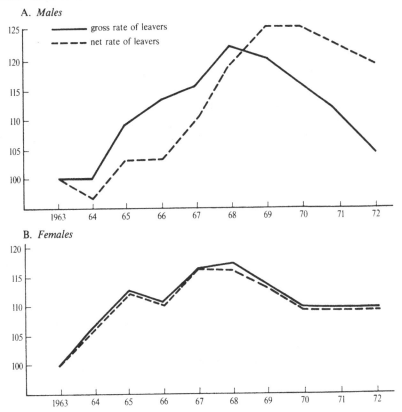

Figure 6.1   *Rate of leavers from the profession* (1963 = 100).
Note: The index is of the proportion of teachers in service at the beginning of the year who had left teaching by the end of the year.

effect, as can be seen from the evolution of the net rate of leavers, although there is still some decline, this appears much later and it is much weaker than when transfers are not excluded.

So far we have considered only the overall rate of leavers. However, teachers whose training is specifically orientated towards teaching probably have fewer opportunities of work elsewhere than those who are more generally trained, and are therefore likely to be less inclined to leave the teaching profession. In terms of human capital theory, teachers with specific training will have a considerably higher productivity inside teaching than outside, and the wages they will be able to obtain in the profession will be larger than those offered by alternative employments. For teachers with more general training, on the other hand, earnings opportunities inside and outside teaching will be similar. It is difficult to find instances of workers with either purely specific or purely general training. All workers embody in their training both specific and general elements, the difference between them being a matter of degree. Non-graduate teachers are probably those with the highest component of specific training, followed by trained graduates, and finally by untrained graduates. If this argument is correct, we should expect to find the lowest rates of leavers for non-graduates, and the highest rates for untrained graduates.[2] As can be seen in Table 6.1, this is precisely what the empirical evidence shows. The leaving rate of trained graduates is always closer to that of non-graduates than of untrained graduates; for men, while the first two categories have rates which oscillate between 4 and 6 per cent, the latter category reaches levels as high as 12 per cent. Another interesting feature brought out in Table 6.1 is the relatively

TABLE 6.1   *Leavers from the profession by category of training, 1963–72 (percentages)*

	1962–63	1963–64	1964–65	1965–66	1966–67	1967–68	1968–69	1969–70	1970–71	1971–72
					Males					
Non-graduate	3.7	3.4	3.8	4.0	4.1	4.4	4.3	4.3	4.2	3.9
Trained graduate	4.5	4.7	5.3	5.4	5.8	5.7	5.6	5.6	5.4	5.1
Untrained graduate	9.7	10.8	11.7	11.4	11.7	12.5	12.2	10.7	10.2	9.5
					Females					
Non-graduate	10.0	10.7	11.3	10.9	11.6	11.5	11.1	10.8	10.7	10.8
Trained graduate	10.1	10.6	11.6	11.6	11.3	12.6	12.7	12.8	13.7	13.2
Untrained graduate	21.3	21.8	21.8	23.0	23.8	24.1	23.3	22.1	21.4	19.1

Source: DES (annual – a).
Notes: Only teachers younger than 60 have been considered.

small decrease in the leavers rate for non-graduates and trained graduates since 1967–68 as compared with that of untrained graduates.

A negative relationship between worker mobility and age has been clearly established across very different occupations. Reynolds (1951) explains this regularity in terms of the concept of 'job shopping'. In a world in which information is imperfect, young workers find a satisfactory job only by a process of trial and error. At any moment, therefore, younger people are more likely than older people to be changing jobs. Becker (1964), on the other hand, provides an explanation placing the emphasis on the investment element involved in the decision to move. If

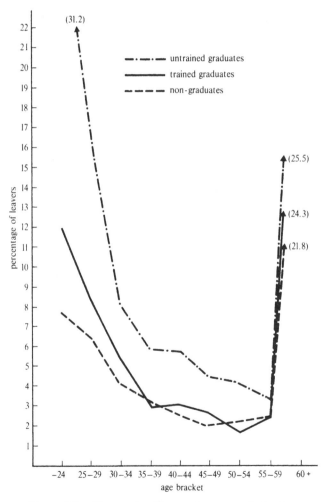

Figure 6.2 *Gross rate of leavers by age: male teachers.*

changing job is interpreted as an investment in human capital, then younger people have a greater incentive to move, inasmuch as they will be able to collect the return over a longer period of time. The second theory does not conflict with the first. The activity of 'job shopping' is after all an act of investment directed to increase the value of one's human capital. This becomes clear as soon as we realise that the objective of the shopping activity is just to find that job in which the individual's human capital will produce the highest return.

Figures 6.2 and 6.3 show, for 1972, leaving rates by age, categories of

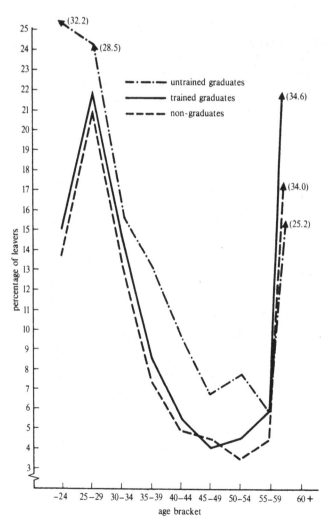

Figure 6.3   *Gross rate of leavers by age: female teachers.*

training, and sex. The expected relationship appears conclusively in the case of men. As can be seen, the age profile of the rate of leavers takes a conspicuous U-shape. The rate declines throughout up to the last (or in some cases the last but one) age bracket and then, due to retirements, rises very sharply again. The figure shows also that untrained graduates have higher rates than the other two categories at all ages. It is worth noting, however, that above the age of 30, the difference is considerably reduced.

The age leaving profile of female teachers does not quite conform to the U-shape. With the exception of untrained graduates, peak leaving rates occur not in the youngest age groups but between the ages of 25 to 29. Subsequently, the behaviour of the profile is similar to that for men, with the only difference that there is a larger proportion of women retiring before the age of sixty. These leaving patterns are strongly influenced by marriage and child bearing, and we know that a large proportion of women teachers seek to return to the profession later on in their life. Untrained female graduates conform more closely to the male pattern. Although the rate in the bracket 25–29 is high (28.5 per cent) the rate in the first bracket is still higher at 32.2 per cent. This seems to confirm the very low degree of attachment of young untrained graduates to teaching found among men.

6.2 Empirical specification and summary of the regression results

Having examined the main characteristics of those teachers who leave the profession, we now turn to the estimation of equations describing the response of those leavers to relative salaries and unemployment. The set of data used consist of a time series (years 1963–72) of cross sections (8 age groups) totalling 80 observations. The dependent variable, leaving rate (RL_{it}), is defined as the proportion of teachers in the ith age group leaving the teaching profession during the year t.[3] If L_{it} is the number of leavers in the age group i during the period t, and S_{it} is the total number of teachers in this age group at the beginning of the period, our dependent variable can be expressed as follows:

$$RL_{it} = \frac{L_{it}}{S_{it}}$$

We used three different measures of relative salaries. The first $(RAW1)$ is an age specific relative average wage. Given that age specific data on alternative salaries do not exist for the period under study, we estimated these data on the basis of information given for the year 1966–67 in the survey of earnings of qualified manpower carried out by the Department of Education and Science (DES, 1971 – b).[4] The second $(RAW2)$ is the relative average wage as defined in Chapter 5, and the third is the two-parameter representation of the earnings profile – starting point (RSW) and slope (K) – and is also defined as in Chapter 5. Alternative job opportunities are represented by the general rate of unemployment (U). To take into account the effect of age on the rate of leaving, we included in the leavers equation a set of dummy variables representing the nine 5-year age groups in which the data was sub-divided (0–24 to 55–59). The first age group – under 24 – was taken as a base; therefore the coefficients on all the other age groups (variables $D2$ to $D8$, in appendix 6B) express the differential effect of age as compared with the youngest teachers. Given that our emphasis is on voluntary terminations of employment other than those due to retirement, we have excluded from our analysis teachers older than 60.

The three variants of equation (4.12) to be used in the regression analysis are:

$$\log (RL_{it}) = d_0 + \text{age dummies} - d_1\log (RAW1_{it}) - d_2\log (U_t) \quad (6.1)$$
$$\log (RL_{it}) = l_0 + \text{age dummies} - l_1\log (RAW2_t) - l_2\log (U_t) \quad (6.2)$$
$$\log (RL_{it}) = f_0 + \text{age dummies} - f_1\log (RSW_t) - f_2\log (K_t) - f_3\log (U_t) \quad (6.3)$$

A first exercise consisted of estimating (6.1), (6.2) and (6.3) using as a dependent variable the 'gross rate of leavers'. The results obtained were extremely poor. Although with the correct sign in most cases, neither relative wages nor unemployment appeared to have much influence. It is not surprising that this first attempt should have proved so unsuccessful. By considering the 'gross rate of leavers' as the dependent variable we were trying to explain at the same time two different flows: the 'net rate of leavers' and the 'rate of transfers' to other educational sectors. While the first may be explained in terms of changes in relative salaries and alternative job opportunities, the second is clearly linked with the expansion of other educational sectors such as Colleges of Education and further education colleges. In fact, these other educational sectors could be considered more as a part of the teaching 'internal market' than as forming an altogether separate market; transfers then could be seen not as a movement out of the profession, but rather as a natural extension of the teachers' careers.

The plausibility of this hypothesis is reinforced by the empirical results obtained when using the 'net rate of leavers' as dependent variable. In effect, as soon as transfers are excluded, the performance of the regressions improves substantially, and relative wages and unemployment become very significant in most of the cases.

In estimating (6.1) to (6.3) we followed the same procedure as with new entrants (Chapter 5).[5] The equations were estimated both by Ordinary and by Weighted Least Squares; equation (6.3) was run with the coefficients of the two slope factors unconstrained, and the validity of the restriction was tested by means of an F-test. A selection of the detailed regressions are shown in Appendix 6B, and the main elasticity results are summarised in Table 6.2.

TABLE 6.2 *Summary of wage earnings profile elasticities for the leaving equation,*

Elasticity with respect to	Male	Female
Trained graduates		
Equation (6.1)		
RAW1	−3.0	−0.7
	(7.2)	(3.8)
Equation (6.2)		
RAW2	−2.4	−0.6
	(7.5)	(4.4)
Equation (6.3)		
RSW	−2.6	−0.7
	(7.9)	(3.7)
K	−1.2	−0.1
	(6.6)	(2.1)
Untrained graduates		
Equation (6.1)		
RAW1	−1.0	−0.1**
	(2.5)	(0.6)
Equation (6.2)		
RAW2	−0.6	−0.1**
	(1.9)	(0.5)
Equation (6.3)		
RSW	−1.4	−0.2**
	(4.4)	(0.8)
K	−0.2**	0.1**
	(1.2)	(1.1)
Non-graduates		
Equation (6.1)		
RAW1	−2.1	−0.2*
	(7.5)	(1.6)
Equation (6.2)		
RAW2	−1.5	−0.1**
	(7.4)	(1.1)
Equation (6.3)		
RSW	−1.6	−0.1**
	(6.6)	(0.5)
K	−0.9	0.1**
	(8.8)	(1.1)

Note:
Figures in parentheses are absolite values of the *t*-statistic. Coefficients with one asterisk are *not* significant at the 5 per cent level and with two, at the 10 per cent level (one-tail test).

Following the method described in the previous chapter, several lag structures were tried for both the salary and the unemployment variables. For male leavers, however, employment proved to be very insignificant in all specifications and was dropped from the regression. The effect of relative salaries, on the other hand, appears to be felt much more quickly than in the case of new entrants. Only the current value of the salary variable had a significant effect on leavers. In general, the hypothesis is very well corroborated, and practically all the variables appear with the expected sign.

(i) *Men.* Wages have a well determined impact on the rate of male trained graduate leavers. The three alternative measures all support our hypothesis that relative pay is a relevant factor in the decision to leave teaching. The elasticity with respect to the two average measures of salaries (*RAW1* and *RAW2*) is very similar, in the region of -2.5. When using the two-parameter representation of the earnings profile (equation 6.3), the elasticity with respect to the level of the profile is practically equal to that using average salaries alone, but in addition we have a very significant effect of the relative slope variable, with an elasticity above unity. This result corroborates our contention that the shape of the salary profile is a relevant variable, not only in the decision to enter teaching, but also in the decision whether to leave the profession.

For untrained graduates, the fit of the three equations is again very good, but the response to change in salaries shows some differences from that of trained graduates. The size of the elasticities is much smaller; the elasticities with respect to *RAW1* and *RAW2* are respectively -0.97 and -0.57. In the two-variable specification the elasticity with respect to the level is also lower than in the case of trained graduates (-1.40), and the slope elasticity is not significant. These results suggest that salaries have a smaller influence in the leaving decision of untrained graduates, and that furthermore, career prospects do not appear to have any influence.

Despite the more specific nature of their training, and the fewer alternative opportunities open to non-graduate teachers, changes in salaries are also a relevant variable in their leaving decision. In all specifications the wage variables appear with the expected sign and are statistically very well determined. The elasticities with respect to *RAW1* and *RAW2* are -2.11 and -1.54 respectively, and those with respect to level and slope -1.58 and -0.94. Although lower than the elasticities of trained graduates, they indicate that the loss of this category of teacher is more sensitive to wages than that of untrained graduates. These results, together with the ones found for the flow of new entrants, are encouraging, for they constitute evidence that as far as the economic influences on decisions about the profession are concerned, the behaviour of non-graduates is not substantially different from that of their graduate colleagues.

(ii) *Women*. The second column of Table 6.2 presents the earnings elasticities for female teachers leaving the profession. On the whole, we have only been able to detect significant influence of earnings on female trained graduates. For this category at least, we are reasonably certain that, once age effects have been taken into account, economic variables play a role in their decision to leave. On the other hand, their wage elasticity is much lower than that for men. The elasticities with respect to the two measures of relative average salaries are approximately a quarter of those of male trained graduates (-0.74 and -0.59). In the two-variable specifications, the level of the profile exerts a similar influence (-0.75), but relative career prospects, as measured by the variable K do not appear to have a strong influence, the effect being much smaller than for entrants.

The other two categories of female leavers appear even more insensitive to changes in earnings, giving the poorest results as far as our theoretical hypotheses are concerned. The belief that family reasons may play an important role in women's decisions is supported by the present evidence, and could explain, to some extent, the poorer performance of the equations.

Unlike male teachers, female teachers appear to be quite strongly influenced by unemployment elsewhere, this being so for all categories of training (an elasticity around the level -0.2). We believe that this result is related to the position of women as secondary earners in the present social organisation. When unemployment increases and job opportunities for their husbands are scarce, decisions concerning marriage or child-birth can be postponed; furthermore, even if these sorts of questions are not envisaged, depressed economic conditions will make the wife's salary an element of insurance against the possibility of a loss of the husband's earnings. These factors are likely to be quite specific to married women teachers, which means that in addition to the normal effect that changes in unemployment may have on the probability of finding an alternative job, the leaving decision of female teachers will *also* be influenced by their accommodating role within the family unit.

6.3 Conclusions

Looking at the leavers exercise as a whole, we may conclude that earnings variables have an important effect, in particular as far as male teachers are concerned. Among this group we find that trained graduates are more sensitive to changes in salary variables than either of the other two categories; this is true not only of relative salaries, but also of earning prospects. The two-year period which on average had been used to renegotiate salaries during the period under study fits very neatly with such behaviour and explains the oscillatory pattern of leaving rates described in Section 6.1. After each renegotiation the relative improvement in the level of teachers' salaries induces a decline in leavers; this improvement, however, deterio-rates progressively during the settlement period, due to the rise in alternative salaries, and causes the number of leavers to increase in the following year. Untrained male graduates particularly, and non-graduates to a lesser extent, also exhibit high elasticities with respect to wages. It is interesting to note the pattern in which the level of training and the level of wage elasticities are related. The absolute value of the wage elasticities always follows the ordering: trained graduates, non-graduates, untrained graduates. In prin-ciple, given the low level of specificity involved in their training, we would have expected untrained graduates to display the highest elasticity, followed by trained graduates and non-graduates. The fact that this is not so com-bined with the high level of leavers for this category leads us to believe that many untrained graduates simply considered teaching merely as a stepping stone towards other employment. However, with the change in regulations since 1969 this category of teacher is rapidly disappearing.

Women teachers show in general a much lower response to wages than men. With the exception of trained graduates, female teachers appear in-sensitive to salaries in their decisions about leaving teaching, be it in terms of changes in the slope of the earnings profile or in terms of changes in its level, but we suspect that this is partly due to a misspecification in the equa-tion. Even for trained graduates, the level of the elasticities is very small; in particular that with respect to career prospects, which although significant is not very different from zero (-0.1). However, the effect of unemployment is marked. We have suggested that this result may be related to the secondary earner role played by women within the context of the family. It is difficult to be more precise about this question on the basis of our present exercise; however, the consistency of this pattern for all categories of training sug-gests the existence of a very well rooted behavioural difference between men and women teachers in situations of widespread unemployment.[6]

One of the theoretical results of Chapter 4 was that the difference between the level and the slope effect on the discounted return of an individual should be larger at the entry point than at any other point in his career. Although strictly speaking we cannot apply this conclusion to elasticities, it is interesting to look at what our estimates indicate in this respect. The category of teachers for which this conclusion most clearly holds is non-graduate teachers. Both for males and for females the difference between these two effects is much smaller for leavers than for new entrants, not only in an absolute sense, but also in relative terms. For graduate teachers the results are somewhat more ambiguous. In absolute terms the difference, as predicted, is always larger for new entrants than for leavers, but in relative terms the difference is about the same for both categories. One possible explanation for this result could be the much larger proportion of young leavers among graduates (especially untrained) than among non-graduates. If this is taken into account, then it is quite plausible to expect that the effect of changes in the slope of the profile relative to the effect of changes in its level, should be similar for the flows of new entrants and leavers.

7

Inter-school and inter-regional mobility of teachers

There is an ambiguity about the economic and educational value of mobility. Within the context of a competitive market the economic function of labour mobility is to ensure that workers move to those assignments where they are most productive. According to this view, teachers would move to the schools where they are most needed. In some respects such a mechanism is fairly obviously in operation. If a particular school has vacancies in senior posts it may recruit junior staff from other schools to fill them. If we assume that seniority is in some way related to the value of the post to the education service, this kind of mobility has the effect of improving the efficiency of utilisation of the stock of teachers available at any point in time. The ambiguity occurs because changes in staffing may have detrimental effects on the education of pupils. It is widely believed, though the empirical evidence is slight, that pupils in schools which experience frequent changes of teaching staff perform less well for that reason than pupils in schools where the composition of the staff is more stable.

A study of internal mobility of teachers is therefore both an aspect of our overall examination of the supply of teachers *and* a subject that is worth studying in its own right since, if institutional arrangements or salary scales can be organised so that the same degree of efficiency in the distribution of the stock of teachers is achieved with less movement, there would probably be an educational gain. There is, however, an added complication in that, even from an educational point of view, some mobility may be useful in encouraging movement of ideas and reducing the self-centredness of staff common rooms.

In essence, our hypothesis is that, as with teachers entering and leaving the profession, changes in the numbers moving within the profession can be explained at least in part by economic incentives and particularly by differentials in salaries and career prospects.

7.1 Inter-school mobility

7.1.1 *Some facts about inter-school mobility*

Throughout the period we are studying, approximately 1 in 5 teachers left their school each year (Table 7.1). It is difficult to judge this level in terms

TABLE 7.1   *School turnover, 1963–72 (percentages)*

	1962–63	1963–64	1964–65	1965–66	1966–67	1967–68	1968–69	1969–70	1970–71	1971–72
Remained in the same school	84.6	80.7	81.1	73.5	79.1	77.3	77.4	79.3	78.4	79.3
Moved school	8.2	9.6	10.0	16.7*	11.0	11.2	12.2	10.9	11.0	11.2
Leavers and transfers	7.1	9.7	9.0	9.4	9.8	11.4	10.4	9.7	10.5	9.5
Total stock at the beginning of the year (= 100%)	2,708	2,726	2,754	2,808	2,845	2,918	2,974	3,104	3,273	3,436

Source: 1 per cent sample.
Note:
*School turnover figures for the year 1965–66 are distorted because of local government reorganisation in the London region (creation of the GLC). During this year, many teachers were coded as having changed school because their school code number changed, the school having come under a new Local Education Authority.

of strictly objective criteria, although from an educational point of view it was usually regarded as too high. However, taking into account the growing concern up to 1974 about the high rate of school turnover,[1] it is somewhat surprising to find that turnover rates only marginally increased over the ten-year period. This 20 per cent of teachers who leave their school in any one year is divided equally between those leaving the maintained school sector and those simply moving school. It is the latter 10 per cent that we are investigating in this chapter and Table 7.2 shows that this group again divides equally between those who stay in the same local education authority (*MSCH*) and those who move further afield (*MLEA* and *MREG*).

Table 7.3 breaks down the rates of school mobility in primary and secondary schools by sex. Over the whole period the rates of school mobility showed an upward trend for all categories, with female teachers showing the largest increase.

It is somewhat surprising to find that men moved school more than women in primary schools, whereas women moved more than men in secondary schools; furthermore, when graduate teachers only are considered, these relationships are completely reversed. It would appear plausible to expect the behaviour of men and women over a reasonable span of time to follow some definite and stable pattern irrespective of sector and qualifications. We would expect women to move more than men – married women in particular might be expected to orientate their movements not only in accordance with their own interests but also in accordance with the interests of their husbands, who are usually the main source of earnings in the family. At least, this would be so if other factors affected both men's movements and women's

TABLE 7.2 *The components of school movement, 1963–72 (percentages)*

Category of movement	1962–63	1963–64	1964–65	1965–66	1966–67	1967–68	1968–69	1969–70	1970–71	1971–72
				Primary sector						
MSCH	52.7	56.9	57.6	29.1	54.2	63.1	50.5	58.6	51.4	53.9
MLEA	16.1	19.0	22.3	38.0	24.5	17.9	28.1	16.6	24.9	16.5
MREG	31.3	24.1	20.1	32.9	21.3	19.0	21.4	24.8	23.7	29.6
Total number of school movers (= 100%)	112	137	139	234	155	168	192	181	185	206
Above as percentage of the stock at the beginning of the year	8.1	10.3	10.5	17.6*	11.2	11.8	13.1	11.7	11.1	11.7
				Secondary sector						
MSCH	45.0	51.6	43.6	18.4	42.8	57.9	41.2	46.2	49.4	48.0
MLEA	19.8	23.0	21.1	36.6	30.2	25.8	29.4	15.8	22.2	20.7
MREG	35.1	25.4	35.3	45.3	27.0	16.3	29.4	38.0	28.4	31.3
Total number of school movers (= 100%)	111	126	133	234	159	159	170	158	176	179
Above as percentage of the stock at the beginning of the year	8.4	9.0	9.3	15.8*	10.8	10.7	11.3	10.2	10.9	10.7

Source: 1 per cent sample.
Notes:
1. * School turnover figures for the year 1965–66 are distorted because of local government reorganisation in the London region (creation of the GLC). During this year, many teachers were coded as having changed school because of local government changed, the school having come under a new Local Education Authority.
2. *MSCH* = those who moved school within the same Local Education Authority (LEA).
   MLEA = those who moved LEA but stay in the same region.
   MREG = those who moved region.

TABLE 7.3 *Rates of school mobility by sector and sex (percentages)*

	1962–63	1963–64	1964–65	1965–66*	1966–67	1967–68	1968–69	1969–70	1970–71	1971–72
Primary sector										
Male	9.3	12.2	11.4	20.1*	12.0	13.1	15.1	12.3	9.5	12.9
Female	7.7	9.7	10.2	16.7*	11.0	11.3	12.4	11.4	11.7	11.4
Total	8.1	10.3	10.5	17.6*	11.2	11.8	13.1	11.7	11.1	11.7
Secondary sector										
Male	7.7	7.9	7.8	14.1*	10.9	10.1	10.3	8.7	10.3	9.8
Female	9.1	10.5	11.2	18.3*	10.8	11.6	12.6	12.3	11.8	12.9
Total	8.4	9.0	9.3	15.8*	10.8	10.7	11.3	10.2	10.9	10.7

Source: 1 per cent sample.
Note:
* School mobility figures for the year 1965–66 are distorted because of local government reorganisation in the London region (creation of the GLC). During this year, many teachers were coded as having changed school because their school code number changed, the school having come under a new Local Educational Authority.

movements in the same way. We know that one such 'other factor' is the career prospects that the profession offers to each teacher. If these prospects interact with the *a priori* relationship between men's and women's movements in a different manner depending on the sector and on the qualifications of teachers, then results such as those commented on above become perfectly plausible. In effect, if we split movements between those involving immediate promotion and those not, we find that over the whole ten-year period men move more than women in order to obtain promotion, and women move more than men when such movement does not involve promotion; furthermore, we find this relationship both in primary and secondary schools, and also among graduate and non-graduate teachers. Table 7.4 gives the figures for 1970–71. The data for other years during the period under review are similar.

We turn now to the evolution of promotions as compared with mobility. Since promotions are the most obvious way in which career prospects materialise, we would expect to find some relationship between the rate of promotions and the rate of school mobility. The second row of Table 7.5 indicates the percentage of teachers promoted,[2] the third and fourth split this percentage between those which are internal to a particular school and those which are external, and the fifth shows the total percentage of teachers changing school. A superficial glance at the table does not show a very clear association between school mobility and promotions, and this is not surprising once we take into account the way in which overall and internal promotions are related. If we look at the second and third rows of Table 7.5, it can readily be seen that most of the increases in total promotions are absorbed

TABLE 7.4   *School mobility for 1970–71 split by promotion and non-promotion (percentages)*

Category of mover	All teachers (1 per cent sample)		Graduate teachers (5 per cent sample)	
	Promoted movers	Non-promoted movers	Promoted movers	Non-promoted movers
Men – primary	4.4	5.6	6.6	5.7
Women – primary	2.8	10.3	1.9	11.8
Men – secondary	4.7	6.2	7.0	7.0
Women – secondary	4.2	10.3	1.7	9.4
Total movers	3.8	8.5	5.6	7.7

Source: 1 per cent and 5 per cent graduate sample.

TABLE 7.5   *Promotions and school movements, 1963–72*

	1962–63	1963–64	1964–65	1965–66	1966–67	1967–68	1968–69	1969–70	1970–71	1971–72
Total number in stock at the beginning of the year	2,708	2,726	2,754	2,808	2,845	2,918	2,974	3,104	3,273	3,436
Total promotions during the year as a percentage of stock	4.8	6.2	10.3	9.1	9.2	10.2	8.8	14.7	10.5	15.9
Internal promotions as percentage of stock	2.7	3.9	7.6	5.7	5.7	7.2	5.5	10.6	7.1	12.2
External promotions as percentage of stock	2.1	2.3	2.7	3.4	3.4	3.1	3.3	4.1	3.4	3.7
Percentage of stock changing school during the year	8.2	9.6	9.9	16.7*	11.0	11.2	12.2	10.9	11.0	11.2

Source: 1 per cent sample.
Note:
*School mobility figures for the year 1965–66 are distorted because of local government reorganisation in the London region (creation of the GLC). During this year many teachers were coded as having changed school because their school code number changed; the school having come under a new local Education Authority.

by increases in internal promotions. In fact, there is a clear relationship between those two variables: whenever there is an increase in the total level of promotions, the increase in internal promotions is more than proportional;[3] thus, the larger part of short-run changes in career prospects are taken up by internal promotions and do not directly affect the rate of mobility. Naturally, there is a much closer relationship between external promotions and school mobility, but this tells us very little about the causes of mobility. It merely reflects the fact that a sizeable part of movements were made by teachers gaining promotion from their schools.

A potentially more promising way of investigating the determinants of school mobility is to apply the same general hypothesis that has been used to study occupational decisions in the previous three chapters. An individual will change his or her place of work if the expected net advantage of doing so is positive. We would then expect that inter-school mobility would be influenced by the existence of differentials, both pecuniary and non-pecuniary, between the schools of the system. Due to the nature of our data, it is difficult to identify non-pecuniary differentials, but we can obtain a measure of pecuniary differentials between schools. We explore this question in the next section.

7.1.2 *Inter-school mobility and differentials in career prospects*

Because of the administered salary system in force in England and Wales, pecuniary differentials between schools generally appear in the form of differential promotion prospects between schools.[4] The school system can be characterised by two main features: first, schools differ in size and in the ages of their pupils; second, the scope for promotion within a particular school is

	School Burnham group				
salary scale	1	2	3	4	5
5	p_{51}	p_{52}	p_{53}	p_{54}	p_{55}
4	p_{41}	p_{42}	p_{43}	p_{44}	p_{45}
3	p_{31}	p_{32}	p_{33}	p_{34}	p_{35}
2	p_{21}	p_{22}	p_{23}	p_{24}	p_{25}
1	p_{11}	p_{12}	p_{13}	p_{14}	p_{15}
	$\sum_{i=1}^{5} p_{i1} = 1$	$\sum_{i=1}^{5} p_{i2} = 1$	$\sum_{i=1}^{5} p_{i3} = 1$	$\sum_{i=1}^{5} p_{i4} = 1$	$\sum_{i=1}^{5} p_{i5} = 1$

Figure 7.1 *The school size–career structure matrix.*

related to the number and age of its pupils by means of a complex weighting procedure.[5] This means that promotion prospects differ between schools.

A convenient way of representing a system like this is by the matrix shown in Figure 7.1. The columns of the matrix represents schools ordered by their corresponding weight (Burnham group), while the rows represent the different salary scales. In each cell we indicate the corresponding proportion of teachers serving in each scale within a given type of school. Let us assume for the sake of simplicity that only five Burnham groups exist (five types of schools), and also that there are five different scales; then p_{ij} will be the proportion of teachers serving in schools of Burnham type j who are paid according to scale i.

The information displayed by such a matrix gives an approximate idea of the promotion characteristics of the system and, most importantly, of the differences in prospects between types of school. If all schools offered similar promotion prospects for their teachers, we would expect to find a roughly similar distribution of the ps; that is, the proportion of teachers in each scale would be approximately equal in all schools. If this is not the case, some school types will have much larger proportions of teachers in the high salary scales than others.

Assuming that teachers behave in a wealth maximising manner, the fact that schools are similar or differ in their distribution of ps has definite implications as far as school mobility is concerned. If schools were identical in their promotion prospects (and for a uniform set of non-pecuniary characteristics), there would be little reason for a teacher to leave his school. His expected earnings would be the same whatever type of school he is teaching in. However, if there exist differentials in the promotion prospects among schools, it will pay him to move school even though this may not entail immediate promotion because by doing this his expectation of future earnings will be higher. We would therefore expect that increases in the range of variation of promotion prospects among schools will induce an increase in the level of school mobility.

Since we have school-specific data on the proportion of teachers in each salary scale (the ps of Figure 7.1), we constructed a school-specific index of promotion prospects (*IPP*) which takes into account the distribution of posts in each type of school, and the pecuniary remuneration associated with such posts. With reference to Figure 7.1, the form of this index for, say, type 1 schools was as follows:

$$IPP_1 = w_1 p_{11} + w_2 p_{21} + w_3 p_{31} + w_4 p_{41} + w_5 p_{51} = \sum_{i=1}^{5} w_i p_{i1}$$

where the ws correspond to the maximum wage attainable within each salary scale. To facilitate comparisons over time, we standardised the set of maximum wages with respect to its first element ($w_1 = 1$); in this manner, the other ws measure, for any given year, the relative pecuniary benefits attainable in each of the higher scales. The index will be bounded between the range $[1, (w_5/w_1)]$. A low *IPP* indicates that the school has few posts in the higher salary scales, and therefore that it cannot offer many opportunities of promotion. A high *IPP* indicates that the school has more posts in the higher scales, and that potentially it can offer a much wider range of promotion opportunities. It should be noted that this index ignores differences in the age structure of teachers. Since promotions are positively related to age, the *IPP* index possibly underestimates the promotion prospects of teachers in schools with a young teaching force, and overestimates those of teachers in schools with an older teaching force. The magnitude of this bias depends both on the extent to which age is an influencing factor in facilitating promotions, and on the extent to which types of schools differ in the age structure of their teaching force.

We obtained for each year a set of *IPP*s, each corresponding to the different types of school considered. If N_j is the number of teachers serving in type j schools, and $N = \Sigma_j N_j$ is the total number of teachers in the system, we can interpret the set of *IPP*s as a discrete distribution of promotion prospects among types of schools, the frequency of each value of the distribution being N_j/N. Then, the range of variation of promotion prospects among schools may be represented by some measure of dispersion of this distribution, such as its standard deviation (SD_{IPP}).

Until 1974 the number of school types defined by their Burnham group was 14 and the number of scales was 5, plus extra scales for heads and deputy heads.[6] The salaries paid in each of the first 5 scales are the same irrespective of the type of school in which the teacher is serving. The salaries paid in the last scales vary according to the Burnham group of the school; the larger the Burnham group, the higher are the salaries paid in these two scales. The total number of posts in any given school is calculated in accordance with the Burnham group to which the school belongs, by means of the point system described in Chapter 3. At one end of the spectrum we find small schools where, apart from the post of head, only posts in scale 1 are available; at the other end, large schools where posts in all scales are available.

Since the data comes from a 1 per cent sample of the total population of teachers, the 14 different size categories of schools were aggregated into 6 groups, so that the proportions of teachers in each scale could be calculated on the basis of a reasonably large absolute number. We considered three groups for each sector (primary and secondary) which we called respectively small (S), medium (M), and large (L).[7] The results are given in Table 7.6. For each sector, the first three columns show the value of *IPP* in each of the three categories of schools considered, and the fourth gives the value of the standard deviation (SD_{IPP}) of the distribution (weighted by the numbers of teachers in each category).

The most obvious feature in the distribution of this index is the difference in promotion prospects between primary and secondary schools; while the

TABLE 7.6 *The distribution of the index of promotional prospects (IPP)*

Primary					Secondary			
Year	S	M	L	SD_{IPP}	S	M	L	SD_{IPP}
1963	1.058	1.038	1.057	0.0093	1.091	1.128	1.182	0.0367
1964	1.058	1.040	1.052	0.0083	1.090	1.127	1.194	0.0421
1965	1.075	1.075	1.058	0.0040	1.090	1.141	1.198	0.0442
1966	1.070	1.076	1.054	0.0052	1.096	1.140	1.204	0.0450
1967	1.064	1.080	1.054	0.0079	1.092	1.145	1.208	0.0477
1968	1.064	1.070	1.069	0.0026	1.094	1.153	1.201	0.0438
1969	1.059	1.065	1.066	0.0033	1.091	1.150	1.203	0.0463
1970	1.076	1.085	1.088	0.0050	1.099	1.148	1.200	0.0405
1971	1.051	1.069	1.074	0.0092	1.088	1.136	1.190	0.0408
1972	1.050	1.075	1.085	0.0137	1.094	1.145	1.189	0.0371

Source: 1 per cent sample.

mean of the index for primary in 1972 was 1.07, the mean for secondary was 1.16, similar differences also being observed in previous years. The second point concerns the distribution of the indices within each sector. In secondary the value of *IPP* follows a monotonic pattern; it is higher the larger the Burnham group of the school. In primary, however, this was not true until 1969; in previous years the values were not ordered in accordance with the size of the school. The explanation lies in the large proportion of heads in small primary schools; although paid at lower rates than heads in large schools, this large proportion results in the index being heavily weighted upwards. Expanding intermediate promotion prospects in larger primary schools has subsequently produced an index which now follows the same pattern as that for secondary schools.

To what extent is the dispersion in promotion prospects related to the level of inter-school mobility? Before attempting to answer this question it should be noted that school mobility usually takes place within primary and secondary, with few movements between these two sectors. We therefore investigate separately the existence of this relationship *within* each sector. Figure 7.2 shows, for primary and secondary, the time evolution of the rate of school mobility (*RSM*) and of the dispersion of career prospects (SD_{IPP}). In primary the two variables do not appear to be related in any systematic manner. If anything, their relationship is negative rather than positive as expected; in effect, in five out of the ten years considered a decline in the standard deviation of promotion prospects between schools coincided with an increase in the rate of school mobility. In secondary, on the other hand, these two variables appear to be strongly associated. The rate of school mobility shows a discernible upward trend, but once this is taken into consideration the oscillations of this variable are clearly accounted for by the oscillations of the standard deviation of promotion prospects. In all the ten

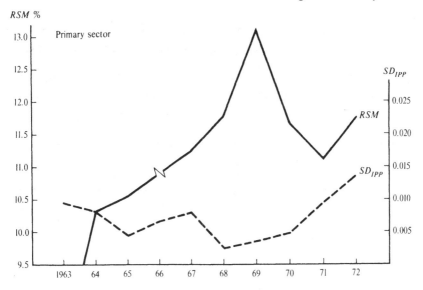

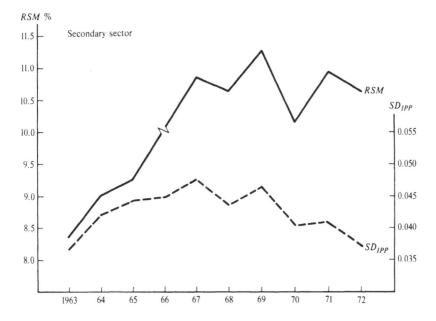

Figure 7.2   *Inter-school mobility and dispersion of promotion prospects.*
Note. The rates of mobility in 1966 are 17.6 in primary and 15.8 in secondary; these values are not shown in the graph because they are distorted due to the redefinition of local authority boundaries in that year.

years considered the movements of both variables were positively related: whenever there was a widening of the dispersion of promotion prospects, the rate of inter-school mobility experienced a corresponding increase, and vice versa.

In Table 7.7 we show the results of regressing the rate of school mobility on the standard deviation of promotion prospects. Both variables were entered in logarithmic terms and we added a dummy variable to capture the spurious effect on school mobility caused by the redefinition of local authority boundaries in 1966, and also a time variable to take into account the increasing trend of the dependent variable. For each sector we run the regression for all teachers and also for male and female teachers separately.

As expected from the above discussion, the hypothesis is not corroborated by empirical data on the primary sector. In all three equations the estimated sign of the coefficient is negative. It is difficult to rationalize these results in terms of our theoretical explanation of mobility; probably other factors not considered here are relevant in explaining inter-school movements in the primary sector. In secondary, on the other hand, the hypothesis that inter-school mobility is influenced by the dispersion of promotion prospects between schools is largely confirmed by the data. In all cases the variable takes the expected positive sign and, except for female mobility, is statistically significant. According to the last equation of Table 7.7, a 10 per cent increase in

TABLE 7.7   *School mobility regressions, 1963–72. Dependent variable log (RSM)*

| | \multicolumn{4}{c}{Independent variables} | $\overline{R}^2$ | $F(3, 6)$ | DW |
	Intercept	Dummy	Time trend	SD_{IPP}			
Primary sector							
Male	−2.9510	0.5288	0.0167**	−0.1422	0.5983	5.47	2.65
	(6.36)	(3.54)	(1.07)	(1.62)			
Female	−2.9724	0.4951	0.0377	−0.1023	0.9158	21.74	2.54
	(12.84)	(6.64)	(4.85)	(2.34)			
Total	−2.9622	0.5045	0.0323	−0.1121	0.8502	18.02	2.63
	(11.80)	(6.24)	(3.82)	(2.36)			
Secondary sector							
Male	0.2057**	0.4187	0.0270	0.8688	0.7819	11.75	1.83
	(0.19)	(4.36)	(2.76)	(2.55)			
Female	−1.4711	0.5101	0.0310	0.2777**	0.9210	35.96	2.03
	(2.32)	(9.04)	(5.38)	(1.39)			
Total	−0.6042*	0.4584	0.0282	0.5834	0.9759	122.40	1.79
	(1.83)	(15.55)	(9.40)	(5.58)			

Notes: 1. The variable SD_{IPP} is entered in logarithmic terms.
2. Figures in parentheses indicate absolute *t*-statistic values. Coefficients with one asterisk are *not* significant at the 5 per cent level, and with two asterisks at the 10 per cent level.

the standard deviation of promotion prospects between secondary schools would result in a 6 per cent increase in the rate of school mobility in that sector. The effect would be much larger on male mobility – almost a 9 per cent increase – and much lower on female mobility – only a 3 per cent increase.[8] This is consistent with our previous results on supply, which also show that men are much more sensitive to pecuniary differentials than women. It is also consistent with the widely acknowledged fact that a large part of female movements are not a response to the economic factors specifically faced by individual female teachers, but the result of decisions taken within a family context. It should be noted that the performance of the aggregate regression is much better than the performance of either the male or female regressions. This could be due to the fact that our measure of the dispersion of promotion prospects is not sex-specific. Since promotion prospects and their dispersion among schools may differ between male and female teachers, a sex-specific measure of the standard deviation may have been more appropriate. To obtain that measure, however, a larger sample than the one used here would have been needed.

Our results show that in the secondary sector the dispersion of promotion prospects between schools is a significant contributor to the rate of inter-school mobility. We cannot claim the same for the primary sector, nor can we say that this is the only variable that affects inter-school mobility. Even for the secondary sector we have only managed to explain the deviations of the rate of inter-school mobility from an increasing time trend. The time trend itself, however, has been left unexplained. We believe that probably other factors concerning non-pecuniary differences between schools or areas, or even concerning pecuniary differences between schools or areas, or even concerning pecuniary differences not directly related to the teaching career structure, may also be relevant determinants of school mobility. In the following two sections we attempt to take into consideration some of these factors.

7.2 Inter-regional mobility

Although based on a small number of observations, the above results indicate that there exists a relationship between school mobility and the variation in promotion prospects between schools. They suggest that teachers, in orientating their movements, respond to both actual and expected pecuniary differentials arising within the profession. We now want to look at the same question, this time analysing inter-regional rather than inter-school movements. This exercise, apart from providing information on the determinants of inter-regional flows, will produce additional evidence on the responsiveness of teachers, derived from a data base larger than that of the previous analysis.

7.2.1 *The hypothesis*

We wish to test the hypothesis that inter-regional mobility is responsive to regional earnings differentials and to investigate the direction and magnitude of any response. Our dependent variable is the flow of teachers from one region to another, relative to the total stock of teachers in the region of origin. That is, M_{ij}/T_i, where M_{ij} is the number of teachers who, in a given period of time (one year), move from region i to region j, and T_i is the total stock of teachers in region i at the beginning of the period.

As pointed out before, the rates of pay in teaching are uniform over the whole of England and Wales. However, this does not mean that actual salaries are the same in all regions. Differentials may arise for several reasons: the most important are age structure, mix of school types, qualification mix, and the London allowance. We will standardise for most of these factors and retain only the London allowance and any remaining unidentified factor. By retaining the London allowance we will be able to estimate the influence of this allowance on the inter-regional flows of teachers. The remaining differentials, we presume, indicate divergences among regions in long-term career prospects. We denote these salary variables by W_i and W_j, and we expect that high levels of W_i will be associated with low rates of movements out of region i, and high levels of W_j will be associated with high rates of movements into region j.[9]

The above variable incorporates the only explicit differential between geographical areas allowed by the salary structure, but also captures differentials in promotion prospects. In the context of a profession such as teaching, this second aspect is very important because the promotion system is the only element of flexibility within a rigidly fixed salary structure. Differentials in career prospects are thus a relevant factor in evaluating the return to the decision to move. The consideration of the variable W (wages), however, is unsatisfactory for two reasons. First, due to the way in which it is defined, it is bound to reflect mainly the effect of the London allowance differential. Second, even if it manages to capture differentials in career prospects, these will only be measured in a long-term sense. The standardised salary differential between regions reflects the different distribution of their respective teaching forces between posts, and this is the result of past promotion policies. It is then necessary to introduce another variable which measures the regional differentials in short-term career prospects, and which therefore complements the long-term career prospects represented by the standardised salary differentials. In this respect, we consider the proportion of teachers promoted during the current year as a proxy of the relative short-term promotion opportunities offered by regions. We expect that teachers will tend to move away from regions in which promotion prospects are poor, and into regions with good opportunities. In terms of the dependent variable used in this chapter, we expect that the higher the level of promotions in the region of origin (P_i),[10] the lower will be the proportion of teachers who move out. Conversely, the higher the level of promotions in the region of destination (P_j), the higher will be the proportion of teachers moving into that region.

In addition to the variables W and P, a third important pecuniary element is the differential cost of living between regions. The higher the cost of living in a given region, the lower will be the real value of the teacher's salary. In the absence of any official regional cost of living indices, we concentrate here on a particular element of the cost of living which may be expected to be directly relevant to the moving decisions: house prices. It has been frequently reported that movements out of 'expensive' regions are to some extent due to financial pressures related to the increased personal responsibilities of young teachers as they face marriage and build up families.[11] Adequate housing then may be a crucial variable to consider. We denote this variable for the region of origin by HP_i, and that for the region of destination by HP_j.

The three pecuniary factors considered above, wages, relative promotion prospects and house prices $(W, P$ and $HP)$ are the basic economic variables with which the present hypothesis is tested. The rest are essentially standardising variables called for by the specific form of the model. The distance between the two regions i and j (D_{ij}) is the first obvious standardising factor, although it has usually been interpreted as a proxy for costs of moving, cultural differences and levels of job information. Under any of these interpretations, it is expected that the larger the distance, the smaller will be the amount of movement between regions.

With respect to the region of destination, we consider, as a standardising variable, first the stock of teachers serving there (T_j), and second, the rate of expansion of the pupil population in the region (RE_j). It is evident that more teachers will move into large than small regions and also that expanding regions will attract more teachers than contracting ones.

Finally, we standardise regions with respect to the age structure of their teaching forces (A). Most of the people who change regions are less than 30 years old,[12] consequently we measure the age structure by the proportion of teachers younger than 30 serving in the region. We expect the sign of A_i to be positive, and that of A_j to be negative.

The functional relationship used to test the hypothesis belongs to the 'gravity models' class – cf. Weeden (1973). Together with the expected signs, it can be summarised as follows.

$$M_{ij}/T_i = f(\underset{+}{T_j}, \underset{+}{RE_j}, \underset{-}{D_{ij}}, \underset{+}{A_i}, \underset{-}{A_j}, \underset{-}{W_i}, \underset{+}{W_j}, \underset{-}{P_i}, \underset{+}{P_j}, \underset{+}{HP_i}, \underset{-}{HP_j})$$

where

M_{ij} = Number of teachers moving from region i to region j

T_i = Number of teachers serving in region i

RE_j = Rate of expansion of pupil population in region j
D_{ij} = Distance between region i and region j
A_i = Proportion of teachers younger than 30 in region i
W_i = Standardised teacher salary in region i
P_i = Percentage of teachers promoted in region i
HP_i = Housing prices in region i

See Appendix 7A for further details of the calculation of these variables and their sources.

7.2.2 *Empirical results*

Between 1 April 1971 and 31 March 1972, 10,060 teachers moved region in the maintained primary and secondary sector, about 3 per cent of the total teaching force. Of those, 3,458 were men (2.4 per cent of the male teaching population) and 6,602 were women (3.2 per cent of the female teaching population). A multiplicative form of the above function was estimated by regression analysis on the basis of all the possible flows between the 10 standard statistical regions of England and Wales (90 observations) during that period. The estimated equation is linear in logarithms.

Table 7.8 shows the final selected equations for male, female and all teachers.[13] Although the estimated coefficients can be directly interpreted as elasticities, the different variances of the variables involved tend to give a distorting picture of their actual effect on the rate of regional mobility. In order to evaluate their relative contributions more clearly, we standardise these coefficients to take into account the degree of variability of the independent variables.[14]

The hypothesis that inter-regional mobility of teachers is responsive to spatial earnings differentials is supported by the present set of data. Although smaller than the influence of factors such as age and distance, the three pecuniary variables considered in this exercise (W, P and HP) do have a significant effect on the rate of regional mobility. In general (see column 6) the effect of salary differentials is only marginally larger than that of promotion prospects, and both variables show a pulling and a retention effect of similar magnitude. The effect of housing prices, on the other hand, is smaller and only significant in the region of origin. Among the standardising variables, the age structure of the region of origin has the strongest effect; the younger the teaching population in a given region, the larger is the movement of teachers out of that region.

In general, these results hold for both male and female flows, thus suggesting that the two sexes behave in a similar fashion as far as inter-regional mobility is concerned. There are, however, some interesting differences which deserve a more detailed consideration. A first thing to notice is the much larger effect of age on male than on female mobility.

TABLE 1.8 *Inter-regional flows, 1971–72. (Dependent variable log (M_{ij}/I_i))*

Variable	Male Regression coefficient (1)	Male Standardised coefficient (2)	Female Regression coefficient (3)	Female Standardised coefficient (4)	Total Regression coefficient (5)	Total Standardised coefficient (6)
Intercept	-5.3028 (1.65)	—	-3.9866** (1.28)	—	-5.9733 (2.26)	—
T_j	0.7030 (5.09)	0.3545	0.7243 (4.39)	0.4429	0.7544 (6.66)	0.4495
RE_j	1.3943 (5.71)	0.3855	1.5695 (5.85)	0.4867	1.4195 (6.45)	0.4454
D_{ij}	-0.7411 (6.74)	-0.3938	-0.7165 (8.12)	-0.4271	-0.7002 (8.00)	-0.4223
A_i	4.2454 (5.78)	0.6236	1.8795 (4.88)	0.3095	3.1989 (6.28)	0.5332
W_i	-9.2590 (2.55)	-0.2694	—	—	-6.0926 (3.73)	-0.2016
W_j	—	—	9.2429 (4.11)	0.3022	6.0926 (3.73)	0.2016
P_i	-0.3292 (3.86)	-0.2389	-0.1827 (1.71)	-0.1062	-0.2717 (3.19)	-0.1828
P_j	0.3292 (3.86)	0.2389	0.3441 (1.75)	0.2001	0.2717 (3.19)	0.1828
HP_i	0.6531 (2.70)	0.1809	0.2597* (1.45)	0.0806	0.4546 (2.55)	0.1429
	$\bar{R}^2 = 0.7231$ $F(7, 82) = 34.20$		$\bar{R}^2 = 0.7780$ $F(7, 82) = 39.98$		$\bar{R}^2 = 0.7813$ $F(8, 81) = 46.42$	

Notes:
1. All independent variables are in logarithmic form.
2. Figures in parentheses are absolute values of the t-statistic. Coefficients with one asterisk are *not* significant at the 5 per cent level, and with two asterisks at the 10 per cent level (one-tail test).

The main differences, however. concern the coefficients of the promotion variables and the effect of salary differentials. Whereas in the case of men, both promotion variables affect movements in a similar way, in the case of women, the pulling effect of promotions from the region of destination is much larger than the retention effect of promotions in the region of origin. Similarly, for women, salaries have a pulling effect while for men they show a retentive effect. Another interesting difference is the much lower coefficient on housing prices for women than for men. This is consistent with the fact that the burden of higher financial outlays mainly affects the moving decisions of household heads who are, in general, men.

An important result worth emphasising is the relatively large effect and significance of the salary differential variable. In practice, this variable is dominated by the salary differential between London and the rest, created by the London allowance. It therefore gives an indication of the power of retention for men, and of attraction for women, of this allowance, and of the potential use of salary differentials in redistributing the supply of teachers. This conclusion is largely based on the flows in and out of London, but we believe that a similar result would be obtained in the presence of more regional wage differentials.

Given the exceptional characteristics of London as compared to the rest of the regions, other coefficients apart from the wage variable may have been heavily influenced by the inclusion of this area in the regression exercise. We therefore repeated the regressions reported above, this time excluding flows in and out of London. The results of this exercise were practically the same as those shown in Table 7.8.[15]

7.3 Mover or stayer: a discriminant analysis

So far in this chapter we have been concerned with the determinants of the aggregate levels of mobility. We now focus our attention directly on the individual teacher and attempt to answer the question: what factors make a teacher more likely to be a stayer or a mover?

The methodology we use is similar to that used by Greenberg and McCall (1974) in their study of the movements of teachers in the San Diego school system of the United States. We estimate, by means of multiple regression analysis, that linear combination of independent dummy variables which produces the highest discrimination between a mover and a stayer. The dependent variable is '0' for a stayer and '1' for a mover. A positive sign on any of the independent variables implies that this characteristic raises the probability of being a mover while a negative sign implies that this characteristic lowers the probability.[16]

The variables used are explained in Table 7.9 while the results are presented in Table 7.10. However, before analysing these results, it is worth commenting upon the Greenberg and McCall analysis which, to a large extent,

TABLE 7.9 *Variables used in the discriminant analysis*

Variable	Definition	Hypothesised sign
Dependent variables		
MTOT	Mover between year 1 and year 2	
MSCH	Moved school within the same LEA	
MLEA	Moved school and LEA but within the same region	
MREG	Moved region	
Standardising variables		
AGE1	Over 30	−
AGE2	Over 40	−
SEX	Men	?
SEX2	Married women	+
GRAD	Graduate	+
GRAD2	Good honours graduate	?
Pecuniary variables		
POST	Holder of a post above scale 1 (except Heads) in year 1	−
HEAD	Head teacher in year 1	−
PROM	Promoted between year 1 and year 2	+
PROM2	Promoted between year 1 and year 2 but already holding a promoted post in year 1	+
Non-pecuniary variables		
RURAL	In: Wales, East Anglia, the North, or the South West in year 1	−
GRAM	In a grammar school year 1	−
MOD	In a secondary modern school year 1	+
COMP	In a comprehensive school year 1	−
OTHER	In an 'other secondary' school year 1	?
LARGE	In a 'large' school in year 2 (Burnham group > 8 in secondary and > 4 in primary)	?
SMALL	In a 'small' school in year 2 (Burnham group < 6 in secondary and < 4 in primary)	?
SED	In a school of 'exceptional difficulty' in year 2	−

Notes:
1. All variables take the value '1' for the category of teacher indicated and '0' otherwise.
2. Primary schools are taken as the base group from which the secondary school categories are defined.
3. Medium sized schools (6, 7 and 8 in secondary; 4 in primary) are taken as the base group from which these school size variables are defined.
4. The hypothesised signs should be interpreted as expressing our initial information concerning the level of mobility found among that category of teachers with respect to the base group. For instance, we have previously found that over-40-year old teachers move less than 30-year olds who in turn are expected to move less than the under-30-year olds. Therefore the hypothesised signs for *AGE1* and *AGE2* are negative. Similarly we have previously found that secondary modern teachers move more than primary teachers while teachers in grammar and comprehensive schools move less; then, the hypothesised signs on the school type variables follow from this (all defined with respect to the primary group base.)

TABLE 7.10   *Discriminant analysis of movers and stayers, 1970–71*

Independent variables	Dependent variables MTOT	MSCH	MLEA	MREG
(i) *Standardising variables*				
(CONSTANT)	0.144	0.041	0.044	0.060
AGE1	−0.024 (2.2)	0.035 (7.8)***	−0.015 (3.1)*	−0.044 (23.4)***
AGE2	−0.055 (12.6)***	−0.030 (6.8)***	−0.011 (1.9)	−0.014 (2.5)
SEX	0.004 (0.1)	−0.004 (0.1)	0.001 (0.0)	0.007 (0.6)
SEX2	0.034 (4.1)**	0.004 (0.1)	0.012 (1.4)	0.018 (3.6)*
GRAD	0.034 (2.2)	0.019 (1.3)	−0.009 (0.6)	0.024 (3.5)*
GRAD2	−0.033 (1.5)	−0.032 (2.5)	0.017 (1.6)	−0.018 (1.5)
(ii) *Pecuniary variables*				
POST	−0.070 (20.3)***	−0.034 (8.3)***	−0.023 (8.4)***	−0.013 (2.3)
HEAD	−0.051 (4.3)**	−0.037 (3.9)**	−0.014 (1.2)	−0.000 (0.0)
PROM	0.137 (28.6)***	0.104 (29.1)***	0.031 (5.4)**	0.002 (0.0)
PROM2	0.102 (7.6)***	0.010 (0.1)	0.031 (2.6)	0.061 (8.9)***
(iii) *Non-pecuniary variables*				
RURAL	−0.036 (6.9)***	−0.010 (1.0)	−0.011 (2.4)	−0.015 (3.8)**
GRAM	−0.025 (0.9)	−0.026 (1.6)	−0.010 (0.5)	0.010 (0.4)
MOD	0.033 (3.7)*	0.028 (4.6)**	0.008 (0.9)	−0.003 (0.1)
COMP	−0.001 (0.0)	−0.024 (3.9)**	0.013 (1.4)	0.011 (0.9)
OTHER	0.050 (3.2)*	0.033 (2.5)	−0.003 (0.5)	0.020 (1.6)
LARGE	0.018 (1.7)	0.029 (7.6)***	−0.001 (0.0)	−0.009 (2.3)
SMALL	0.083 (15.3)***	0.058 (13.2)*	0.007 (2.0)	0.018 (2.3)
SED	−0.014 (0.1)	−0.010 (0.1)	−0.000 (0.0)	−0.004 (0.0)
R^2	0.086	0.045	0.027	0.037
$F(18, 2772)$	14.4	7.3	4.3	5.9

Notes:
1. Figures in parentheses are the F-statistics of the variable; those marked with one asterisk are significant at the 10 per cent level ($F > 2.7$), those with two at the 5 per cent level ($F > 3.8$) and those with three at the 1 per cent level ($F > 6.6$).
2. This analysis was performed on all those teachers from our 1 per cent sample who were in service on both 31 March 1970 and 31 March 1971 (2,791). Teachers serving in schools with Burnham group '0' were excluded because this group also included: unattached, visiting and supply teachers who are not attached to any particular school and therefore cannot be classified as a mover or a stayer.
3. All equations are significant at the 1 per cent level as measured by their respective F-statistics ($F > 1.9$).

inspired this section. A wide range of non-pecuniary factors[17] including socio-economic status, race, reading ability, and IQ of pupils were found to have a significant effect on the mobility of teachers. Teachers moved away from those schools with pupils of low socio-economic status etc. and into more 'middle class' schools. In consequence, new and less experienced teachers became concentrated in the 'difficult' schools.

The system is more complex in England and Wales. We have already demonstrated that pecuniary factors are highly relevant in the moving decision of teachers. However, only 30 per cent of all movements are associated with immediate promotion, and although some of the remaining 70 per cent may be due to pecuniary factors there must still remain a significant proportion of movements to be explained by non-pecuniary factors. Apart from 'schools of exceptional difficulty' (see below), our data do not enable us to identify any socio-economic characteristics of the school in which a teacher is located. We can only identify its type (primary, modern, grammar, comprehensive, or other secondary) and its Burnham group. This difficulty would have been partially overcome if we had been able to identify the Local Education Authority of the teacher. Although still a wide area, socio-economic variables corresponding to the LEA could have been used as a reasonable proxy for the non-pecuniary characteristics of individual schools. Unfortunately this information, although available, is considered to be confidential by the DES.

The school of exceptional difficulty (henceforth SED)[18] then offers us the only means of identifying some of those teachers who are in schools with pupils from disadvantaged backgrounds. If the Greenberg and McCall findings are relevant to teachers in England and Wales, and we believe that they are, then teachers in these schools will be more likely to move (i.e. they will move to non-SED schools). This is indeed demonstrated to be the case in our detailed investigations of SED teachers presented in the following chapter and based on a specially extracted 100 per cent sample of such teachers.

However, as far as our present analysis is concerned, the number of teachers recorded on our 1 per cent sample as being in SED schools is so small (42) that it is possible that even if there is an effect on mobility, it will not show as statistically significant. A second problem concerning the definition of both this variable and the school size variable is that we can only associate them with the school a teacher moves into, not, as we would ideally like, the school a teacher leaves. Because of this, interpretation of their coefficients is ambiguous. All that we are able to say in the case of a negative sign is that such schools are less likely to attract teachers than other schools. It is unfortunately impossible to be sure that this implies more movements out of such schools.

After several experiments with other variables, we finally settled on the list in Table 7.9. The independent variables are split into three categories: standardising variables, pecuniary variables and non-pecuniary variables.[19] We have also indicated on this list the sign, if any, that we predicted the coefficients to take, based on the foregoing discussion and on our knowledge of teacher mobility developed in earlier sections of this chapter.

The results presented in Table 7.10 support our hypothesis concerning the signs of the coefficients with only one or two exceptions. All the equations are statistically significant, but the extremely low percentage of the variation explained (only 9 per cent) is rather disappointing. It is not uncommon in such analyses to obtain low R^2 values but these are so low that we will strictly confine our comments to the statistically significant variables. We can at least be sure (sometimes at the 1 per cent confidence level) that these variables do affect the probability that an individual will be a mover or a stayer.

(i) *Standardising variables.* Age affects the probability of being a mover in the hypothesised manner; however, for the total only the over 40-year-olds show a significant negative effect. Contrasting results are found when the dependent variable is split into its three categories; teachers aged between 30 and 40 years are the most likely to move school within the LEA (*MSCH*) while it is the under 30-year-olds who are the most likely to move region.

There are no significant differences between men and single women but married women teachers are more likely to move than others, this being particularly so as far as moving region is concerned. This result fits very well with our earlier suggestion that the secondary earnings role in the family unit of most married women significantly affects their mobility patterns.

(ii) *Pecuniary variables.* Head teachers, and teachers holding scale posts, are less likely to be movers than those on the bottom scale, even after standardising for age. This is a reasonable behaviour pattern for two main reasons: firstly, such teachers would feel greater responsibility to the school in which they obtained their promotion and secondly, the further the teacher has reached in the career structure the fewer are the promotion opportunities available. In this context it is interesting to note that while the general promotion variable (*PROM*) is the most significant of all our independent variables and produces the largest 'net' addition to the probability of an individual teacher moving, promotions from intermediate scales (as opposed to those from scale 1) add a further significant 'net' amount of this probability. External promotions of this latter nature must be relatively more frequent in the profession than those from scale 1.[20]

In general, pecuniary variables are less important for movements between LEA and between region than for movements within an LEA. One important exception, however, is that promotion from an intermediate post makes a teacher more likely to move region while promotion from scale 1 does not affect the probability of a teacher moving region in any way. This result is consistent with what we would expect in a hierarchical labour market. As promotions to the highest posts in the system are harder to obtain, they involve widening the area of search beyond that necessary to obtain promotion to intermediate scales (for scale 1).

(iii) *Non-pecuniary variables.* Teachers in predominantly rural regions are less likely to move than others, and in particular they are less likely to move region.

The influence of school type on movements almost follows the pattern found from simple tabulations (in descending order of magnitude: modern, primary, comprehensive and grammar). Teachers in primary, grammar and comprehensive schools have approximately the same probability of moving (except comprehensive teachers moving school within the LEA, whose probability is lower) while teachers in secondary modern schools and those in other secondary schools are more likely to be movers.

Given that the school size variable refers to the position of the teacher after the move has been made, the results obtained indicate that both small and large schools attract movers. Unfortunately we cannot say whether this means that teachers are attracted into these schools from medium sized schools or whether it simply means that teachers in small and large schools are more likely to move within their respective size categories.

The school of exceptional difficulty (SED) variable takes the correct sign but is not significant. However, when the equation was estimated separately for primary school teachers (the great majority of SED teachers are in primary schools) a significant negative result was obtained for movements within the LEA. Considering that there is a monetary gain involved in teaching in these schools (£75 in 1971) this result is quite strong. Other things being equal, this allowance would attract teachers into such schools (i.e. the SED variable would have a positive sign). Thus, the significant negative sign implies that these schools are perceived by teachers to have adverse non-pecuniary characteristics which greatly outweigh the monetary gain involved in moving into them. This question is taken up further in the following chapter.

Despite the difficulties posed by our data, the results obtained indicate the relevance of non-pecuniary factors. We have not been able to use specific school or pupil characteristics, but differences between school type in the secondary sector and between the schools of exceptional difficulty and others in the primary sector reflect differences in socio-economic status between schools. In general we have shown that teachers in schools usually associated with low socio-economic status are more likely to be movers than those in higher status schools; this probably, but not necessarily, implies that teachers move from lower to higher status schools. Naturally, and for the reasons already mentioned, this is only a tentative result; a great deal of further work needs to be done in order to study the socio-economic characteristics of schools and their influence on teacher movements, but for this task a more sociologically oriented data base would be needed.

A further point of interest is that the effect of school characteristics on mobility is only significant within the Local Education Authority. This is consistent with intuitive reasoning which would expect school movements within an LEA to be influenced by non-pecuniary characteristics of the school, movements of LEA within a region to be influenced by non-pecuniary characteristics of the LEA (which we are unable to identify), and finally movements of region to be influenced by non-pecuniary characteristics of the region.

8

The effect of special allowances

In the previous chapter we considered inter-school mobility and suggested that the promotion system could be used as a policy instrument to re-orientate teachers to areas of relative undersupply or to areas where priority of supply is desired. So far this policy option does not appear to have been consciously used.

An alternative policy instrument designed to serve the same purpose has been adopted in a number of cases – namely the use of 'school based' salary allowances. In this chapter we examine the London allowance[1] and the Social Priority allowance or the School of Exceptional Difficulty allowance, as it was then called, which are paid to teachers within specified schools or groups of schools. We are concerned in particular with the effectiveness of these two allowances as policy instruments to redirect the stock of teachers.

Localities with high cost of living, accommodation difficulties, unpleasant environment, and unpleasant or difficult working conditions, will, other things being equal, be less attractive to workers than places without such problems. The supply price of labour will differ between areas and if the demand for a particular category of labour is uniformly distributed, wage differentials will appear which, at the margin, will compensate for these pecuniary disadvantages.

The above prediction is valid when the market is not subjected to any control or regulation which prevents it from reaching its equilibrium state. In particular, wage levels have to result from competitive pressures. This is obviously not the case for teachers, nor for most categories of labour in present conditions. Salary scales are negotiated on a national basis and apply throughout the country. Even if they accurately reflect aggregate supply and demand conditions, they will fail to take into account specific circumstances of particular geographical areas or of particular groups of schools. This is likely to lead to alternative market adjustments: schools or areas with good 'working conditions' will find it easier to attract teachers and schools or areas with bad 'working conditions' will tend to have difficulties.

The aim of the two allowances we are examining is to avoid this sort of disequilibrium situation. Unless it is desired to create specially favourable conditions in certain schools, the ideal allowance structure would result in a similar supply of teachers being available throughout the whole labour market.

This refers to a hypothetical situation[2] but it provides a guide for the analysis of the effects of school allowances in the teaching profession. To the extent that an allowance actually compensates for the non-pecuniary differences between schools, we should expect to find a similar number with similar characteristics of teachers in schools receiving the allowance and those not receiving it. The existence of different supply conditions in the two categories of schools would constitute *prima facie* evidence of an inappropriate level of allowance.

For several reasons, however, this comparative analysis can only be taken as a first approximation to a more comprehensive study of the effects of these types of allowances. First, the allowances themselves are not the only factor that differentiates the schools or areas studied. We have attempted to control for as many other factors as possible, but we have probably left out relevant variables, especially those (social or economic) that characterise the external environment of the place of work. Second, given the nature of our data, we have assumed that the observed differences in number and characteristics of teachers are mainly due to supply forces, while it is perfectly possible that demand considerations have also played an important role. Finally, we have had to confine ourselves to describing the differences in characteristics of the teaching force between schools or areas, without being able to assert what these differences imply in terms of teaching effectiveness. In this respect, we have occasionally applied criteria widely used in the profession (e.g. a more experienced teaching force is more productive from a pedagogical point of view than a less experienced one), but we must point out that we have no empirical support for these presumptions.

Despite these shortcomings, however, we believe that the analysis carried out in this chapter can be a useful description of supply conditions in different geographical areas and in different types of schools. In addition, the study of the social priority allowance provides a unique opportunity to examine the before and after situation with respect to the introduction of a salary differential.

Section 8.1 examines the London allowance bringing in, where relevant, other regional differences in teacher supply and characteristics. Section 8.2 examines the Social Priority allowance or the School of Exceptional Difficulty allowance, as it was then called. Finally, section 8.3 presents some general conclusions which we believe may be of use beyond the limits of these two particular allowances.

8.1 The London allowance and regional differences in supply

In this case study, we analyse the differences in several aspects of supply between the Greater London region and the remainder of England and

Wales. We have also analysed the general regional heterogeneity of the labour market for teachers. It may well be that some of the special market features which necessitate an additional salary allowance for Greater London are also characteristic of other areas. This approach is admittedly limited. It would be more orthodox to analyse the effect of a given allowance by comparing the situation in a given area before and after the allowance had been implemented. However, this is impossible for the London allowance since London teachers have enjoyed some form of salary differential in their favour for many years. In 1971 the allowance was £118 for all teachers in schools within the Metropolitan Police district.[3] At the time this represented 7.1 per cent of the teacher's average salary, but since then a three-tier allowance structure has been introduced. Inner London (including some of the Outer London boroughs) receives the highest rate, the remainder of the area formally receiving an allowance receives the medium rate, and the so-called 'fringe' area in the surrounding South East region the lowest rate.[4] In 1974 and 1975 these allowances stood at £351, £267 and £141 respectively, and in 1974 represented 15 per cent, 11 per cent, and 6 per cent respectively of the teacher's average salary.

The data we were able to use does not permit the identification of geographic areas smaller than the standard economic planning regions of England and Wales. Consequently, we are unable to make direct comparisons between urban and rural areas. The only totally urban area we can identify is Greater London; all the other regions are a mixture of urban and rural. This fact does not, in itself, prevent us from making comparisons

TABLE 8.1   *Population density of the regions, 1971*

Region	Population (millions)	Area in square kilometres (thousands)	Population density: people per square kilometre (thousands)
Greater London	7.45	1.58	4.72
North West	6.74	7.99	0.84
West Midlands	5.11	13.01	0.39
South East	9.78	25.83	0.38
Yorkshire and Humberside	4.80	14.20	0.34
East Midlands	3.39	12.18	0.28
North	3.30	19.35	0.17
South West	3.78	23.66	0.16
East Anglia	1.67	12.57	0.13
Wales	2.73	20.76	0.13
Total: England and Wales	48.75	151.12	0.32

Source: 1971 Census.

between London and the rest of the country, but it makes it difficult to draw conclusions about teacher supply in other big cities.

Taking into account this difficulty, we have characterised the standard regions according to a measure of their degree of urbanisation. The index we used is the density of population of the region. As we can see from Table 8.1, London has a much higher density than any other region and we define this as the only fully urban region. It is more difficult to characterise the rest of the regions, but in general the ranking defined by the densities is consistent with what casual observation would suggest. At the bottom of the scale are Wales, East Anglia, the South West, and the North, with densities ranging from 130 to 170 inhabitants per square kilometre. These we characterise as predominantly rural regions. The other regions: East Midlands, Yorkshire and Humberside, South East, West Midlands, and North West, show a substantial increase with respect to the first group, with densities ranging from 280 to 840 inhabitants per square kilometre. This is consistent with the fact that some big cities can be found in all of them. This regional division is obviously less useful than the identification of specific districts but, as is shown below, it did enable us to discern some pattern of teacher supply related to the degree of urbanisation, enabling problems affecting areas other than London to be evaluated to some extent.

8.1.1 *Stock comparisons*

In 1971 the pupil population in London was 1,115,464 distributed in the following way: 671,816 in primary, 408,816 in secondary (first five years) and 34,832 in the sixth form (DES, annual – a). If we apply to these numbers the 'desired' pupil–teacher ratios (NACTST, 1965), the total number of teachers required for the London area in that year was 53,911. Since the actual number of teachers was 53,729[5], on these terms London was short of only 182 teachers. In terms of global pupil–teacher ratios the conclusion reads as follows: while the desired global pupil–teacher ratio for London was 20.7, the actual ratio was 20.8. By any standard, this shortage compares very favourably with the situation in any other region. In the best of them – East Anglia – the desired ratio was 21.1 and the actual 21.6, in the worst – the North West – these ratios were respectively 21.1 and 23.0. London was the best staffed region in the whole country.

Does this mean that the allowance is working properly, or even possibly that it was too high? It is perhaps premature on this superficial examination to claim that all those who were pointing to teacher supply problems in London were wrong. We must first turn our attention to other aspects of teacher supply.

Table 8.2 shows the age distributions in each of the 10 regions together with the national average. Three features need to be mentioned. First,

TABLE 8.2   *Age distributions of teachers by region, 1971 (Percentages)*

Region	Age group				Total numbers teachers (=100 per cent)	Percentage of the teaching force in each region
	Less than 30	30–39	40–49	50 and over		
North	32.0	18.5	25.9	23.6	259	7.5
Yorkshire and Humberside	34.6	25.6	21.3	18.6	376	11.0
North West	35.6	25.8	20.2	18.3	480	14.0
East Midlands	39.5	20.6	21.4	18.5	243	7.1
West Midlands	35.2	23.9	23.1	17.7	355	10.4
East Anglia	30.2	25.6	22.9	21.1	109	3.2
Greater London	43.5	16.5	18.5	21.4	471	13.7
South East	34.9	21.7	21.5	21.9	649	18.9
South West	28.6	25.2	23.3	22.9	266	7.8
Wales	27.5	19.6	23.4	28.4	218	6.4
Total	35.1	22.3	21.7	20.9	3,426	100.0

Source: 1 per cent sample.

regions which are predominantly rural tend to have fewer young teachers (younger than 30) and more old teachers (older than 50) than the national average; on the other hand, regions which are predominantly urban employ about the same proportion of young teachers as the national average and, with the exception of the South East, a smaller proportion of older teachers. Secondly, all regions other than London employ a larger proportion of middle-aged teachers (brackets 30–49) than the national average. Thirdly, London constitutes the exception of the group: it employs a much larger proportion of young teachers and a much smaller proportion of middle-aged teachers than other regions.

The absence of an overall shortage needs then to be qualified. London has relatively few experienced teachers. However, as Table 8.3 shows, the proportion of male teachers under 30 in London was only slightly higher than in the other regions, and the proportion of male teachers in the 40–49 brackets was higher than in the rest of the country. On the whole, except for men aged 30–39 the difference between London and the other areas, as far as male teachers are concerned, is not very dramatic. The major cause of the overall difference between London and the other regions appears to be caused by an even more severe difference between the age distribution of women teachers in London and elsewhere. This is particularly apparent for the under-30s – 51 per cent of London women are under 30 compared with 38 per cent in other regions. Furthermore, a greater proportion of teachers in London than in other regions are single women: 33 per cent compared with 21 per cent. This is not an age effect; the table shows that

TABLE 8.3   *Age distribution of teachers by sex, 1971 (Percentages)*

Sex and region	Age group				Total number of teachers (= 100 per cent)
	Less than 30	30–39	40–49	50 and over	
Men and women					
London	43.5	16.5	18.5	21.4	471
Other regions	33.8	23.1	22.1	21.0	2,955
Total	35.1	22.3	21.7	20.9	3,426
Men					
London	29.0	18.2	23.9	28.9	159
Other regions	27.8	26.3	22.6	23.3	1,239
Total	27.9	25.4	22.7	24.0	1,398
Women					
London	51.0	15.7	15.7	17.6	312
Other regions	38.2	20.9	21.9	19.0	1,716
Total	40.2	20.1	21.0	18.8	2,028
Single women as a percentage of all women in each age group					(all ages)
London	61.0	44.9	26.5	41.8	49.7
Other regions	50.8	27.7	23.9	33.1	36.8

Source: 1 per cent sample.

London has not only more young women but also more single women teachers *of all ages* than other regions.

Teachers are not the only group of London workers whose characteristics differ from those in the rest of the country. In other occupations also, London has larger proportions of young and old people than the national average at the expense of those in the middle-age brackets and also a much higher proportion of single women of all ages than the rest of the country. However the discrepancies are not so great as for teachers, particularly in the case of women under 30.

In order to examine some of the other differences in teacher characteristics between London and other regions, we carried out a discriminant analysis as in Chapter 7. The results from this analysis confirmed our previous findings concerning age, sex and marital status distribution. They further indicated that the larger proportion of graduate teachers in London can be attributed to a larger proportion of untrained graduates.

8.1.2 *Flow comparisons*

The above analysis was concerned with the distribution of the stock of teachers. We now consider teacher mobility and turnover in the various regions. The most important facts are that London has a higher rate of recruitment of new young teachers and also that recruits are younger in London than in other regions. As far as turnover is concerned, Table 8.4 shows that London has the highest rate for both men and women with 23 per cent of men teachers and 32 per cent of women changing their jobs in the course of a year. The West Midlands has an equally high rate for women and the third highest for men. Yorkshire and Humberside also have a high rate of turnover for women and the North West has a high rate for men. Nevertheless, both components of turnover, teachers moving schools and those leaving the profession altogether, are higher than average in London.

(i) *Leavers.* Two aspects of the 'loss' of female teachers are of some interest. First there exists quite a wide fluctuation between regions, ranging from 7.5 per cent in the North to 16.2 per cent in the South West; secondly, this variation does not appear to follow any pattern in relation to the level of regional urbanisation. For males, however, there is some evidence of a

TABLE 8.4   *School turnover by region, 1970–71*

Region	Those remaining in* teaching on 31 March 1971				Those who left teaching by 31 March 1971		Total number in service on 31 March 1971 (= 100 per cent)	
	Same school		Movers					
	Men %	Women %	Men %	Women %	Men %	Women %	Men	Women
North	92.7	84.9	6.3	7.5	1.0**	7.5	96	146
Yorkshire and Humberside	85.5	71.4	7.8	13.3	6.6	15.2	166	210
North West	81.8	73.5	15.9	14.2	2.4**	12.4	170	275
E. Midlands	84.0	83.1	13.0	8.1	3.0**	8.9	100	124
W. Midlands	82.6	67.6	11.2	18.1	6.2	14.2	161	204
East Anglia	87.5	74.5	7.5	15.7	5.0**	9.8	40	51
Greater London	77.0	68.0	13.0	16.2	9.9	15.8	161	291
South East	85.7	77.4	12.0	11.0	4.0	11.6	251	363
South West	87.2	78.2	9.2	5.6	3.7**	16.2	109	142
Wales	83.5	75.8	12.9	10.5	3.5**	13.7	85	124
Total	84.2	74.6	11.1	12.5	4.8	13.0	1,339	1,930

Source: 1 per cent sample.
Notes:
  *Including transfers to other educational establishments.
  **Based on less than five observations.

systematic pattern. London has a level of male loss about twice the national average; other urban areas like Yorkshire and Humberside, and West Midlands, also have higher than average rates. In contrast, predominantly rural areas like North, Wales and South West have a substantially lower male leavers rate. Although there exist some exceptions, it would appear that male teachers are more likely to leave the profession in places where numerous alternative job opportunities exist than elsewhere.

When the figures for women are split by marital status, it becomes apparent that for single women the difference between London and the rest of the country is of the same order as for men (about twice as high). In contrast the leavers rate for married women is only slightly higher in London than elsewhere. This supports the alternative job opportunities explanation of the high male leavers rate in London since, on the whole, married women are undoubtedly less career conscious and, in many cases, domestic circumstances will determine their job decisions.

When the leavers rates are disaggregated by age, it is in the middle age groups where the difference between London and the rest is most severe. It is about 50 per cent higher in the under-30 age group, but in the 30–39 and 40–49 age groups it runs at almost 100 per cent higher than the rest of England and Wales.

(ii) *Movers.* London does not have the highest proportion of teachers moving between schools: for men it is exceeded by the North West, and for women it is exceeded by the West Midlands. Nevertheless, inter-school mobility rates in London are higher than the national average, and indeed the top four regions in our population density–urbanisation league table – London, North West, West Midlands, and South East – all have a much higher mobility than the average. The two regions with very low levels of mobility are both rural (South West and the North). When disaggregated by marital status it is again clear that single women behave similarly to men.

As explained in Chapter 7, movers can be disaggregated into various categories. There are those who transfer to other educational establishments and those who stay in maintained primary and secondary schools. The latter group can in turn be split into: those who move school within the same LEA; those who change LEA within the same region; and those who change region. A comparison of London with the other regions was carried out for each of these categories and the following main points emerged:

(a) London had a much larger proportion of movers who transferred to other educational establishments. (This seems plausible given that such opportunities are much more common in London.)

(b) Movements of school within London involve a much more frequent change of LEA than within any other region (again this is plausible given the relatively small geographical area covered by LEAs in London).

TABLE 8.5   *Age distribution of region leavers and profession leavers, 1970–71*

	Age group					Total number of teachers (=100%)
	Less than 25	25–29	30–39	40–49	50 and over	
*Region leavers**						
London	36.4	45.5	18.1	0	0	22
Other regions	23.5	38.3	23.5	12.3	2.4	81
Profession leavers						
London	29.0	35.5	16.1	8.1	11.3	62
Other regions	23.4	15.1	21.5	8.8	31.2	205
Total out of region						
London	31.0	38.1	16.7	6.0	8.3	84
Other regions	23.4	21.7	22.0	9.8	23.1	286

Source: 1 per cent sample.
Notes:
*Teachers who remain in teaching but change region, including transfers to other educational establishments between 31 March 1970 and 31 March 1971. Figures given under 'other regions' are aggregate figures for individual regions and not simply movements into London.

(c) The proportion of teachers changing region was much greater for London than for any other region: 29.4 per cent of London movers changed regions (i.e. moved out of London) compared with only 22.7 per cent for the rest of England and Wales. Thus even though London does not have the highest overall mobility level, it does have a much larger loss of teachers to other regions than other parts of the country.

Obviously the high rates of teacher turnover in London are associated with the high proportion of young teachers in the capital. 69 per cent of those leaving teaching in London were under 30 compared with only 45 per cent for other regions. Table 8.5 indicates that this was equally true of those leaving the region for another teaching job and of those giving up teaching altogether.

8.1.3 *Earnings and promotion rates*

Our discussion on the role of salary allowances was based on the assumption that national salary scales prevent unconstrained market wage adjustments from taking place. Although this is true on broad terms, Chapter 9 will demonstrate that some limited earnings adjustments do take place. The flexibility for these limited adjustments comes through promotion. In this section we will therefore investigate regional wage differentials and variations in promotion rates.

We aim to assess the extent to which, other things being equal, teachers obtain higher earnings in regions that find it relatively difficult to recruit and retain teachers, and lower earnings in those which find it relatively easy. We have previously shown that teachers in predominantly rural regions are older than those in urban regions, and in particular older than those in London. These age distributions dominate average salaries in the regions because of the incremental salary scales on which teachers with more experience are paid higher salaries. Column 1 of Table 8.6 shows in index form the average teacher salary in each region in 1971. London earnings were high because of the allowance but earnings in Yorkshire and Humberside and West Midlands were also higher than their age structure would have led us to expect. The second column of Table 8.6 standardises these average earnings for age and other relevant factors.[6] Teachers in London are now, as expected, well at the top of the league table earning 6.1 per cent more than the national average. The previous leading region, Wales, now drops to the bottom, demonstrating once more the influences of age and/or experience on salaries. The second highest standardised earnings are found in Yorkshire and Humberside and the West Midlands and the lowest standardised earnings are found in Wales and the South West.

It could then be said that there exists evidence of wage adjustments in

TABLE 8.6 *Regional earnings, 1971*

| Region | Teachers' salary index | | Index of earnings of full-time non-manual workers | Teachers' relative earnings index** |
	Actual (1)	Standardised* (2)	(3)	(4)
North	99.2	97.4	90.1	108.1
Yorkshire and Humberside	102.4	99.7	92.9	107.3
North West	97.3	98.5	95.1	103.6
E. Midlands	98.5	98.4	93.8	104.9
W. Midlands	100.3	99.6	97.2	102.4
E. Anglia	100.4	98.8	94.7	104.3
London	103.9	106.1	115.4	92.0
South East	97.8	97.8	98.5	99.3
South West	98.4	96.1	94.8	101.4
Wales	104.2	96.0	95.7	100.3
Total	100	100	100	100

Source: 1 per cent sample and UGC, *New Earnings Survey*, 1971.
Notes:
  *Standardised for age, qualifications, sex and sector using the earnings function method developed in Chapter 9.
** $\left(\dfrac{\text{Column (2)}}{\text{Column (3)}}\right) \times 100.$

regions like Yorkshire and Humberside, and West Midlands. But what about London? Or, more specifically, to what extent is the London differential a result of the allowance, and to what extent a result of labour market adjustments? To answer this question we repeated the standardisation exercise, after first subtracting the London allowance from the salaries of all London teachers.[7] This exercise showed that all of the differential in London was due to the existence of the allowance; in effect, after accounting for this area addition, London teachers do not exhibit significantly higher earnings.

In contrast, wage adjustments were in evidence in Yorkshire and Humberside, and the West Midlands, and local authorities in these regions seem to compensate their teachers to some extent (through better promotion) for the expense and inconvenience involved in living in urban areas. But is the London allowance adequate? Columns 3 and 4 of Table 8.6 reveal another dimension of the issue. London non-manual workers in general in 1971 earned 15 per cent more than the national average compared to the teachers' 6 per cent. We can thus compute a relative earnings index of 92, which is by far the lowest of any region and 16 points lower than that for teachers in the North. Thus, even after the 6 per cent London allowance, London teachers were by far the worst paid relatively to their white collar neighbours.

One of the ways in which local authorities may compete for teachers is through more rapid promotion. However, we have shown that if age standardised earnings are taken as a criterion, this mechanism does not seem to be operating in London. We can also examine the issue by looking directly at the promotion prospects of the region as compared with the rest of the country.

Table 8.7 shows that the probability of promotion in London for a teacher was higher than average but was not the highest of all regions. In London 12.8 per cent of those remaining in the teaching profession were promoted but in Yorkshire and Humberside and in West Midlands the proportion was 14.2 per cent. We find then additional support for our previous finding: the two regions which had higher earnings than the rest also had higher promotion rates than the rest.

The table also shows the proportions of teachers promoted among movers and stayers. Again London did not by any means have the highest proportion promoted in either category; however, when movers were split into the three categories used in the previous section, an interesting pattern emerged. The proportion promoted was higher in London for those school movers who remained in the same local education authority (45.5 per cent against 31.8 per cent). The proportion promoted of those who changed LEA and of those who changed region was much lower in London than in the other regions (26.3 per cent against 32.3 per cent, and 20 per cent against 26 per cent, res-

TABLE 8.7 *Teachers remaining in maintained primary and secondary schools from 31 March 1970 to 31 March 1971: promotions by region and movement*

| Region | Percentage promoted | | | Number of teachers in service 1970 and 1971 |
	Teachers who stayed in the same school	Teachers who changed school	All teachers	
North	6.1	31.3	7.9	229
Yorkshire and Humberside	12.0	30.8	14.2	331
North West	10.0	28.8	12.7	400
East Midlands	8.0	22.2*	9.3	205
West Midlands	9.6	37.0	14.2	325
East Anglia	9.6	27.3*	11.9	84
Greater London	9.3	31.1	12.8	383
South East	8.9	30.5	11.2	555
South West	8.3	25.0*	9.5	222
Wales	7.3	30.4	10.1	188
All teachers	9.1	30.6	11.7	2,922

Source: 1 per cent sample of teachers.
Note:
*Based on less than five observations.

pectively). Putting it simply, this indicates that the movement of teachers out of London was less motivated by promotion than the movement out of any other region (or out of a local authority within any other region). It would seem that, to a larger extent than in other regions, many teachers move out of London irrespective of promotion considerations. Although we cannot identify LEAs it seems probable that the lower figure for those changing LEA in London could be caused by a similar movement out of inner London to outer London schools.

On examining promotion rates by age group, we found that rates were higher in London than in the rest of the country for teachers less than 30 and for those over 40. London teachers aged 30–39, however, had a substantially lower promotion rate. Considered together with our previous finding concerning the relatively fewer numbers of 30–39 year-old teachers in London, this is a striking finding. It would appear that in 1971 teachers not only left London as they approached their 30s, but also those who remained appeared to have fewer promotion opportunities than their counterparts outside London. One would expect that if fewer people are in a given group, their chances of climbing the promotion ladder would be better, but this did not seem to be the case in London. Two possible explanations spring to mind to account for this phenomena. Either a promotion bottleneck existed for teachers aged 30–39 or the best teachers had already moved out of the region and those remaining were less suitable for promotion.

8.1.4   *Summary of findings on the London allowance*

Although in aggregate terms London had the most favourable pupil–teacher ratio in the country, there appear to be fewer experienced teachers in mid-career. Most other indicators also show that London may have had a poorer 'quality' teaching force in 1971 than other regions. London also had a significantly higher rate of teacher turnover, 29 per cent compared with 20 per cent in the rest of the country. The outflow of teachers from the London area, both because of leavers from the profession and because of movements to other regions, is higher and more heavily concentrated in the 20 to 30 age group than in the rest of the country. The causes of this large and young outflow are almost certainly financial. There was no evidence of any adjustment above the payment of the London allowance that would compensate teachers for the higher costs of living in the capital, and the greater availability of alternative employment. Despite the allowance, teachers in London were the worst paid of any region in relation to earnings in other white collar occupations. Furthermore, promotion prospects do not appear to be higher in London than in other regions that could be characterised as predominantly urban.

There are differences between the sexes in our findings. In general London attracted only a slightly higher proportion of male recruits but the rate of male leavers was much higher than in the rest of the country. On the other hand, the rate of recruitment of female teachers was much higher than elsewhere, while the rate of female leavers was not much different from the other regions. As a result, London had the highest proportion of female teachers of any region. Furthermore, and given the high rate of loss of married women, London also has a higher proportion of single female teachers in all age groups.

The aggregate nature of our data meant that it was impossible to study other regions in any detail since all of them were a mixture of urban and rural areas. However, a comparison of the overall density of population in each region with the main characteristics of teacher supply in the region suggests that the problems of London are not exclusive to that area, though they are probably more acute there. Other education authorities do appear, however, to have made more use than those in the London area of what flexibility is possible under existing salary arrangements.

8.2 The school of exceptional difficulty allowance[8]

The overt rationale of the School of Exceptional Difficulty allowance (henceforth SED) is rather different from that of the London allowance. However it can be studied in similar terms. Schools which were designated for this allowance when it was first introduced in 1968 were by the nature of the criteria used in their selection (see next section) less attractive to teachers than other schools. This must be expected to have led to a poorer quality teaching staff and higher rates of staff turnover. The introduction of the SED allowance should have reduced if not eliminated these differences. It is the purpose of this section to discover the extent to which it succeeded in meeting this objective.

8.2.1 *Background*

The contemporary history of educational policies of 'positive discrimination' began in the United States during the early 1960s. The 'Headstart' educational programmes for underprivileged and underachieving children and the 'Coleman Report' (Coleman, 1966) being notable examples. The theme was given powerful support in Britain in the influential Plowden Report published in 1967 (DES, 1967b). This report recommended that 'Educational Priority Areas' (EPAs) should be set up in socially deprived areas. A multitude of extra educational and social resources were to be channelled into those areas, one of which, it was proposed, would be a £120 Salary Allowance for teachers serving in schools within these EPAs.

Reaction was initially favourable to the EPA policy. A provision was quickly made by the Burnham Committee with the active support of the Government for a £75 allowance to be paid to teachers in 'Schools of Exceptional Difficulty' from 1 April 1968. The final designation of schools was not made until November 1968 at which time it included 572 schools containing 145,801 children, or 1.8 per cent of the total pupil population in maintained primary and secondary schools (Halsey, 1972). This was very close to the 2 per cent recommended by Plowden, though the size of the allowance was less than the recommended £120.

The final designation of SED schools was made by the DES from lists of schools submitted by local authorities. A major problem was to find a criterion which was socially acceptable and administratively workable. The criteria for designation were laid down by the Burnham Committee as follows (DES, 1969 – b):

(i) The social and economic status of the parents of children at the school.

(ii) The absence of amenities in the homes of children in the school.

(iii) The proportion of children in the school receiving free meals or belonging to families in receipt of supplementary benefits under the Ministry of Social Security Act 1966.

(iv) The proportion of children in the school with serious language difficulties.

Local authorities were given no further guidance on how to measure items (i) and (ii) nor how to weight the four criteria into an objective index. Each local authority was left to work out its own subjective assessment of their schools and, furthermore to decide for itself how many schools to include

on the list submitted to the DES. (One unplanned but important consequence of the fact that all this had followed the Plowden Report on primary schools was that the great majority of schools on the submitted lists
were primary.) Finally, since the total amount of money made available for
the SED allowance was limited, only the top few from each submitted list
were finally chosen (not necessarily equal proportions from each list) by
the DES.

After the introduction of the SED allowance the Teachers Unions and
Local Authorities came increasingly to the opinion that a more flexible
system of attracting and retaining high quality teachers in EPA schools was
required.[9] Consequently the 1973 salary agreement incorporated a new
open-ended provision for EPA schools (DES, annual –b). Under this clause
a local education authority could at its discretion increase the unit total
which determines the number of higher paid posts in certain schools by up to
20 per cent. To qualify, the schools had to fall under the previously mentioned criteria for Schools of Exceptional Difficulty, but need not necessarily
be the same as those receiving the SED allowance.

This new provision was quickly seized upon by urban authorities experiencing teacher shortages and for the first time a substantial number of
secondary teachers benefited from policies of positive discrimination. By
1974, 9.1 per cent of the total teaching force in England and Wales were in
schools benefiting from this new clause. These were mainly concentrated in
inner city areas with, for example, the Inner London Education Authority
having 37 per cent of its teachers in schools which benefited from this provision.[10] Unfortunately no data exists as to how many individual teachers benefited from this new policy and furthermore no study has been undertaken or
commissioned to examine the relative effectiveness of the flexible system
versus the flat rate salary allowance system.

By 1974 the original 572 SED schools had fallen to 511 containing 5,728
teachers.[11] The allowance remained at £75 until 1971 when it was raised to
£83, again raised to £105 in 1972 and to £114 on 1 April 1974. The incoming
Labour Government, however, reaffirmed their belief in a flat rate allowance
and a new higher and more extensive allowance was introduced from 1 June
1974. This new 'Social Priority' allowance of £276 for teachers with three or
more years service in the same social priority school and £201 for the rest,
replaced the old allowance, absorbing the old SED schools and including a
great many more. 3,444 schools, both primary and secondary, containing
some 12.5 per cent of the teaching force were designated.

The educational and social effects of the EPA allowance have been
mentioned by Halsey *et al.* (1972). However little work has been done on the
effect on teachers. One exception was a short survey by ILEA (ILEA, 1972a
and b). This compared teachers in SED schools with those in other schools
on the EPA list which did not receive the allowance. They found a consider-

able reduction in resignations from the SED schools during the first year (1968–69) but in the following year resignations were up again to the level of the non-SED schools. They also found considerable resentment among teachers not receiving the allowance but this was tempered by the fact that most teachers (SED and non-SED) considered that the allowance was too small to have any effect on staffing.

The only other available data on EPA teachers comes from Halsey (1972) though this concerns only a small subset of EPA teachers in four localities not all of whom were receiving the SED allowance. They conducted an attitude survey of these teachers and compared it with a similar national survey of primary school teachers. The most striking finding was that EPA teachers were *less* interested than others in teaching less-able children while a second survey found, not surprisingly, that they had more of such children than the national average. The EPA teachers also considered that on the following four items they were worse off than teachers in non-EPA schools: support from parents; physical conditions of work; neighbourhood in which they work; and the ability of the children they teach. Off-setting these items, they considered that their job was more worthwhile and brought greater satisfaction.

8.2.2 *The SED teachers as designated in 1968*

A list of 563 SED school numbers (coded so as to prevent identification of particular schools) was supplied to us by the DES; although this does not correspond to the 572 quoted by Halsey (1972), we have assumed that all the schools designated in 1968 were included on our list. Subsequently we extracted the records of all teachers in these schools from each of the data files: 1966 through to 1972. This gives us information covering three years prior to the introduction of the SED salary allowance and four years after. Simultaneously to this data extraction we took a sample of all teachers in a 1 per cent sample of non-SED primary schools (primary, because the vast majority of SED schools are primary). Apart from the obvious inadequacy of not possessing any direct information on the social and economic characteristics of SED teachers, schools, or localities, our data base presented several other problems which are discussed below.

The distribution of SED teachers by type of school is shown in Table 8.8. SED teachers were to be found in primary, secondary and special schools and represented 1.3 per cent of the total teaching force in such schools. The vast majority, nearly 90 per cent, of these teachers were in primary schools and comprised 2.4 per cent of the primary teaching force or approximately 1 in every 40 teachers. Most of the remainder were to be found in secondary modern schools but only comprised 1 in every 200 of such teachers. An analysis of SED teachers by region shows that the North West of

TABLE 8.8   *SED teachers by type of school: 1968*

Type of school	SED teachers No.	Per cent	SED teachers as a percentage of the total teaching force in the school type
Primary	3.519	89.6	2.4
Secondary modern	330	8.4	0.5
Comprehensive	39	1.0	0.1
Other secondary	18	0.5	0.1
Special schools	20	0.5	0.3
Total	3,926	100.0	1.3

Source: SED sample and DES (annual – a).

England, the West Midlands and London contained nearly 70 per cent of all SED teachers, but less than 40 per cent of the total teaching force. In terms of density of SED teachers per 100 teachers, these three regions had a density of more than 2 being closely followed by the North with a figure of 1.8. Two regions, Yorkshire and Humberside and East Midlands, had intermediate densities of 1.4 and 1.1 respectively, while the South East, South West, and Wales had negligible numbers of SED teachers, and East Anglia had none.

We have restricted further analysis to primary teachers because of the small numbers of SED teachers in other types of schools. In looking for any effects of the allowance in the following two sections, the timing of the payment of the allowance should be borne in mind. The final designation of schools was not made until November 1968 (Halsey, 1972) and thus came too late to have had any effect on the main intake of teachers for 1968–69, which occurs in September. It may still have influenced some components of the turnover of teachers but the main effect, if any, of the allowance would not be felt until 1969–70. We should not, therefore, notice any major change in the distribution of the stock of teachers until 1970.

8.2.3 Stock comparisons

As we are unable to make calculations of pupil–teacher ratios, the direct effect of the introduction of the allowance on staffing standards in SED schools cannot be deduced from our data. The analysis had therefore to be restricted to comparisons of the characteristics of teachers in SED and non-SED schools. Even here difficulties arose because of the substantially different regional distribution of the two. As we have seen, the vast majority of SED teachers are in predominantly urbanised regions (London, West Midlands, North West) and most of the remainder are situated in cities within the less urbanised regions. Urban areas, and in particular the above three urban regions differ in several teachers characteristics, as shown in the first case study of this chapter. As a consequence, the comparisons between SED and non-SED teachers will be biassed as far as these characteristics are concerned (for example, there are more graduates in urban regions and turnover is higher).

This does not, however, present a problem in our analysis of changes over time since we can assume fairly confidently that any bias in a single year's comparison will have remained constant during the relatively short time period being considered.

Table 8.9 presents some comparisons of the teaching force in SED schools and in our non-SED sample by means of what we have termed 'Relative Quality Indices'. These are simply the percentage of SED teachers with a given characteristic divided by the equivalent percentage for non-SED teachers. An index value greater than one indicates that there were more of such teachers in SED schools while a value less than one indicates that there were less. We must however bear in mind that regional biases have not been removed from these indices and apart from casual interest they are useful only from a time-series point of view.

We can, however, on the basis of various assumptions, eliminate bias and simultaneously summarise the overall differences between SED and non-SED teachers by means of the discriminant analysis technique used in previous chapters. In the present case we 'discriminate' between SED and a non-SED sample of teachers standardising for region and school size. The results of the analysis are contained in an appendix to this book which is available upon request from the Centre for Labour Economics at the London School of Economics. The results are drawn on in the following paragraphs.

Table 8.9 indicates that in 1968 there were more unqualified teachers in impending SED schools, more young teachers under 30, more over 50, more untrained graduates,[12] and fewer teachers having attended supplementary training courses. On the other hand there were just as many men, slightly fewer married women, just as many graduates and good honours graduates and fewer married women re-entrants. On the basis of criteria widely accepted within the profession, it could then be said that SED schools had poorer quality teaching staff.

The large and significantly higher proportion of unqualified teachers, which stood at its highest in 1967 at 8.1 per cent, appears to be the most striking indicator of lower quality teaching staff in SED schools. In 1968, new regulations were introduced restricting the employment and recruitment of such teachers, and their numbers rapidly fell to only 0.6 per cent by 1971. For this reason we cannot hope to pick up any influence of the allowance on this quality indicator.

We now seek any indication of a change in the relative characteristics of SED teachers after the introduction of the allowance by looking at the main variables one at a time.

TABLE 8.9   *Relative 'quality' of SED teachers by: age group, qualification sex, and marital status, 1966–72*

	Pre allowance			Post allowance			
Category for index	1966	1967	1968	1969	1970	1971	1972
Age group							
1. Under 30	1.15	1.19	1.16	1.16	1.18	1.13	1.19
2. 30–49	0.89	0.86	0.84	0.81	0.81	0.83	0.83
3. 50 and over	1.00	1.00	1.05	1.13	1.09	1.12	1.03
Qualifications							
4. Graduates	1.48	1.34	1.28	1.07	1.20	1.25	1.37
5. Trained graduates (out of all graduates)	0.75	0.74	0.72	0.66	0.85	0.84	0.79
6. Trained good honours graduates (out of all trained graduates)	1.24	1.17	0.88	0.88	0.86	0.81	0.97
7. Attended supplementary course	0.84	0.76	1.04	0.96	0.89	0.87	0.70
8. Unqualified	1.48	1.76	1.47	1.93	1.56	(*)	(*)
Sex and marital status							
9. Men	1.07	1.05	1.02	0.95	1.00	0.97	1.00
10. Single women (out of all women)	1.12	1.20	1.19	1.18	1.17	1.18	1.21
11. Men with a break in service (out of all men)	1.64	1.87	1.48	1.55	2.00	(**)	(**)
12. Single women with a break (out of all single women)	1.75	1.69	1.34	1.23	0.88	(**)	(**)
13. Married women with break (out of all married women)	0.90	0.98	0.88	0.86	0.82	(**)	(**)

Source: SED sample.
Notes:
The relative quality index is the relevant SED percentage divided by the equivalent percentage for non-SED teachers.
(*)Numbers were too small to calculate a reliable index here.
(**)Data not available.

(i) *Age distribution.* Subsequent to the introduction of the allowance, and despite the virtual elimination of unqualified teachers, more and more younger teachers were attracted into SED schools relative to teachers in all the other age groups, but particularly in relation to the 30–49 age group. This U-shaped relative age distribution, which was apparent but non-significant before, immediately became significant in 1969 and gradually increased in severity. It appears then that the allowance did not improve the experience mix of teachers in SED schools because of its relatively greater attractiveness to younger teachers.

A separate analysis by sex reveals that this is more true among men than among women teachers. Within the regions, SED schools in London and the West Midlands in particular showed a growth in the proportion of young teachers subsequent to the introduction of the allowance.

The distribution by length of teaching experience (not shown) reveals a similar pattern to that indicated above: proportionally more SED teachers with less than 5 years experience and more than 30 years, and proportionally fewer with 5 to 29 years service.

(ii) *Qualifications*. We have already commented upon unqualified teachers in SED schools. Among graduates there were some noticeable changes. The standardised results show that there was a temporary increase in the number of trained graduates in 1970 but this disappeared afterwards (perhaps only a transitory influence of the allowance when it was first introduced). The proportion of untrained graduates shows a steadily increasing trend from 1966 to 1972 interrupted by a sharp drop in 1970 corresponding to the previously mentioned trained graduate increase for that year. From 1970 onwards, there also appears to have been a sustained increase in the overall proportion of graduates in SED schools. Once again there are differences in the behaviour of the indices when calculated separately for men and women. The sustained increase in the proportion of graduates was confined to women SED teachers while the temporary 1970 rise in trained graduates shows up for both, but more strongly for women.

(iii) *Sex, marital status of women and re-entrants*. There are no indications of any influence of the salary allowance on the sex composition of the SED teaching force. There were more single women and slightly fewer married women and men. This is true even standardised for the younger age distribution of SED teachers.

The last three rows of Table 8.9 present the indices corresponding to the percentage of men, single women and married women who have had a break in service of more than two years during their teaching career. Once again there is no evidence of any effect of the salary allowance, but the indices do not conform to our initial expectations and need further comment.

The relevant percentages for men and single women are of the order of 10 per cent but for married women they are as high as 40 per cent. This high figure for married women is, of course, due to the large number who re-enter the profession after bringing up their families. Ollerenshaw and Flude (1974) have demonstrated that the distribution of such re-entrants far from matches the distribution of the areas of greatest teacher shortage.[13] Our figures show the highest concentration of married women re-entrants in the North, Yorkshire and Humberside, East Midlands, East Anglia and Wales, and these are not by any means the regions with the highest proportion of SED schools. However, the data show a lower proportion of married women returners to SED schools within each and every region. Possibly the localities within each region which have substantial numbers of married women re-entrants or potential re-entrants (the outer city suburbs) are not the localities in which the SED schools are largely situated (inner-city). This hypothesis might also explain why there are fewer married women of all kinds in SED schools and more single women.

8.2.4 Earnings

We now examine the earnings of SED and non-SED teachers by means of the age standardised earnings functions developed in Chapter 9. The results of this analysis indicated that there was no discernible differential between the earnings of SED and non-SED teachers either before the introduction of the allowance or after (net of the allowance). Of course, inclusive of the allowance, SED teachers earned more (about 5 per cent) but there was no detectable effect on their residual earnings.

Somewhat different results were obtained when this analysis was repeated separately for men and women. The results for women were similar to the overall pattern with no discernible difference in earnings net of the allowance and approximately 6 per cent inclusive of the allowance. In contrast the corresponding figures for men were -3 per cent and $+2$ per cent. In other words, but for the allowance, men SED teachers would have been earning 3 per cent less than their colleagues (standardised for age, qualifications, region, etc.) in non-SED schools. Furthermore, a distinct time trend was apparent from 1966 to 1972 which appeared to have been unaffected by the introduction of a salary allowance. The earnings differential in favour of non-SED men teachers stood at slightly over 1 per cent in 1966 but steadily rose to nearly 3 per cent by 1972 (net of allowance).

As explained in Chapter 9, when allowances and other structural factors are accounted for, any residual earnings differentials can be attributed to differential promotion performance. On this interpretation the evidence indicates no overall difference between women SED and non-SED teachers, but a significantly poorer promotion performance for men in SED schools both before and after the introduction of the allowance. It also shows that this differential for men has increased significantly since the allowance. Looked at in another way, men still did better than women, career wise, within SED schools but the differential was smaller than in non-SED schools and has been narrowing.

Our general analysis of earnings differentials in Chapter 9 shows that there is considerable scope within the salary structure (via preferential promotion) for schools and local authorities to adjust salaries in response to shortages and surpluses. At first sight therefore it is somewhat surprising to find no such adjustment to have taken place in SED schools prior to the introduction of the salary allowance.[14]

Many local authorities, however, were reluctant to use monetary induce-ments to overcome supply problems preferring instead to rely on the national 'quota' system to redirect teachers into their areas. Within each school, however, no such reluctance can apply. Teachers are allocated to the various levels of responsibility posts according to some perception of merit. The foregoing earnings function results therefore indicate that there was a downward adjustment of promotion prospects for male SED teachers since the introduction of the salary allowance. A plaus-ible explanation for this result is that the quality of men teachers in SED schools relative to both men in other schools and to women in all schools was lower throughout the period and, furthermore, deteriorated after the allow-ance was introduced. By quality in this sense we are not referring simply to age or qualifications, which have been standardised for in the earnings function, but to some more general measure of teaching performance or ability as assessed directly by those responsible within the schools.

8.2.5 *Flow comparisons*

Our analysis of SED teacher flows was beset by two major data problems. The first concerned an inability to identify movers out of SED schools directly. A method of calculating the numbers concerned was, however, derived. The second data problem concerned a suspected error on the data files. For some reason the total number of West Midlands teachers recorded in SED schools for 1969 was about 200, or 30 per cent down on what it should have been. Some of the figures in the following tables were therefore calculated excluding the West Midlands.

Table 8.10 reveals that before the payment of the allowance, SED schools experienced substantially higher turnover rates than non-SED schools. All the indices except that corresponding to 'movers in' are greater than one. The total loss of teachers from SED schools in 1967–68 was 32.2 per cent or almost 1 in every 3 teachers.

The allowance seems to have considerably reduced this turnover after 1968, particularly the leavers component.[15] The relative number of leavers dropped considerably in the first year after the introduction of the allowance and dropped even further in 1969–70 but rose slightly again after this. However, discriminant analysis standardising for age, qualifications, sex, marital status and region revealed no residual difference in the leavers rate between SED and non-SED schools for any year except 1969–70 when the standardised leaver rate was lower in SED schools than in non-SED schools. This suggests that the allowance had only a temporary effect in reducing the number of leavers from SED schools, thus supporting the findings of the ILEA Study (1972a) concerning London SED teachers, which also found that the allowance temporarily reduced turnover and

TABLE 8.10   *Relative flows into and out of SED and non-SED schools, 1966–67 to 1971–72*

Category of flow	Pre allowance		Post allowance			
	1966–67	1967–68	1968–69	1969–70*	1970–71	1971–72
Flows out						
1. Leavers	1.24	1.23	1.09	0.88*	1.13	0.98
2. Movers out	1.38	1.18	1.06*	1.63*	1.45	1.16
3. Total turnover	1.30	1.20	1.08*	1.20*	1.29	1.08
Flows in						
4. Entrants	1.58	1.38	1.23	0.98*	1.05	1.20
5. Movers in	1.31	0.97	1.00	0.94*	0.88	1.02
6. Net loss of experienced teachers (see below)	1.30	1.38	1.06*	1.53*	2.08	1.12

Source: 1 per cent sample.
Notes:
1. *Leavers*: Those leaving the teaching profession during the year.
2. *Movers out*: Those leaving their school but remaining in teaching. Transfers to other educational establishments are also included here.
3. *Total turnover*: Total numbers of teaching leaving their school during the year $[= (1) + (2)]$.
4. *Entrants*: Includes both new entrants and re-entrants to teaching.
5. *Movers in*: Those moving into the sampled schools from other schools or from other educational establishments.
6. *Net loss of experienced teachers*: Total loss minus the movers in $[(3) - (5)]$. Represents the net loss of teachers who have to be replaced by new entrants.
* These indices have been calculated from percentages based on the total excluding the West Midlands (see text for explanation).

attributed this to a psychological effect. The ILEA report concluded that the SED salary allowance was too marginal to have any permanent impact on teacher turnover.

The index for movers-in does not seem to show any improvement after 1968. The entry index cannot be interpreted simply in terms of the relative attractiveness of the schools. On the whole entrants are only recruited to fill vacancies created by net movements of teachers out of the schools, together with any planned expansion. The low entry rates for SED schools in 1969–70 and 1970–71 has therefore probably been due to the slower growth rate of the teaching force in SED schools and not to any effect of the allowance. Indeed the final row of Table 8.10 reveals that the net loss of experienced teachers from SED schools was highest in these same two years. This index furthermore reveals that the allowance may have had only a temporary effect (1968–69 this time) although the index does also drop again in 1971–72.

The analysis of flows for each of the three major SED regions does not reveal any different pattern from that of the above. The drop in leavers is apparent for all three regions, while for London and the North West there is also a temporary drop in movers-out. In addition the North West also shows evidence of a temporary increase of movers-in for 1968–69.

On examining the composition of the flows represented in Table 8.10, several interesting points were revealed. We have already shown that SED schools attract fewer experienced recruits from other schools (movers-in) and more direct entrants. However, the proportion of re-entrants among the entrants (i.e. those with previous teaching experience) was also lower for SED schools and the only evidence of any effect of the allowance on this proportion was a temporary increase in 1969–70.

In general, men comprise between 15 to 20 per cent of entrants and leavers and between 20 and 30 per cent of movers in and out. However, in comparison with non-SED schools they comprise a higher proportion of the former and a lower proportion of the latter, thus maintaining a fairly constant balance in the proportion of men in the SED teaching force.

After the introduction of the allowance there was a sustained increase in the proportion of men among entrants to SED schools and a sustained drop in the proportion among movers-out. However, only a temporary increase was evidenced among movers-in (for 1969–70) and the leavers index was more complex, showing two drops corresponding to 1968–69 and to 1971–72.

The indicators of the age of entrants and leavers show that SED teacher flows are considerably younger on all counts that the corresponding non-SED flows. The fact that this is true of both in-flows and out-flows means it cannot simply be a consequence of the younger age of the SED teaching force.

Prior to 1969–70 promotion rates had been slightly and consistently higher in SED schools, but in 1969–70 when promotion rates in all primary schools dramatically increased, both the overall rate and the stayers rate were substantially lower than the corresponding ones for non-SED schools. All primary schools should theoretically have benefited equally from the 1969 decision to increase the number of promoted posts in primary schools. The fact that SED schools did not promote as many teachers implies that headmasters of SED schools could not find as many teachers whom they considered worthy of promotion. This was particularly true of the teaching staff already in SED schools of whom only 9.4 per cent were promoted compared with 13.7 per cent in non-SED schools. Even though more 'movers-in' were promoted in SED schools, headmasters were still unable to use up all the available promotions. Furthermore, among these 'movers-in' it was only married women who benefited to any greater extent than movers into non-SED schools. The same was true among the stayers.

These findings on promotion for this exceptional year can only be interpreted as indicating a lower quality of teachers in SED schools and furthermore a lower quality among men than among women. In both cases there was less potential available for promotion in SED schools, and this was more true of men than of women. Furthermore the SED schools could only attract candidates considered suitable for promotion in larger numbers among married women.

Despite the allowance, SED schools were obviously still suffering from teacher supply problems in 1969–70. The figures for 1971–72, however, which was also a year of exceptionally high promotion rates, indicate a much improved situation. Just as many promotions were made in SED schools as in non-SED schools both among stayers and movers-in. Although married women again did proportionally better, the difference between the sexes was not as severe as in 1969–70.

8.2.6 *Summary of findings on the School of Exceptional Difficulty allowance*

In this case study we have tried to ascertain the differences in staffing provision between 'Schools of Exceptional Difficulty' and other 'normal' schools, and to discover to what extent the introduction of the salary allowance for SED teachers in 1968 influenced these differences.

We were not able to attempt to answer the more important questions as to whether or not poorer staffing provision contributes to the lower educational achievements of children in socially disadvantaged schools. This is a complex sociological question which we are not qualified to answer. Clearly, however, staffing provision is one important item of general educational provision which might influence this underachievement. The salary allowance was specifically introduced to improve staffing standards in SED schools and we have consequently attempted to ascertain its effectiveness in doing just that.

Prior to the introduction of the allowance, it could be said that on three very important counts quality was lower in SED schools than in non-SED schools: teacher turnover was much higher, there was a much larger proportion of unqualified teachers (nearly twice as many), and more untrained graduates. This indicates that the schools were clearly experiencing difficulties in recruiting and retaining qualified and trained teachers. On the other hand, there were just as many men and more single women. The relative age distribution of SED teachers prior to the introduction of the allowance showed evidence of the same U-shape found when London teachers and others were compared in the previous case study. There were relatively more younger teachers under 30 and relatively fewer experienced teachers aged 30 to 50. These differences were not, however, statistically significant until after the introduction of the allowance.

Further analysis suggested that although there were just as many men teachers in SED schools, their 'quality' was probably lower. The earnings differential in favour of men was smaller in SED schools than in non-SED schools, so much so in fact that men SED teachers earned significantly less than men elsewhere (excluding the SED salary allowance). Similar smaller differentials were discovered between married women and single women and between graduates and non-graduates. For men in particular this situation seems to have got worse since the introduction of the SED salary allowance, implying that the allowance has raised the quality of women SED teachers relative to that of men. Further evidence supporting this conclusion was found in an analysis of promotions during 1969–70. In a year which saw promotion rates generally more than double, a much smaller rise occurred within SED schools. This suggested that they contained insufficient teachers judged worthy of promotion. Furthermore, this was more true among men than among women and more true among single women than among married women.

The age structure also reveals evidence of a possible deterioration in quality since the introduction of the allowance (for both men and women). There were fewer middle-aged teachers and more younger teachers, accentuating the previously mentioned U-shaped relative age distribution. We were not able to ascertain the effect of the allowance on the high proportion of unqualified teachers in SED schools because they were quickly phased out of all schools after 1968. The proportion of untrained graduate teachers did however show a drop after the introduction of the allowance, but this proved only temporary.

The analysis of teacher flows indicated that although there was a substantial drop in teacher turnover in SED schools, only a small and temporary part of this could be attributed to the allowance. Furthermore, this effect was confined to women teachers and against our expectations was to be found among the teachers who left the teaching profession altogether and not among those who were simply moving schools. The high rates of turnover evidenced in SED schools prior to the introduction of the allowance was found mainly to be caused by the high proportions of unqualified teachers and untrained graduate teachers in SED schools. Such teachers would comprise an unstable element in any school often intending or being recruited to teach for only a temporary period.

There were also some other temporary effects of the allowance but the main permanent effects consisted of an increase in the flows of certain categories of teachers into SED schools. More men were recruited among movers-in and new entrants, while more graduates (mainly women) were recruited among movers-in and re-entrants.

In conclusion the analysis showed, despite the allowance, a continuing gap between the relative attractiveness of SED and non-SED schools. All the inflows of teachers to SED schools were considerably younger than those into non-SED schools, and furthermore those flows representing more experienced teachers, movers-in and re-entrants comprised a smaller proportion of all in-flows to SED schools.

8.3 General conclusions

In this chapter we have examined the effects of two school-based salary allowances. With SED schools we were able to study the situation before and after the introduction of a new allowance. The similarity of the post-allowance situation with that existing in London in 1971 gives us confidence that we can reliably extend our conclusions to relate to the effectiveness of school-based salary allowances in general.

The most important of our findings relates to the effects of school-based salary allowances on the age structure of the teaching force in schools receiving the allowance. At the time to which our study relates, both allowances were a flat rate addition to the salary of all teachers in designated schools. Such a flat rate addition necessarily represents a greater percentage addition to the salary of younger teachers who are on the bottom of the incremental salary scales. We observed that both allowances seem to have the effect of reducing the average age and experience of teachers in schools that qualify for the allowance. In our view, if equalisation of experience levels is considered desirable, a case can be made for a percentage allowance rather than the flat rate system.

The Social Priority allowance introduced in 1974 to supersede the SED allowance has moved in this direction. In 1974 it had two levels, £276 for a teacher with three or more years of experience in that particular social priority school and £201 for the rest. In view of our findings concerning the lack of experienced teachers in both SED and London schools, it is doubtful if the differential between these two levels is sufficient. Furthermore the restriction of the higher allowance to only those who have served three years in the particular school seems of dubious value. The intention clearly is to retain present teachers in social priority schools by the higher allowance rather than to attract new ones. Our data suggest, however, that there is a need to attract more experienced teachers into such schools and the higher allowance could, if available, help in this respect.

The second finding emerging from these case studies is that despite the allowance, there was a residual 'quality' gap between teachers in schools receiving allowances and others. This suggests that the level of both allowances (at the time) was inadequate to equalise net advantages and that probably a higher differential was needed. The SED allowance was set at about 5 per cent of average teacher earnings in 1968 and subsequently declined. In 1971 the London allowance represented 7 per cent of average teacher earnings. Both allowances have been substantially revised in relative value since then, but our analysis suggests that even current values of around 10 per cent are inadequate. The actual level necessary for any particular school-based salary allowance will of course depend on the circumstances of the particular group of schools in question.

The need for such high earnings differentials to achieve the necessary redistributions of supply seems to point to the conclusion that flat rate salary allowances paid to *all* teachers in a *minority* of schools could be more effectively spent by paying some teachers much larger premiums via improved promotion prospects. In the case of London, such a system could not entirely replace the allowance because of the higher cost of living, but in SED or social priority schools it could.

Just such an alternative system was introduced in 1973 for socially disadvantaged schools in addition to the SED allowance, and if our findings are any guide it is likely to have been a more effective means of improving the quality of teachers in disadvantaged schools. Unfortunately, no study of this policy initiative has so far been attempted.

9

Personal characteristics and the earnings of teachers: an earnings function approach

9.1 Introduction

Because of a lack of suitable data we were not able to specify and estimate a demand function in the same way as for teacher supply. In this chapter, we examine some aspects of the demand for teachers by considering the factors which influence the earnings of individual teachers.

Multiple regression analysis was used to estimate an earnings function which related the earnings of each individual teacher to a number of selected characteristics. The results show that despite the existence of rigidly fixed salary scales in the teaching profession, the existence of senior posts which some teachers obtain more quickly than others, and the slight flexibility local authorities have in appointing teachers to new posts, result in some variability of earnings that must be due to differences in demand and supply relationships. Two particularly interesting general results are that the differential in favour of graduates has fallen over time, while the relative disadvantage of women, especially married women, has increased.

The earnings function technique. An earnings function is a mathematical relationship, relating individual earnings or income to various individual characteristics such as age, experience, sex and educational qualificationn. An example involving only threee variables is:

$$SALARY = \alpha_0 + \alpha_1 \, `AGE' + \alpha_2 \, `SEX' \qquad (1)$$

The 'α' coefficients represent constants for a particular group of workers and have to be estimated from empirical data (usually by multiple regression analysis) and it is upon the relative sign, size and statistical significance of these estimated coefficients that interpretation of the earnings function rests. 'α_0' represents the constant term, or intercept in graphical terminology. If the variable 'AGE' is continuous, then 'α_1' in equation (1) represents the 'slope' of a straight line relationship (see Figure 9.1) between salary and age. Since there are only two sexes, it is convenient to code such variables as 'SEX' as '0' or '1' (it does not matter which is associated with which sex). These variables are generally known as 'dummy' variables and the coefficient 'α_2' in equation (1) represents the estimated differential between the salary

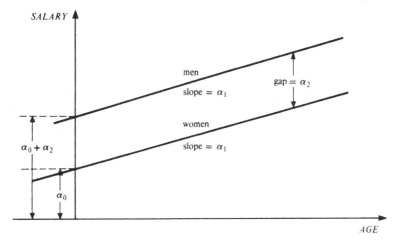

Figure 9.1   *Graphical representation of equation (1).*

of a man and that of a woman, holding only age constant. Figure 9.1 presents a graphical representation of the crude model of equation (1), which is seen to take the form of two parallel straight line relationships between salary and age, one for women and one for men. It conveniently illustrates the assumptions implicit in adopting such a linear additive model, the estimated differential between the sexes is assumed constant for all ages. If in the actual data this were not so, then the value of 'α_2' derived from estimating equation (1) would only represent an average of the varying differentials over all ages.

Similarly, if the age/salary relationship were not a straight line (and it usually is not), then estimating equation (1) might give us some confusing, if not erroneous, results.

The above discussion serves to illustrate the crucial nature of the basic assumptions implicit in the earnings function model which it is chosen to estimate, and how important it is to get the basic functional form relating salary to age or experience at least to approximate to reality.

Earnings functions were originally developed by economists for estimating the extra earnings associated with various levels of schooling. Since then, however, the increasing availability of individualised data on the earnings of various groups of workers have made them almost commonplace. A comprehensive survey of earnings functions has recently been undertaken by Psacharopoulos (1973), but some recent British studies relevant to our analysis of school teachers are worth mentioning. They include studies of university teachers in Metcalf and Bibby (1972) and in Williams, *et al.* (1974). Klinov-Malul (1974) analysed some earnings data on recent graduates in industry, and Westoby *et al.* (1976) looks at social science graduates in all occupations. Ziderman and Morris (1971) is also worth mentioning as an example of earnings functions applied to graduates in general. A relevant study of school teachers in the United States is to be found in Levin (1968).

Figures 9.2 and 9.3 present age–earnings profiles in graphical form for the teaching profession. These figures demonstrate, for all eight sub-divisions, the typical convex shape of well behaved age–earnings profiles for non-manual employees; rising steeply at early ages, the rate of increase gradually easing off until a peak is reached sometime prior to retirement. After this peak, earnings either remain constant until retirement or in some cases actually drop.

Given the shape of this age–earnings profile, the pattern of the earnings differentials associated with the eight sub-groups is not always consistent. Male graduates in secondary schools are the highest paid at all ages; however, male non-graduates would appear to do better in primary schools than

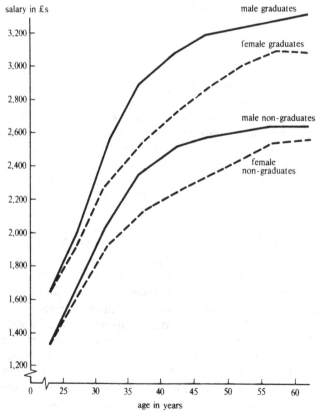

Figure 9.2 *Age–earnings profiles of full-time teachers in maintained secondary schools at 31 March 1973.*
Source: DES (annual – a).

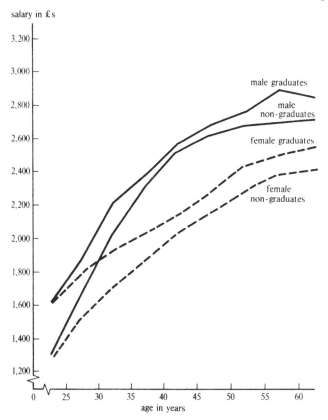

Figure 9.3 *Age–earnings profiles of full-time teachers in maintained primary schools at 31 March 1973.*
Source: DES (annual – a).

secondary. Women graduates do better than male non-graduates in secondary schools, but less well in primary schools. Furthermore, these relativities have remained stable throughout the period. Clearly there are a number of interacting factors at work here which will have to be allowed for in the analysis.

The regression equation. In an earlier paper (Turnbull and Williams, 1974) we considered four possible functional equations relating salary to age (or experience) and concluded that a form relating the logarithm of salary to a quadratic expression in age (or experience) was not only the most realistic from our *a priori* expectations about age–earnings profiles, but also gave the best fit to the data in terms of explanatory power.[1] This preferred form, shown below, is accordingly used in this chapter as the basic regression equation for salary with dummy variables added to represent various categories of teacher (for a discussion of the theoretical aspects of dummy variable regression analysis, see Johnston, 1972, or Drapper and Smith, 1967).

$$\log (SAL) = \alpha_0 + \alpha_1 x + \alpha_2 x^2 + DUMMY\ VARIABLES + ERROR \quad (2)$$

The continuous variable 'x' represents either age or length of service, depending on which of these two variables is being standardised for at the time.

All the dummy variables take the value 0 or 1 depending on whether a certain teacher characteristic is absent or present. For example, the dummy variable '$GRAD$' takes the value 1 for a graduate teacher and 0 for a non-graduate teacher. An estimated regression equation, containing only this one dummy variable, might look like the following:

$$\log (SAL) = \delta_0 + \delta_1 x + \delta_2 x^2 + \delta_3 (GRAD) \quad (3)$$

where the δ_i are estimated values of the α_i coefficients in the assumed underlying salary estimating model represented by equation (2). Because the variable '$GRAD$' takes the value 0 or 1, the coefficient δ_3 represents an estimated addition to log salary experienced by a graduate teacher over a non-graduate teacher, similar in all the other characteristics that we are standardising for (in this example only length of service). A positive coefficient would indicate a higher salary for graduates while a negative coefficient would indicate a lower salary. Differences in log salary are difficult to interpret so we have converted all our results into their percentage equivalent[2] and these are the figures reported in this chapter.

Interaction. The earnings function, or regression model, specified above is linear and additive. Because of this, it estimates fixed percentage differentials between the different categories of teachers represented by the dummy variables. Figures 9.2 and 9.3, together with the discussion on page 146, point quite clearly to the presence of interactions between the three major characteristics being considered: sex, graduate status and sector. Interactions are best understood by means of an example; the simple version of the model would estimate the same earnings differential between graduates and non-graduates whatever their sex and whatever sector in which they were teaching. However, the differential is not the same for men as for women, and it is not the same in primary schools as in secondary schools. The easiest and most common way of dealing with interactions is to ignore them. A more satisfactory and quite simple method is to estimate the regressions independently for different subsets of the whole population and compare coefficients on each variable. An alternative method is to introduce additional dummy variables obtained by multiplying two dummy variables together. If the two variables interact to produce an effect on the dependent variable these 'cross product' dummy variables would have a statistically significant coefficient attached to them. However, with large numbers of original dummy variables this method becomes cumbersome and difficult because there are so many two-way cross-product terms to be introduced.[3]

Obviously such an approach is unnecessarily complex for our purposes and we have not used it extensively (but see Turnbull and Williams, 1974). However, we thought it important to detect at least the major interactions and to achieve this we used the simpler but very effective split-sample method of detection. In particular all regressions were estimated separately for primary and secondary teachers. They were also estimated independently from our 1 per cent sample of teachers and from a second 5 per cent sample of graduate teachers. Not all of these results are presented, but wherever they differ significantly from the results shown they are commented upon.

Age or experience standardisation?[4] Age is one obvious factor influencing the earnings of a teacher and its inclusion in the earnings function lends the results greater intuitive appeal. Figures 9.2 and 9.3 indicate that earnings rise steadily with age until after 55 when they level off, sometimes even dropping after 60. This is the normal pattern. The incremental system in teaching under the 1969 Burnham Report (DES, 1969–6) consisted of 14 annual salary increments of between £30 and £60 each awarded for one full year's teaching service. Once the last increment has been paid and the maximum basic salary reached, no further automatic increments in salary are paid. The existence of this length of service related incremental scale explains why, as is demonstrated later, higher explanatory power (i.e. a better statistical fit) is obtained from those regressions using length of service[5] instead of age as the standardising variable. Service standardisation also increases the significance levels of most of the other variables. This means that, for these variables, actual individual earnings exhibit a smaller variation about the estimated differential when standardised for length of service rather than for age.[6] We have, therefore, concentrated on service standardisation in this paper. Some 'age' regressions are, however, reported and whenever age standardised results differ significantly from the corresponding service standardised results reported, this is mentioned in the text.

Career progression and income variation. The complex hierarchical structure of the school teaching profession prior to the 1971 restructuring is described in full in Chapter 3. Table 9.1 however shows that nearly 55 per cent of teachers were receiving some kind of salary allowance above the basic scale in 1971. For historical reasons, and also because of differences in the size of schools, these posts were not evenly distributed between the primary and secondary sectors. Furthermore, the salaries of heads and deputy heads in the primary sector were much lower than the corresponding posts in secondary schools. The overall result was, and still is, much lower average earnings in this sector.

The salary for which any individual teacher is eligible is closely determined by the Burnham agreements. Under these, length of service, qualification and post held are practically the only factors determining the salary of a teacher. Thus, including these three variables in the regression should leave practically nothing further to explain.[7] It must be obvious, therefore, that for the purposes of this study, grade or post held must not be introduced as an explanatory variable into the regressions.[8]

In essence, post held is the main dependent variable we are explaining in these earnings functions. Salary standardised for service and qualification is simply a convenient numerical scale on which to classify the career hierarchy in teaching. In the subsequent analysis, whenever we talk about higher or lower earnings associated with a particular characteristic, it should be borne in mind that we could just as well talk about better or worse career performance. What we are measuring in fact, is how well any individual teacher's career is progressing in relation to others of similar age or experience. The results of our analysis are discussed in the next section.

9.2 Regression results using 1971 data

Sex differentials. Published statistics show that in all age groups, women teachers earn less than men. However, school teachers have had equal pay since 1961 and it is generally argued that average earnings are lower only because of the large numbers of married women re-entering the profession with shorter lengths of service than men or other women of the same age. If

TABLE 9.1   *Post held in school on 31 March 1971 (Percentages)*

Post held	Sector		Total
	Primary	Secondary	
Head	13.6	3.2	8.4
Deputy Head*	9.6	4.4	6.4
Head of department	3.5	29.1	17.1
Graded post scales 2 and 3	0.5	10.7	5.8
Graded post scale 1	13.8	18.2	15.9
Unpromoted teachers	58.8	34.4	46.4
Total in schools (thousands) (= 100 per cent)	172.3	170.5	342.8

Source: DES (annual – a).
Note: *Including deputy heads who were also heads of department and also including second masters/mistresses.

this is true, then the male/female earnings differential should actually be composed of a differential between married women and all other teachers, single women being little more likely than men to have had a break in their service record. Furthermore, since the incremental salary scale is tied to length of service, standardising for service instead of age should remove the differential altogether. If any differential remains, it can only be attributed to the group with the higher earnings being more successful in obtaining promotion.

Table 9.2 shows, as hypothesised, that when salaries are standardised for

TABLE 9.2 *Estimated percentage extra salary differential associated with: sex, marital status, sector and class of degree*

Differential	Age standardisation		Serivce standardisation	
	(i)	(ii)	(iii)	(iv)
Men over single women	1.6	1.6	1.4	1.4
	(5)	(5)	(8)	(8)
Single women over	10.8	10.9	3.3	3.3
married women	(221)	(221)	(40)	(41)
Secondary over primary	4.6	4.6	3.8	3.8
	(61)	(61)	(77)	(75)
Graduate equivalent	9.7	9.7	9.4	9.4
over non-graduate	(28)	(27)	(47)	(47)
Graduate (ordinary or pass)	13.6	–	13.6	–
over non-graduate	(133)		(240)	
Graduate (3rd class honours)	17.0	–	15.5	–
over non-graduate	(102)		(154)	
Graduate (2nd class honours)	25.5	–	24.1	–
over non-graduate	(715)		(1,163)	
Graduate (1st class honours)	24.8	–	24.8	–
over non-graduate	(52)		(93)	
Graduate (non-good honours)	–	14.7	–	14.3
over non-graduate		(212)		(364)
Good honours graduate	–	9.4	–	8.7
over other graduate		(65)		(100)
n	3,414	3,414	3,414	3,414
R^2	0.760	0.760	0.857	0.867

Source: 1 per cent sample, 1971.

Notes:

1. *F*-statistics for the original regression coefficients are shown in brackets (to the nearest whole number).
2. — = not applicable.
3. As explained in the text, figures reported in this and subsequent tables represent percentage differentials in earnings calculated from the original log linear regression equations. A paper containing all the original regression results plus others not reported is available on request (see Bibliography).

age, the sex differential is in fact composed almost entirely of a difference between married women and men, single women doing nearly as well as men. The coefficient representing this latter difference is only just significant at the 5 per cent level. When length of service is the controlling variable, we see that the pattern repeats itself, the greater difference being that between single and married women. Changing from age to service standardisation reduces the differential between single and married women but leaves the single women/men differential unaltered.

Thus it appears so far, that single women in general earn very nearly, but not quite, as much as men, while married women earn 3.3 per cent less than their single colleagues even after standardising for their length of teaching experience.

This differential, though significant, appears small in comparison to some other recent studies; none of which distinguished between married and single women. For example, a study of US urban school teachers (Levin, 1968) estimated a differential of $440 between white male and female teachers after standardising for length of teaching experience (approximately 6 per cent).

An earnings function analysis of British university lecturers (Williams, et al., 1974) which also standardised for experience, found a differential of £166 (approximately 7 per cent) between men and women. Other recent estimates of the sex differential among qualified manpower only used age standardisation (compare with our 11 per cent); they include: 14 per cent for British graduates entering industry and commerce (Klinov-Malul, 1974); 11 per cent for US university teachers (Gorden, et al., 1974); and 9 per cent for British graduates with social science degrees (Westoby, et al., 1976).

Our initial hypotheses have thus been supported by the data. However, a differential of 3.3 per cent still remains unaccounted for explicitly. It we distinguish those teachers who have had a break in service from those who have had continuous service, we may get some idea as to whether the remaining differential applies to married women as a whole, or only those with an interrupted service record.

Accordingly, three dummy variables were introduced into the regression representing men, single women and married women who have had breaks in service of more than two years in total since their initial date of entry into teaching.[9]

The break variable for married women was statistically significant and negative at −1.7 per cent, indicating lower earnings for such married women. However, it only reduced married/single women differentials from 3.3 per cent to 2.7 per cent (still highly significant) indicating that even married women with continuous teaching service have lower earnings than single women.

In contrast to this result, men teachers who have had a break in service earn approximately 6 per cent *more* than those who have not (the corresponding result for single women is also positive but not significant). Men are of course more likely to have been gainfully employed during any such absence and it may be that this 6 per cent represents a premium paid for their outside experience, possibly also as compensation for their lost increments in salary.[10]

Qualification differentials. Regressions (i) and (iii) in Table 9.2 indicate that there is very little difference between the earnings of 1st and 2nd class honours graduates, both earning about 25 per cent more than a non-graduate teacher. Similarly, the other two classes of graduates earn approximately the same at about 15 per cent more than non-graduate teachers. Graduate equivalents (who do not possess a university degree but receive allowances as if they did) earn only about 10 per cent more than non-graduates.

The above results contrast strongly with those for university teachers where very large differences in career performance were found between 1st and 2nd class honours graduates, this being especially true at the highly competitive recruitment stage (Williams, *et al.*, 1974; Metcalf and Bibby, 1972). A recent study of social science graduates entering all occupations also found a major difference between 1st and 2nd class honours graduates (about 10 per cent higher earnings for the former – Westoby, *et al.*, 1976).

Despite this lack of a differential between 1st and 2nd class degrees, as a whole, graduates are receiving a considerably greater earnings differential than can be accounted for by the graduate allowances (about 6 per cent for graduates and a further 7 per cent for good honours graduates). We must conclude that graduates have more successful careers than non-graduates in the school teaching profession.

The sector differential. It is often claimed that primary school teachers suffer in their career prospects as a result of a bias in the awarding of senior posts, towards schools with older pupils. As shown in Table 9.1, nearly 60 per cent of primary school teachers were on the basic salary scale in 1971 compared with only 35 per cent of secondary school teachers. However, when standardised for length of service, sex and qualification, the earnings differential is reduced to about 4 per cent. Most of the larger absolute differential[11] is accounted for by the qualification variables. The larger proportion of senior posts in secondary schools are in the main filled by the larger proportion of graduates in these schools (37 per cent compared with 4 per cent in primary schools).

The problem of interactions. The estimated differentials in Table 9.2 give an overall picture of the pattern but it is not necessarily true that each differential is the same for each sub-category of teacher. Thus, for instance, the male/ single women differential may be different for graduates and non-graduates or for primary teachers and secondary teachers. As explained in Section 9.1,

TABLE 9.3   *Estimated increases in salary associated with various factors for subsets of the whole sample*

Differential	Factor split by						
	Sector		Sex			Graduate status	
	Primary	Secondary	Men	Single women	Married women	Graduates	Non-graduates
Men over single women	4.6 (45)	−1.3* (2)	−	−	−	0.2* (0)	1.9 (11)
Single women over married women	2.5 (18)	3.8 (18)	−	−	−	3.4 (6)	3.2 (34)
Secondary over Primary	−	−	0.7* (1)	6.7 (54)	5.3 (74)	9.2 (41)	3.0 (46)
Graduate equivalent over non-graduate	10.3 (6)	9.7 (39)	8.4 (17)	8.3 (7)	13.2 (32)	−5.0 (10)	−
Graduate (non-good honours) over non-graduate	7.8 (27)	16.2 (316)	14.9 (190)	13.8 (62)	12.5 (90)	−	−
Good honours graduate over other graduate	10.4 (23)	8.0 (63)	9.2 (55)	8.2 (15)	9.0 (33)	8.3 (70)	−
n	1,754	1,660	1,395	781	1,238	773	2,641
R^2	0.880	0.851	0.823	0.885	0.876	0.817	0.870

Source: 1 per cent sample, 1971
Notes:
1. F-statistics for the original regression coefficients are shown in brackets (to the nearest whole number). Those marked with an asterisk have an F-value less than 3.8 and are *not* significant at the 5 per cent level.
2. − = not applicable.
3. All regressions in this table are service standardised. Age standardised results are not presented here, but show no deviation from the above pattern.
4. The graduate equivalent variable is defined relative to a non-good honours graduate for the graduate only regression.

the simplest and most effective way of examining the data for interactions of this kind is to split the sample by each factor in turn and estimate the regression separately for each sub-sample. This is done in Table 9.3 for the 1 per cent sample, and also for three age categories in Table 9.4. The age categories are young teachers (under 30), middle-aged teachers (30–50) and older teachers (over 50). Table 9.5 presents results for graduates only from our independent 5 per cent graduate sample.

TABLE 9.4 *Estimated increases in salary associated with various factors for three age subsets of the sample*

Differential	Age standardisation			Service standardisation		
	Younger teachers	Middle-aged teachers	Older teachers	Younger teachers	Middle-aged teachers	Older teachers
Men over single women	−0.7* (1)	0.9* (1)	−0.5* (0)	0.7* (2)	1.8 (5)	−0.9* (0)
Single women over married women	1.2 (4)	19.6 (179)	13.7 (61)	1.5 (8)	5.1 (32)	4.5 (8)
Secondary over primary	4.5 (72)	4.7 (19)	1.9* (20)	4.4 (87)	3.5 (26)	3.2 (3)
Graduate equivalent over non-graduate	11.5 (53)	10.0 (10)	−1.5* (0)	9.4 (48)	8.9 (20)	6.1* (1)
Graduate (non-good honours) over non-graduate	14.8 (242)	14.5 (71)	8.6 (13)	13.7 (279)	14.2 (161)	10.4 (24)
Good honours graduate over other graduate	7.6 (49)	10.5 (28)	14.8 (24)	7.2 (58)	9.3 (53)	12.2 (22)
n	1,199	1,500	715	1,199	1,500	715
R^2	0.743	0.510	0.313	0.807	0.795	0.480

Source: 1 per cent sample, 1971.
Notes:
1. F-statistics for the original regression coefficients are shown in brackets (to the nearest whole number). Those marked with an asterisk have an F-value less than 3.8 and are *not* significant at the 5 per cent level.

Before going on to analyse interactions for each factor in turn, it is worth commenting on the very poor explanatory power achieved for the over 50 age group in Table 9.4. Only 31 per cent and 48 per cent of the variation in earnings is explained by the age and service standardised regressions respectively. This compares very unfavourably with figures of 76 per cent and 87 per cent for the full sample. These poor results are due in the main to the failure of the age variables to explain any of the variation (F values are nearly zero), and to the length of service variables explaining only a little. This means that age is not relevant to the earnings of these older teachers, while the other variables, though still relevant, leave a much greater residual of unexplained variation. By this late stage in their career then, other variables that we are not able to identify on our data are assuming a more important role in explaining the career performance of teachers. We can perhaps

TABLE 9.5   *Estimated increases in salary associated with various factors for the 5 per cent graduate sample*

Differential	All teachers	Primary	Secondary
Men over single women	2.2	3.6	2.2
	(16)	(10)	(14)
Single women over married women	2.8	1.2*	2.7
	(19)	(1)	(14)
Secondary over primary	7.0	–	–
	(108)		
Graduate equivalent over graduate (non-good honours)	−4.0	0.1*	−4.7
	(30)	(0)	(34)
Good honours graduate over other graduate	9.0	8.7	9.0
	(402)	(103)	(330)
n	3,896	451	3,445
R^2	0.812	0.895	0.799

Source: 5 per cent graduate sample, 1971.
Notes:
1. *F*-statistics for the original regression coefficients are shown in brackets (to the nearest whole number). Those marked with an asterisk have an *F*-value less than 3.8 and are *not* significant at the 5 per cent level.
2. – = not applicable.
3. These regressions are service standardised.

speculate and indeed, for the benefit of the education service, hope that one, at least, of these variables is 'teaching ability' or 'teaching efficiency'.

Interactions: sex differentials. The most interesting result here is that the male/single women differential is insignificant (in fact negative) in secondary schools indicating that single women do as well, career-wise, as men in this sector. In contrast, single women in primary schools are worse off, with more of the overall male/female differential being attributed to this split than that of single/married women.

The married/single women differential shows no large variation when the sample is split by sector or by graduate status (though it is smaller in primary schools especially for graduates). However, when the sample is split into three age groups, marked differences do emerge.

The age standardised results show a small but significant differential of 1 per cent for the under 30s, rising to nearly 20 per cent for the 30 to 50 age group, and decreasing slightly to 14 per cent among the over 50s. It is, of course, the 30 to 50 group in which most married women re-entrants will be located; their much shorter length of teaching service and missed promotion opportunities putting them far behind the rest of the teaching profession. Service standardising produces the same result, but with much smaller differentials.

Interactions: qualification differentials. The graduate/non-graduate differential in primary schools is only about one half that in secondary schools, however the additional differential of a good honours graduate over other graduates is maintained at about the same level. No differences emerge when the sample is split by sex and marital status, except for an increase in the graduate equivalent differential among primary school teachers and among married women.

Important differences once again appear when the sample is split by age. With increasing age, non-graduate teachers consistently catch up both on graduates and on graduate equivalents. However, at the same time good honours graduates increase their differential over other graduates, effectively allowing their overall earnings differential over non-graduates to remain almost constant.

Interactions: sector differentials. While a significant earnings differential between primary and secondary teachers of the order of 6 per cent exists for both married and single women, it is insignificant and practically zero for men. This confirms our earlier claim that men do relatively better in primary schools with respect to women teachers than in secondary schools. For graduate teachers the differential between the sectors is either 7 or 9 per cent, depending on which sample, but in either case it is much wider than that for non-graduates which is only 3 per cent.[12] This result concurs with the smaller graduate differentials found in primary schools.

Splitting the sample by age indicates that by the time they reach the over-50 age group, primary teachers have caught up a little, the differential being reduced to only 3.2 per cent (service standardised).

Graduate training and 'in-service' training of teachers. Similar salary allowances are paid to teachers undertaking either of these training courses. The graduate teacher training qualification[13] is, of course, relevant only to graduate teachers, but the supplementary course qualification is awarded to any teacher who has successfully completed certain approved one-year courses. However, these in-service courses are mainly taken by non-graduates.

Table 9.6 shows that graduate teacher training increased the subsequent earnings of graduates by about 7 per cent (age standardised); however, this was reduced to only 4 per cent when standardised for length of service. Such a reduction implies that trained graduates have on the whole a longer service record than untrained graduates of the same age.

Completing a one-year supplementary course increases the subsequent earnings of teachers by 10 per cent (age standardised) dropping to only 5 per cent for service standardisation. Once again we can conclude that the service record of these teachers must be considerably greater than those of the same age who have not attended such courses. This time, the difference is even

TABLE 9.6.   *Estimated increases in salary associated with graduate training and in-service training for teachers (Percentages)*

Differential	Age standardisation		Service standardisation	
	All teachers	Graduates only	All teachers	Graduates only
Trained graduate over untrained graduate	6.0 (22)	7.4 (177)	3.2 (12)	4.3 (58)
Supplementary trained teachers over other teachers	10.0 (63)	1.6* (1)	4.7 (26)	0.3* (0)
n	3,414	3,896	3,414	3,896
R^2	0.766	0.761	0.869	0.815

Sources:
Columns 1 and 3 – 1 per cent sample, 1971.
Columns 2 and 4 – 5 per cent graduate sample, 1971.
Notes:
1. F-statistics for the original regression coefficients are shown in brackets (to the nearest whole number). Those marked with an asterisk have an F-value less than 3.8 and are *not* significant at the 5 per cent level.
2. Other variables included in these regressions are: x, x^2, *SEX*, *SEX2*, *SECTOR*, *EQUIV*, *GRAD*, *GRAD2*, where x is either *AGE* or *SERV* depending on which factor we are controlling for. The values of the coefficients on these variables are little different from those shown in Tables 9.2 and 9.5.

greater and probably reflects a greater commitment to teaching as a career by those who are willing to attend in-service training courses.

Subject studied by graduate teachers.[14] Although most graduates have only one main subject of study recorded, some of them have up to three. Because all of these are main subjects, not subsidiary subjects, it would have been unsatisfactory to classify graduates on the basis of first subject only. Consequently, an overlapping set of dummy variables were used which were set equal to 1 if a graduate had that particular subject or subject grouping recorded as one of his three subjects of study. Thus, a graduate could be included into up to three subject classifications although over two thirds of them only fall into one category.

Most graduates who enter school teaching come from the subject disciplines which have traditionally dominated the academic secondary school curriculum, namely: mathematics, physics, chemistry, biology, history, English, classics, geography, and French. These are the clearly defined subject classifications we have used, except that the less frequently taught modern languages (German and Spanish mainly) were included with French. Other smaller groups of graduates who enter school teaching include many with miscellaneous science and technology degrees, and these have been classified under the heading 'other science'. Economics is a subject which has recently been expanding its foot-hold as a school subject (mainly 6th form) and because there were considerable numbers with this subject, it was included in our list. Other social science graduates (sociology, social administration, and law) were included as a separate category, as were 'education' graduates, most of whom had obtained the recently introduced four year B.Ed. degree from colleges of education.

Table 9.7 shows the estimated earnings differentials of graduates in each of these subjects defined relative to the quite large category of 'other arts' and miscellaneous subjects which are not included in the list. Although the subjects in the table are shown in descending order of salary differentials, too much notice should not be taken of the specific order. Only three of the subjects are statistically significant from zero. Mathematicians and chemists receive 3.2 per cent and 2.2 per cent higher earnings, while modern language graduates receive 1.6 per cent lower earnings. The superior earnings of

TABLE 9.7   *Estimated increases in salary associated with the subject studied by graduate teachers (in descending order)*

Subject	Percentage increase	
Mathematics	+3.2	(16)
Chemistry	+2.2	(9)
History	+0.7	(2)*
English	+0.5	(1)*
Classics	+0.5	(0)*
Physics	+0.4	(0)*
Biology	+0.2	(0)*
Other arts	0	(Base)
Other science	−0.1	(0)*
Economics	−0.1	(1)*
Geography	−0.2	(0)*
Other social science	−0.2	(0)*
Education	−0.8	(0)*
Modern languages	−1.6	(7)
R^2	0.817	
n	3,896	

Source: 5 per cent graduate sample, 1971.
Notes:
1. *F*-statistics for the original regression coefficients are shown in brackets (to the nearest whole number). Those marked with an asterisk have an *F*-value less than 3.8 and are *not* significant at the 5 per cent level.
2. Variables included in these regressions for standardisation purposes, but not shown above are, *SERV*, *SERV*^{2}, *SEX*, *SEX2*, *EQUIV*, *GRAD*, *GRAD2*, *SECTOR*, *GRADT*.

maths and chemistry graduates seems to be consistent with the reported shortage of graduates in maths and science subjects. We can assume that this is a labour market adjustment of wages, made possible by quicker and higher promotions for teachers in these shortage subjects. However, it must be pointed out that neither physics, biology nor the 'other science' categories show any significant positive earnings differential.

The age standardised results (not shown here) are very simiiar, the only exception being that all the subjects, except other science and other social science move up in relation to the unclassified base group 'other arts'.

The subject order shown in Table 9.7 indicates that the predominantly male orientated subjects are at, or near, the top. This is, however, not a case of a badly defined regression equation since we are already standardising for sex in the equation, and furthermore, the sex variable does not show any large change after the introduction of the subject dummies.

Region. As already mentioned, we were unable to obtain information on the local authority of each teacher (for reasons of confidentiality). This was unfortunate, since social and economic characteristics of each LEA could have been used as a proxy for the social and economic characteristics of the schools within which the teachers were located. However, not possessing this information, the only indication we have is the 'region'[15] in which the teacher is located. These regions are rather heterogeneous, but in Chapter 8 we roughly characterised them as largely urban or largely rural depending on their population density.

The South East region contains the largest number of teachers, and this was, therefore, used as the base from which the earnings differentials of the other regions were estimated (Table 9.8). London teachers come out clearly on top. However, this is not surprising, considering that all London teachers receive the London allowance on top of the salary they would get in any other region. In 1971, the allowance stood at £118. When the regressions were repeated after first subtracting this amount from the salaries of all London teachers,[16] the extra earnings of London teachers almost disappeared. This indicates that other than the allowance, they receive no extra economic compensation for living in the capital.

In marked contrast to this, teachers in two of the regions which we have characterised as largely urban, and in which no area allowance is paid, receive significantly higher earnings than teachers in the South East (West Midlands and Yorkshire and Humberside). Similarly, teachers in Wales and the South West (largely rural regions) earn almost 2 per cent less than those in the South East, giving a total differential between the highest and the lowest of almost 4 per cent. All this is, of course, after standardising for length of service, sex and qualification.

Type of school and establishment. Regression (i) in Table 9.9 estimates the

TABLE 9.8   *Estimated differences in salary associated with region of teacher (percentages)*

Region	All teachers		Graduate teachers only	
Greater London	+8.5	(160)	+8.1	(136)
Yorkshire and Humberside	+1.9	(8)	+1.6	(4)
West Midlands	+1.8	(7)	+1.7	(5)
East Anglia	+1.0	(1)*	+0.7	(0)*
North West	+0.7	(1)*	+1.9	(7)
East Midlands	+0.6	(1)*	−0.2	(0)*
South East	0	(Base)	0	(Base)
North	−0.4	(0)*	+2.3	(6)
South West	−1.7	(5)	−0.6	(3)*
Wales	−1.8	(5)	−0.6	(3)*
R^2	0.876		0.822	
n	3,414		3,896	

Sources:
All teachers – 1 per cent sample, 1971.
Graduate teachers – 5 per cent graduate sample, 1971.
Notes:
1. *F*-statistics for the original regression coefficients are shown in brackets (to the nearest whole number). Those marked with an asterisk have an *F*-value less than 3.8 and are *not* significant at the 5 per cent level.
2. Other variables included in these regressions for standardisation purposes are: *SERV*, *SERV*^{2}, *SEX*, *SEX2*, *EQUIV*, *GRAD*, *GRAD2*, and *SECTOR*.

earnings differentials found among the major types of maintained secondary school in England and Wales. This regression is age standardised unlike most of the previous results, in order to compare it with regression (ii). Grammar and comprehensive teachers earn about 3 per cent more than those in modern and 'other secondary' schools. However, comprehensive teachers appear to have a slight edge; this being true for both graduate and non-graduate teachers. The service standardised results are similar, but 'other secondary' teachers move up to equality with the grammar school teachers, indicating that age for age, these teachers have a shorter service record than secondary teachers in general.

Regression (ii) is the only regression reported in this chapter for which we have used the full sample of all teachers in grant-aided schools and establishments. We have done this in order to put the earnings of school teachers into a wider perspective. To the 3,445 teachers in maintained primary and secondary schools are added nearly 900 teachers from colleges of education, further education colleges, special schools and direct grant grammar schools. The resulting 4,322 teachers represents a 1 per cent random sample of all teachers in grant-aided schools and establishments. Similarly, the 5,521 graduates represents a 5 per cent random sample of all graduate teachers in

TABLE 9.9 *Estimated increases in salary associated with: (i) type of secondary school for teachers in maintained secondary schools; and (ii) type of establishment for all teachers in grant-aided schools and establishments*

(i) Secondary school teachers			(ii) All establishments		
Type of school	All teachers	Graduates only	Type of establishment	All teachers	Graduates only
Comprehensive	3.2 (9)	3.7 (17)	Colleges of Education	23.6 (201)	12.2 (157)
Grammar	2.6 (4)	2.2 (6)	Further Education Colleges	16.4 (373)	11.0 (346)
Other secondary	(Base)	(Base)	Special schools	5.3 (12)	−2.0 (1)*
Modern	0.3 (0)*	−1.2 (1)*	Others	4.1 (2)*	7.5 (7)
			Secondary schools	(Base)	(Base)
			Direct Grant Grammar schools	−1.3 (1)*	0.6 (0)*
			Primary schools	−4.8 (201)	−9.5 (165)
R^2	0.781	0.747	R^2	0.765	0.738
n	1,674	3,445	n	4,322	5,521

Sources:
All teachers – 1 per cent sample, 1971.
Graduate teachers – 5 per cent graduate sample, 1971.
Notes:
1. *F*-statistics for the original regression coefficients are shown in brackets (to the nearest whole number). Those marked with an asterisk have an *F*-value less than 3.8 and are *not* significant at the 5 per cent level.
2. Other variables included in these regressions for standardization purposes are AGE, AGE^2, SEX, $SEX2$, $EQUIV$, $GRAD$ and $GRAD2$.

such establishments. The variable 'length of service' is not coded accurately for many teachers in these other establishments, and for that reason it was necessary to standardise the regressions by age.

Lecturers in colleges of education come out with exceptionally high earnings, nearly 24 per cent above secondary school teachers after standardisation. These are followed by lecturers in further education colleges earning 16 per cent more than secondary school teachers. Among graduates, there is little difference between these two types of establishment, in both of them graduates earned about 12 per cent more than graduates in secondary schools.

9.3 The effects of mobility and promotion on earnings

In Chapter 7 we examined teacher mobility and demonstrated a relationship between the promotion structure and the level of mobility of teachers. We hypothesised that teachers move school in order to maximise their expected earnings, and hence expect those teachers who move to earn more, other things being equal, than those who do not. We therefore extended our analysis to include various dummy variables representing both promotions and mobility.

At any given point in time, teachers who have been promoted during the previous year will earn more, on average, than those who have not.[17] Since a higher proportion of movers than non-movers are promoted and assuming that the non-promoted movers do not lose in earnings, we should expect to find teachers who have moved during the previous year to earn more, on average, than those who have stayed in the same school. Table 9.10 shows this to be the case with movers earning 1.7 per cent more than stayers. However, when the regressions were repeated separately for each sex, we only found an increase among male teachers (3.7 per cent). This is consistent with our findings in Chapter 7 that a stronger relationship exists between promotion and mobility among men teachers, but we should still, under the previous argument, have found some smaller increase for women.

On economic grounds, we would expect the existence of some specific pattern among different types of movement: in particular, movements which

TABLE 9.10 *Estimated increases in salary associated with the mobility of teachers (percentages)*

Category of movement	(i) All teachers	(ii) Male teachers	(iii) Graduate teachers	(iv) Male graduate teachers
Regression 1				
MSCH	1.2 (4.0)	2.9 (3.9)	1.1 (1.7)*	2.1 (2.7)*
MLEA	3.0 (6.2)	6.3 (7.4)	3.4 (6.0)	5.4 (8.8)
MREG	0.6 (0.3)*	3.5 (2.7)*	5.4 (23.4)	8.7 (29.6)
R^2	0.868	0.825	0.813	0.759
Regression 2				
MTOT	1.7 (7.8)	3.7 (11.5)	2.9 (19.9)	4.8 (27.4)
R^2	0.868	0.824	0.813	0.757
Sample size	3,414	1,395	3,896	2,291

Source:
Data for columns (i) and (ii) are from the 1 per cent sample, 1971.
Data for columns (iii) and (iv) are from the 5 per cent sample, 1971.
Notes:
1. *MSCH* = Move school within the same LEA
   MLEA = move LEA but stay in the same region
   MREG = move region
   MTOT = move school (total)
2. *F*-values are shown in brackets. Those marked with an asterisk have an *F*-value less than 3.8 per cent and are not significant at the 5 per cent level.
3. Other variables included in these regressions for standardisation purposes are: *SERV*, *SERV*^{2}, *SEX*, *SEX2*, *EQUIV*, *GRAD*, *GRAD2*, and *SECTOR*.

involve greater distances, and are therefore associated with greater pecuniary and non-pecuniary costs, should also be associated with greater returns. When we split the overall results by type of school movement, we found that in general this is the case: movements further afield tended to be associated with higher earnings. This is particularly so in the case of graduate teachers, the lowest gain results from moving school within the same local authority (1.1 per cent), the next highest from moving local authority within the same region (3.4 per cent) and the highest of them all from moving region (5.4 per cent). For the total teaching force, however, moving region is associated with the least extra earnings (0.6 per cent). Even for male teachers as a whole, it is only the second highest with 3.5 per cent increase. Since non-graduates comprise 80 per cent of the teaching force, this result suggests that non-graduate teachers have a somewhat different pattern of motivation than graduates when they decide to move.

TABLE 9.11   *Estimated increases in salary associated with mobility and promotions of teachers (percentages)*

Category of teacher	(A) Mover not promoted	(B) Mover promoted over (A)	(C) Mover promoted over a non-mover	R^2	Sample size
1 per cent sample, 1971					
Men	0.5 (0.1)*	7.4 (12.5)	7.9	0.826	1,395
Women	−2.3 (9.0)	12.2 (56.7)	9.6	0.881	2,019
Total	−1.5 (4.2)	10.4 (66.7)	8.8	0.870	3,414
5 per cent graduate sample, 1971					
Men	0.4 (0.1)*	9.3 (29.5)	9.7	0.760	2,291
Women	−2.7 (7.7)	10.4 (30.9)	7.4	0.863	1,605
Total	−1.0 (1.7)*	10.2 (65.3)	9.0	0.816	3,896

Notes:
1. F-values are shown in brackets. Those marked with an asterisk have an F-value less than 3.8 per cent and are not significant at the 5 per cent level.
2. Other variables included in these regressions for standardisation purposes are: *SERV*, $SERV^2$, *SEX*, *SEX2*, *EQUIV*, *GRAD*, *GRAD2*, and *SECTOR*.
3. Figures in column (C) represent the cumulative effects of figures in columns (A) and (B), approximately but not exactly '(A) + (B)'.
4. These percentages are *not* estimates of the actual increases in earnings received by teachers who move school. We are unable to estimate this from our data because we do not have earnings for 1970 on the same data file as those for 1971. They actually show how much extra, on average, a teacher who has moved and has been promoted during the period 1970–71 could expect to earn in 1971 over a teacher who has not moved and has not been promoted but who is similar in all other respects.

The problem of the zero gain associated with women movers is resolved in Table 9.11, where movers are split between those promoted and those not promoted. We found that promoted women movers gained much the same as men (8 or 9 per cent). Thus, if a woman teacher moves school for personal career reasons her financial advantage is similar to that of male teachers in the same situation. The zero average gain in earnings experienced by women movers as a whole, turns out to be a result of two things: first, a far larger proportion of women than men move for reasons other than promotion; second, these women earn, on average, 2.3 per cent *less* than similar women teachers who have not moved school. Since the only way a teacher can earn less is by accepting a lower level post than that previously held,[18] we must conclude that at least some of the women teachers who move do accept a lower grade post. Some married women are constrained to move school because of their husbands' changing work location. Some of them may find it difficult to obtain a post equivalent to the one they had previously held (especially in areas of adequate teacher supply) and be forced to accept a lower level appointment. Support for this interpretation was afforded by running the regressions for single and married women separately. Single women non-promoted movers lost 1.7 per cent in earnings compared to a 3.0 per cent loss for married women. We may speculate that the slight loss experienced on average by the single women was caused by those who moved in order to get married.

Another interesting aspect of the relation between movements and earnings is the comparison of the extra earnings secured by promoted movers with those obtained by promoted non-movers. We estimated that the average gain in earnings experienced by a teacher who is promoted internally was only 5 per cent as compared with the 9 per cent for one who is promoted externally. This, no doubt, partly reflects the greater frequency of internal promotions at the lower end of the salary structure. However, it is also an indication of the limited promotion prospects that a school can offer to its own teachers; the promotion structure is so designed that the gains for a teacher who remains in a school, even if promoted, are less than those he could obtain by looking for promotion outside his school.

When we repeated the exercise shown in Table 9.11 for each of the three categories (*MSCH, MLEA* and *MREG*) we found a similar pattern to that previously described. Among graduate teachers the highest earnings gain was found among those who moved region (11.5 per cent) while among the total sample the highest gain was associated with moving LEA within the same region (12.6 per cent). One possible explanation for this is that graduates find it easier to obtain promotion beyond regional and geographical boundaries than non-graduates, perhaps because of a greater national acceptance of a university degree qualification as opposed to the certificate of a college-trained teacher. The figures in Table 9.12 support

TABLE 9.12   *Movements and promotions of teachers, 1970–71*

Category of movement	All teachers 1 per cent sample		Graduate teachers 5 per cent sample	
	Percentage of stock who move	Percentage of movers who are promoted	Percentage of stock who move	Percentage of movers who are promoted
MSCH	5.6	34	6.1	37
MLEA	2.6	31	2.3	49
MREG	2.9	26	3.4	46
MTOT	11.0	31	11.8	42

Note:
MSCH = move school within the same LEA.
MLEA = move LEA with stay in the same region.
MREG = move region.
MTOT = move school (total).

this hypothesis. Not only do a larger proportion of graduate movers move region, but also a higher proportion of these movers are promoted.

The above hypothesis might explain why fewer non-graduates move region than graduates, but it still does not explain why so many are still willing to move region for non-promotional reasons and why even those who do get promoted gain so little in earnings. This phenomenon occurs among both men and women, and among both primary and secondary non-graduate teachers. It seems probable that there may be identifiable regional characteristics which make a teacher more willing to change region than he would otherwise be. These, and other aspects of regional mobility, were examined in depth in Chapter 7.

9.4 Changes in earnings differentials from 1963 to 1972

So far we have discussed only results for teachers in service on 31 March 1971. In this section, we compare earnings function results for all years for which we have data, including the new version of the 1971 data (salaries as at 1 April) and the 1972 data.

On both of these last two, teachers' salaries are reported as under the 1971 Burnham Report. This involved a radically new salary structure compared with that which had previously been used (see Chapter 3). Unfortunately, the variable which we had previously used to represent 'length of teaching service' was now used to represent the incremental point on any one of five different salary scales. This means that for this new data we could not standardise the earnings functions for 'length of service'. Consequently, we have presented all the results in this section in their age standardised form for all the ten years from 1963 to 1972. The 1971 results reported are slightly different from those of previous sections because of this, and the fact that we have used the new version of the 1971 data in this section.[19]

The equivalent service standardised results (up to 1971) are referred to wherever they differ substantially from the tabulated figures.

Sex differentials. Table 9.13 shows that earnings differentials between the sexes have widened since 1963. The married/single women differential in particular seems to have widened considerably. This result, being age standardised, could be simply a reflection of an increasing gap between average lengths of service of married and single women of the same age (caused by increasing numbers of married women re-entrants). However, this was not the case since service standardised results also show the gap widening from 1.7 per cent in 1963 to 3.3 per cent in 1971.

TABLE 9.13 *Time series results: estimated increases in salary associated with various factors, 1963–72 (percentages)*

Differential	1963	1964	1965	1966	1967	1968	1969	1970	1971	1972
Men over single women	1.6* (4)	1.6 (4)	1.9 (5)	1.2* (3)	1.0* (2)	0.9* (2)	1.6 (5)	1.8 (7)	1.6 (6)	2.1 (8)
Single women over married women	7.4 (73)	7.9 (82)	7.9 (81)	8.5 (136)	9.1 (152)	9.2 (159)	9.6 (161)	9.3 (178)	10.1 (196)	10.8 (194)
Graduate (non-good honours) over non-graduate	13.1 (101)	12.8 (104)	11.3 (86)	14.2 (188)	14.2 (180)	13.7 (174)	14.5 (188)	14.1 (197)	16.9 (282)	16.1 (233)
Good honours graduate over other graduates	16.0 (108)	17.0 (124)	18.1 (146)	15.0 (145)	14.8 (139)	13.5 (117)	12.6 (98)	10.3 (77)	9.4 (65)	11.0 (80)
Graduate equivalent over non-graduate	0.6* (0)	11.6 (21)	11.7 (22)	11.5 (31)	11.4 (29)	8.9 (18)	9.7 (18)	7.2 (15)	11.8 (38)	12.4 (39)
Secondary over primary	2.3 (10)	3.7 (24)	3.3 (20)	4.3 (49)	4.5 (55)	5.4 (79)	4.7 (57)	4.3 (56)	4.6 (61)	4.7 (57)
R^2	0.722	0.729	0.726	0.795	0.790	0.784	0.774	0.765	0.751	0.735
n	2,719	2,744	2,805	2,842	2,914	2,969	3,085	3,258	3,425	3,600

Source: 1 per cent sample.
Notes:
1. *F*-statistics for the original regression coefficients are shown in brackets (to the nearest whole number). Those marked with an asterisk have an *F*-value less than 3.8 and are *not* significant at the 5 per cent level.
2. Other variables included in these regressions for standardisation purpose are AGE and AGE^2.

The male/single women earnings differentials remained fairly small and insignificant until 1969, since then it has risen to a statistically significant 2.1 per cent.

When the sample was split into primary and secondary sectors, it was found that the trend to increased married/single women differentials was detectable in both sectors, but the increasing male/single women differentials was confined to the primary sector. In secondary schools, single women continued to receive earnings equal to those of men.

Results for graduate teachers are, however, slightly different. They show a similar widening of the male/single women differential, but a stable situation as far as the married/single women differential is concerned.

Thus, the overall conclusion seems to be that apart from single women in secondary schools, the salaries of women teachers were deteriorating in comparison with those of men. This is at a time when the general trend had been in the direction of equal pay for women, and in a profession in which officially equal pay already exists.

Qualification differentials. From 1966 to 1970, non-good honours graduates maintained their differential over non-graduate teachers at about 14 per cent. Subsequently, the 1971 salary restructuring resulted in this rising to nearly 17 per cent. Before 1966, there seems to have been a tendency for the differential to narrow, but an increase in 1966 halted this trend. This increase in the differential may have been connected with the introduction in 1965 of the £50 'merit' addition for trained graduates.

The differential between good honours graduates and other graduates has behaved in rather a different manner, consistently decreasing from a high in the early 1960s of 18 per cent[20] to a low of 9 per cent in 1971.

If the much higher relative earnings paid to good honours graduates in the early 1960s (and presumably before that as well) continued into their later careers, while newly recruited good honours graduates received reduced differentials, then we would arrive at the situation reported for 1971 in the previous section; good honours graduates apparently increasing their earnings differential as they progress through their careers. This alternative interpretation of the 1971 results was tested by examining the interactions between graduate status and length of service. As before, it was found that in 1971 a good honours graduate increased his differential with length of service; however, in the early 1960s he did not. This supports the hypothesis that the increasing differential with length of service in 1971 was simply a result of the general decline over the previous 10 years in the size of the differential of graduates in the early part of their careers.

Among other results not shown in Table 9.13, the only major deviation from the above trends occurs among primary school teachers. Here it is not just good honours graduates, but all graduates, who lost some of their earnings differential between 1963 and 1970. This is probably due to the greater contribution which the graduate allowances make to earnings differentials in primary schools. However, good honours graduates in this sector have managed to maintain their differential over other graduates at about 10 per cent.

Sector differential. The primary/secondary teacher differential increased overall between 1963 and 1968, since when it has declined slightly. This trend towards an increasing differential up to the late 1960s is probably related to two interacting forces working in opposite directions. Firstly, in the early 1960s there was a much more rapid growth of middle level posts in secondary schools than in primary schools. Secondly, during the period 1967 to 1969 strong union pressure was exerted on the authorities to equalise opportunities in the two sectors. The drop between 1969 and 1970 was caused directly by the 1969 Burnham salary settlement which upgraded the primary schools in terms of the proportion of promoted posts allowed (see Chapter 3).

In-service training and graduate training (Table 9.14). The £50 'merit' salary allowance introduced in 1965 was payable to those teachers who had successfully completed one year supplementary courses for serving teachers and also to those graduate teachers who had completed a one year course of teaching training. The result of this extra allowance was a jump in the differential between trained and untrained graduates from 5.3 per cent in 1964 to 12.4 per cent in 1965. However, apart from this jump, the overall trend has been to rapidly decreasing differentials which in 1972 stood at only

TABLE 9.14   *Time series results: estimated increases in salary associated with in-service training and graduate training, 1963–72 (percentages)*

Differential	1963	1964	1965	1966	1967	1968	1969	1970	1971	1972
Trained graduate over untrained graduate	6.2 (14)	5.3 (11)	12.4 (61)	8.1 (39)	8.2 (42)	7.5 (33)	7.8 (35)	6.4 (27)	5.5 (19)	5.5 (16)
Supplementary trained teacher over others	−0.8* (0)	3.2 (6)	4.6 (11)	4.7 (16)	5.5 (21)	6.3 (27)	7.4 (33)	8.1 (48)	9.0 (55)	9.7 (56)
R^2	0.723	0.731	0.733	0.799	0.795	0.788	0.776	0.770	0.756	0.740
n	2,719	2,744	2,805	2,842	2,914	2,969	3,086	3,258	3,423	3,600

Source: 1 per cent sample.
Notes:
1. *F*-statistics for the original regression coefficients are shown in brackets (to the nearest whole number). Those marked with an asterisk have an *F*-value less than 3.8 and are *not* significant at the 5 per cent level.
2. Other variables included in these regressions for standardisation purposes are, AGE, AGE^2, SEX, $SEX2$, $EQUIV$, $GRAD2$, $SECTOR$.

5.5 per cent, this being less than the original 1963 differential of 6.2 per cent when the 'merit' allowance did not exist.

In contrast, the subsequent salary rewards associated with attendance at supplementary courses have continued to increase from zero in 1963 to 9.7 per cent in 1972. If this is an indication of the increasing esteem in which these in-service courses are held, then it is an encouraging sign for those who would like to see the recommendations of the James Report implemented.

Subject studied by graduate teachers. The age standardised results shown in Table 9.15 are from the graduate sample and only figures up to 1971 are available. The three subject categories, education, economics, and other social science were not included in these time series results because of the small numbers involved in the early years. Consequently, the uncoded 're-mainder' or 'base' group from which the other subject differentials were estimated are augmented by graduates from these three subject groups.

TABLE 9.15　*Time series results: estimated increases in earnings association with subject of study of graduate teachers: 1963–71 (percentages)*

Subject	1963	1964	1965	1966	1967	1968	1969	1970	1971
Mathematics	4.6	4.8	4.7	4.8	4.3	4.9	5.5	4.6	4.6
	(21)	(24)	(22)	(23)	(21)	(25)	(31)	(26)	(25)
Physics	2.2	2.5	2.2	2.2	1.1*	1.3*	3.1	1.8*	2.4
	(4)	(5)	(4)	(4)	(1)	(1)	(8)	(3)	(6)
Chemistry	3.3	2.8	2.9	3.0	3.3	3.5	3.1	2.6	3.2
	(9)	(7)	(8)	(9)	(11)	(13)	(10)	(8)	(11)
English	1.5	1.4*	1.9	1.2*	0.5*	0.7*	2.3	1.4	2.0
	(5)	(4)	(7)	(3)	(1)	(1)	(11)	(6)	(9)
Classics	0.1*	0.4*	1.7*	1.7*	2.1	2.3	2.5	2.4	2.5
	(0)	(0)	(3)	(3)	(5)	(6)	(6)	(6)	(7)
History	1.2*	1.3*	1.4*	2.3	1.7	2.1	2.4	2.2	2.4
	(3)	(3)	(3)	(10)	(6)	(9)	(12)	(10)	(12)
Biology	4.2	4.0	2.7	3.2	3.3	2.8	3.3	2.3	2.7
	(14)	(12)	(6)	(9)	(9)	(7)	(9)	(7)	(7)
Other science	−2.2*	−0.4*	−1.1*	1.5*	−0.7*	−0.5*	−0.2*	0.7*	0.3*
	(3)	(0)	(1)	(1)	(0)	(0)	(0)	(1)	(0)
Geography	3.0	2.5	3.4	3.8	2.9	2.3	3.0	2.8	2.5
	(11)	(8)	(13)	(16)	(10)	(7)	(9)	(10)	(9)
Modern languages	0.1*	0.3*	−0.5*	0.0*	−0.4*	−0.2*	0.0*	0.1*	0.2*
	(0)	(0)	(0)	(0)	(0)	(0)	(0)	(0)	(0)
R^2	0.784	0.776	0.758	0.752	0.765	0.759	0.749	0.749	0.754
n	2,993	3,079	3,114	3,252	3,321	3,341	3,451	3,692	3,896

Source: 5 per cent graduate sample.
Notes:

1. *F*-statistics for the original regression coefficients are shown in brackets (to the nearest whole number). Those marked with an asterisk have an *F*-value less than 3.8 and are *not* significant at the 5 per cent level.
2. Other variables, included in these regressions for standarisation purposes are, AGE, AGE^2, SEX, $SEX2$, $EQUIV$, $GRAD2$, $SECTOR$.

Throughout the nine year period, mathematics graduates have been the highest earners (although biologists were close behind in 1963/64). Consistently at the bottom of the earnings league table has been 'other science', modern languages and the base group comprising other arts, social sciences, education and miscellaneous. Among the intermediate subjects, physicists, chemists, biologists and geographers were all initially doing better than arts graduates, comprising English, history, and classics. However, by 1969 these latter three had caught up with all the scientists except the mathematicians. This is an interesting finding in a period in which science teachers were believed to have been in short supply.

The service standardised version of these results is entirely consistent with the above, apart from one important exception. Chemistry graduates come out earning significantly more than the rest, and only slightly less than mathematics graduates for all years, and with no apparent deterioration in their position. This contradiction seems to imply that during the period 1963 to 1971, chemistry graduates gradually came to possess shorter teaching experience than other graduates of the same age, hence increasing the earnings differential when standardising by length of service.

Region (Table 9.16). The year 1965/66 was a period of local government reorganisation in London; the London region was greatly extended and renamed Greater London. Our definition of the London and South East regions correspondingly changes between these two years. In 1966, many teachers previously in the original South East region, *who already received the London allowance*, were redefined as being in the new Greater London region. Consequently, the earnings differential between the two regions would necessarily show an increase between these two years.

However, even allowing for the above, there has been a distinct trend to a high earnings differential between London and the South East. Part of this can be accounted for by the increasing relative value of the allowance which stood at about 4 per cent of average teacher earnings in 1963 and rose to about 7 per cent in 1971.[21] However, between 1971 and 1972 the allowance was unaltered, while the earnings differential increased to nearly 9 per cent.

Among the other regions, the table shows a movement in favour of several of the regions which can be thought of as 'largely urban' in character. Since 1967, teachers in the West Midlands region have received the second highest earnings. In fact, as shown in the previous section, they received higher earnings than London teachers once the London allowance was deducted. The Yorkshire and Humberside region also achieved a significant earnings differential over the South East in 1967 which has since been maintained. By 1970, they had been joined by the North West and finally followed by the East Midlands in 1972. Even if these findings are simply interpreted as a slipping in the relative position of South East teachers, they do seem to

TABLE 9.16   *Time series results: estimated increases in salary associated with region: 1963–72 (percentages)*

Region (base is South East)	1963	1964	1965	1966	1967	1968	1969	1970	1971	1972
London	5.8	4.5	5.2	6.4	6.9	7.6	7.7	6.9	7.5	8.9
	(23)	(14)	(20)	(45)	(51)	(66)	(66)	(60)	(68)	(90)
West Midlands	2.4	1.6*	–	1.6*	2.7	3.1	3.6	2.8	3.3	2.8
	(4)	(2)		(3)	(7)	(10)	(12)	(9)	(12)	(8)
East Anglia	−4.5	−0.5*	−1.2*	−0.6*	−0.3*	1.3*	1.7*	0.9*	0.7*	–
	(6)	(0)	(0)	(0)	(0)	(1)	(1)	(0)	(0)	
South West	0.6*	−1.4*	−4.6	−2.3	−1.6*	−0.5*	−1.1*	−1.1*	−1.7*	−1.8*
	(0)	(1)	(15)	(4)	(2)	(0)	(0)	(1)	(3)	(3)
North West	1.7*	0.2*	0.2*	1.7*	1.4*	1.5*	1.8*	1.9	1.6*	2.2
	(2)	(0)	(0)	(3)	(2)	(3)	(4)	(5)	(3)	(6)
Yorkshire and Humberside	1.8*	−0.6*	1.4*	1.4*	2.3	2.7	1.6*	2.2	2.9	2.0
	(2)	(0)	(2)	(2)	(5)	(7)	(3)	(6)	(9)	(4)
East Midlands	0.3*	−0.9*	−1.0*	−0.3*	−1.1*	−0.3*	0.9*	1.5*	1.7*	2.5
	(0)	(0)	(1)	(0)	(1)	(0)	(1)	(2)	(3)	(5)
North	1.1*	0.2*	0.9*	1.5*	1.3*	2.0*	1.0*	1.6*	2.0*	1.0*
	(1)	(0)	(0)	(2)	(1)	(3)	(1)	(3)	(3)	(1)
Wales	−0.6*	−1.4*	−1.0*	−0.7*	−0.5*	0.7*	1.3*	0.3*	0.5*	1.7*
	(0)	(1)	(1)	(0)	(0)	(0)	(1)	(0)	(0)	(2)
R^2	0.726	0.731	0.730	0.801	0.796	0.790	0.780	0.770	0.758	0.744
n	2,719	2,744	2,805	2,842	2,914	2.969	3,086	3,258	3,423	3,600

Source: 1 per cent sample.

Notes:
1. F-statistics for the original regression coefficients are shown in brackets (to the nearest whole number). Those marked with an asterisk have an F-value less than 3.8 and are *not* significant at the 5 per cent level.
2. Other variables included in these regressions for standardization purposes are, *AGE*, *AGE²*, *SEX*, *SEX2*, *EQUIV*, *GRAD2*, *SECTOR*.
3. – = variable with such a low level of significance ($F < 0.01$) that it was not entered into the regression by the regression program.

indicate that changes have occurred in the balance of supply and demand between the regional labour markets for teachers.

Type of secondary school (Table 9.17). It is apparent from the table that little change has occurred in the relative earnings position of the three major types of secondary school: grammar, comprehensive and modern.

There is a very slight indication in the table of a switch between the earnings order of grammar and comprehensive teachers, the latter coming out on top since 1969. These figures from the age standardised results are not very convincing on this point, but the equivalent service standardised results are unequivocal, showing a zero differential between comprehensive and grammar school teachers rising to 2 per cent in 1971. The 5 per cent graduate sample results also confirm this finding (both age and service standardised), with the earnings differential between comprehensive and

TABLE 9.17   *Time series results: estimated increases in salary associated with type of secondary school: 1963–72 (percentages)*

Type of secondary school (other secondary is the base)	1963	1964	1965	1966	1967	1968	1969	1970	1971	1972
Modern	–	−0.3*	−0.1*	0.6*	−0.4*	−1.8*	−1.1*	−0.4*	–	−2.3*
		(0)	(0)	(0)	(0)	(1)	(1)	(0)		(4)
Comprehensive	5.3	3.8	2.7*	2.5*	1.9*	2.1*	3.0	4.2	3.1	2.6
	(5)	(4)	(2)	(3)	(2)	(3)	(6)	(15)	(14)	(5)
Grammar	5.4	4.2	1.8*	2.7	4.4	2.8	2.3*	2.7	2.8	1.7*
	(14)	(10)	(1)	(4)	(11)	(5)	(3)	(5)	(6)	(1)
R^2	0.694	0.809	0.706	0.813	0.797	0.792	0.794	0.786	0.764	0.761
n	1,392	1,426	1,474	1,463	1,487	1,505	1,542	1,607	1,667	1,753

Source: 1 per cent sample.

Notes:
1. *F*–statistics for the original regression coefficients are shown in brackets (to the nearest whole number). Those marked with an asterisk have an *F*-value less than 3.8 and are *not* significant at the 5 per cent level.
2. Other variables included in these regressions for standardisation purposes are, *AGE*, AGE^2, *SEX*, *SEX2*, *EQUIV*, *GRAD2*, *SECTOR*.
3. − = variable with such a low level of significance ($F < 0.01$) that it was not entered into the regression by the regression program.

grammar schools becoming and remaining statistically significant since 1968 at a level of between 1.5 and 2 per cent.

9.5 Conclusions

Early in the chapter we showed how the rigidly administered salary scales for school teachers severely restrict the process of 'wage adjustment' which normally operates in a labour market. Despite this inflexibility, we have been able to demonstrate conclusively that wage adjustments, although small, do take place. We have done this by isolating and measuring earnings differentials between groups of teachers after standardising for other major sources of variation: length of service, qualification and sector being the most important ones.

Several of these earnings differentials can be attributed to the operation of economic forces, one group of teachers having a lower supply price than another. An example of this might be that higher salaries are paid to men teachers because earnings they could receive if they left the profession are generally higher. Similar cases could be made for graduate teachers and for mathematicians and chemists among the graduates.

Lower supply prices may also have a more psychological or sociological explanation, for example married women. The most likely cause of a low supply price for married women teachers is that the area over which they consider it appropriate to search for work is limited by their husbands' employment. It is also possible that married women are less ambitious for the responsibilities outside the home that promotion to senior posts would bring. There could also be a demand side aspect of this. Employers may believe that married women are more likely to have subsequent breaks in service (and also more likely to be absent through family responsibilities) and that the risks of promoting them to senior posts are, therefore, greater.

Evidence on the lack of ambition or, more accurately, career orientation of women teachers (not just married women) can be found in Hilsum and Start (1974) who found far fewer women than men applying for the senior positions in all types of schools, except infants (where there are practically no male teachers). This point was further substantiated by our regression results reported in Section 9.3 which included the teacher mobility variables. A change of school during a one year period was associated with an average increase in salary for men teachers but not for women, thus indicating that a much higher proportion of the male turnover was directed towards promotion and higher pay.

Another group of teachers with apparently a relatively low supply price are those in Wales, this time caused by a long standing excess supply.[22] This oversupply causes intense competition for teaching jobs in Wales, resulting in lower standardised earnings for Welsh teachers compared with most of the English regions.

In the comparisons of results from earlier years, developments over time presented further evidence of the influence of economic forces on earnings differentials. Science graduates were all relatively highly paid in the early 1960s, but by 1971 most of them (except mathematicians and chemists) had slipped back to parity with arts graduates. This must reflect some easing of the science teacher shortage which had existed throughout the 1950s and 1960s.

In the regional comparisons it was found that teachers in the South East have suffered a steady decline in relative earnings (standardised) so that by 1972 they stood about mid-way and below most of the other high density urban regions. This trend is paralleled by the increasing attractiveness of the South East to middle class professionals, like teachers, and of course the increasing relative affluence of this part of Britain. Apart from the London salary allowance, London teachers were not found to earn any more than teachers in other regions.

A more important trend to emerge from the time series comparisons is the increasing earnings gap between men and women teachers. It is hard to think of a satisfactory supply side explanation of this rather unexpected finding. There is, however, a possible demand side explanation which could be of considerable significance in professional labour markets generally, as sex discrimination in jobs is eliminated.

The proportion of women secondary school teachers who are working in single sex girls' schools fell from 48 per cent in 1963 to 28 per cent in 1971. These women often do not come into direct competition with men for promotion to Head Teacher and Head of Department. The result of comprehensive and coeducational reorganisation of secondary education has meant that this reserved labour market is much smaller and women have not done well in direct competition with men. This does not, in itself, explain the differential between single and married women, which has widened. We can only postulate the following possible explanation. In girls-only schools any male/female discrimination is replaced by single/married women discrimination. As the demand for senior staff in such schools has fallen, competition for the few available posts has resulted in further discrimination against married women. This is a hypothesis which is only partially supported by the regression results, but this result clearly needs further investigation, particularly in the light of many naive assumptions that once demand side discrimination is legally ended, equal earnings in the labour market itself will result.

The trend towards smaller differentials between graduates and non-graduates is perhaps easier to explain. The relative value of the graduate allowances has been progressively decreased by successive salary settlements. However, the 1971 restructuring reversed this process, the subsequent increase in differentials being reflected in our data. Nevertheless, superimposed upon these changing allowances has been a steady trend towards smaller earnings differentials (above the allowances) especially for good honours graduates. It seems probable that the teaching profession has shared in a universal trend towards lower earnings differentials between graduates and other qualified personnel (for evidence on this see Williams, 1973).

A final point should be made about the rapidly increasing salary advantages enjoyed by those teachers who have undertaken one-year supplementary training courses. It seems that such in-service training is being increasingly highly valued in a profession, which like many others, is becoming more and more specialised. Paradoxically, another form of extra training has lost most of its economic value to participants. Moves to make graduate training compulsory may have robbed it of its discriminating value to employers while the fact that it is generally undertaken before commencement of a teaching career may also affect the comparison. Supplementary in-service courses are mainly taken by teachers seconded from their schools by local authorities; they will undoubtedly be carefully selected and highly motivated.

10
Some policy implications

Our enquiry has thrown light on the way in which teachers react to economic factors. We can summarise these findings as follows: (a) teachers entering and leaving the profession are influenced by alternative job opportunities and by both immediate and longer-term relative earnings; (b) the pattern and extent of inter-school mobility are influenced by the configuration of the salary and career structure; (c) despite a unified salary system, some teachers earn more than others with similar attributes, which suggests either a different supply price or different demands for different categories of teacher; (d) although specific allowances may be an effective instrument for redistributing supply between geographic areas and between different types of schools, it is not certain that the present level of these allowances is sufficient or that allowances of a fixed amount are a flexible enough instrument to be the most efficient means of redistributing supply. In the light of this evidence we examine in this chapter some of the ways in which salary policy can be used to complement other teacher supply policies. We do not claim to have given final answers to the chronic problems of planning teacher supply, but we do point in a direction which has hitherto been neglected.

10.1 Salary policies directed at the overall level of supply

The planning of teacher supply in Britain has in the past meant manpower forecasting. This approach usually assumes that all training is completely specific so that once someone is trained as a teacher his opportunity cost, or possible earnings elsewhere are very low. This is manifestly not true as we were able to show in our analysis of entrants, leavers and mobility, where we established that salaries and market conditions have considerable influence on teacher supply. Since teachers salaries are more or less under the control of the central government, they can be used as a policy instrument to influence the size and pattern of the supply of teachers. Here is where our findings concerning the different wage elasticities can be useful.

10.1.1 *The shape of the salary profile*

In general, a wage elasticity gives a measure of the proportional effect that a change in the level of wages has on supply. For example, a wage elasticity equal to 2 indicates that a 1 per cent increase in wages results in a 2 per cent increase in the number of people becoming teachers. In our study, the elasticities estimated refer not to the whole stock of teachers but to the different flows that form this stock. Thus, in looking at the consequences of salary changes, we have to take into account the effects of these changes on each of the flows for which elasticities have been estimated. A further complication arising out of our approach is the existence of other variables which also play a relevant role in the determination of these flows, but which are not controllable by the education authorities. We know, for instance, that both new entrants and leavers are affected by changes in the number of people who qualify as potential teachers, salaries in alternative occupations and outside job opportunities. It is important to remember this because changes in the controllable variables may be offset (or reinforced) by changes in the non-controllable ones, and this makes the final outcome of the policy subject to a considerable degree of uncertainty.[1] However, in the initial design of the teachers' salary structure we can assume that all non-controllable variables remain constant at their present levels. We are, then, evaluating a given policy by investigating its effects on supply *under the assumption that the influence of all other factors remains the same*. It is clear that this is not an entirely reliable procedure, but it gives us information on the partial effect of using salaries as a policy in planning teacher supply.

In Chapters 5 and 6 we obtained several estimates of elasticity of new entrants and leavers to changes in relative salaries (see Tables 5.1, 5.7 and 6.2). We would have liked to determine the sensitivity of each of the flows to changes in the pattern of lifetime earnings. However, we have had to work with some approximations to measure this earnings pattern, mainly because of data problems. As a first approximation, we used a single wage variable; this was either *relative starting salaries* or *relative average salaries*. Both suffer from problems since their use effectively collapses the whole profile into a *single* parameter. A better approximation to the measurement of the whole profile is to use two parameters. We have done this by introducing the *level* and *slope* of relative earnings. This is still not perfect since it assumes a linear salary profile (constant slope), but it is more satisfactory because it disentangles two different reactions – the reaction to the starting salaries and the reaction to future prospects. In any analysis of occupational choice, it is of some value to distinguish these two factors. Furthermore, estimates of the separate effects provide policy makers with two instruments to control supply. For a given overall financial budget, different salary structures (i.e. different profile shapes) may have different supply consequences. We thus have to decide not only on the overall level of salaries, but also on the particular relationship between earnings at different points in the teacher's career. It is convenient to develop this point by means of a simplified illustration.

Let us imagine that two different salary structures are proposed. The first is aimed at improving salaries for young teachers relative to those of their more senior colleagues (flatter slope). The second proposes an increase in salaries for more experienced teachers relative to those of the younger age brackets (steeper slope). We can understand the implications by considering a simple example. Let us suppose that protagonists of the first policy (policy i) propose an increase of 10 per cent, say, in starting salaries (W_0) while keeping *average salaries ($\overline{W}$) constant*; the second policy (policy ii), on the other hand, proposes a decrease of 10 per cent in starting salaries but still keeping *average salaries constant.*[2]

Under our simplifying assumptions of constant slopes, the consequences of these policies for the earnings profile are depicted in Figure 10.1. While the first policy would result in a flatter profile (i.e. would redistribute money from teachers earning above the average to those earning less than the average) the second policy would make it steeper (i.e. would redistribute money from inexperienced teachers earning below the average to experienced teachers earning more than the average).

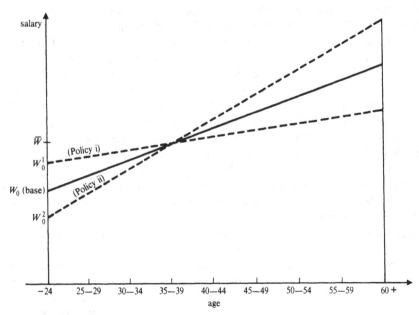

Figure 10.1 *Illustration of the effects of changing starting salaries while keeping average salaries constant.*

Using 1972–73 data as an example, the first policy, a 10 per cent increase in starting salary leaving average salaries constant, would have resulted in an approximate 18 per cent decrease in the slope of the profile for both male graduates and non-graduates. For female teachers, the decrease in slope would have been about 22 per cent for both graduates and non-graduates.[3] Before examining the effects of these changes on supply, it should be noted that elasticities have been calculated for teachers' salaries relative to those in other occupations rather than changes in the money value of teachers' salaries alone. Here, however, we are only interested in the effect of changes in the teaching salary structure, and consequently we assume that salaries in other occupations do not change. This means that the percentage change in teachers' salaries reflects the percentage change in their relative counterparts, and therefore the elasticities can be used directly.

Tables 10.1 and 10.2 summarise the effects of these changes in the profile for the supply of male and female graduates to teaching. Column (1) indicates the type of flow being considered, column (2) specifies the cause of the change as measured by the percentage variation in both relative starting salaries (RSW) and relative profile slopes (K). The elasticities are given in column (3) and the partial effects, resulting from the multiplication of columns (2) and (3) are given in column (4). The net percentage effect for each type of flow is shown in column (5) and its equivalent in terms of

TABLE 10.1   *Hypothetical effects on supply of male teachers of the 'flatter profile' policy (1973)*

Type of flow (1)	Cause (2)	Elasticity (3)	Effects (%) (4)	Net effect on flow (%) (5)	Absolute addition to teacher supply (6)
New entrants					
(i) Graduates	$+10.00\%$ in RSW	$+2.2$	$+22.0$	$+4.01$	$+224$
	-17.99% in K	$+1.0$	-17.99		
(ii) Non-graduates	$+10.00\%$ in RSW	$+1.0$	$+10.00$	$+6.38$	$+444$
	-18.09% in K	$+0.2$	-3.62		
Leavers					
(i) Trained graduates	$+10.00\%$ in RSW	-2.6	-26.00	-4.41	$+60$
	-17.99% in K	-1.2	$+21.59$		
(ii) Untrained graduates	$+10.00\%$ in RSW	-1.4	-14.00	-14.00	$+137$
	-17.99% in K	0	0		
(iii) Non-graduates	$+10.00\%$ in RSW	-1.6	-16.00	$+0.28$	-8
	-18.09% in K	-0.9	$+16.28$		
Total addition to net supply				$+12.32$	$+857$

Note: Estimated elasticities not significant at the 10 per cent level have been assumed to be zero.

TABLE 10.2   *Hypothetical effects on supply of female teachers of the 'flatter profile'*
policy (1973)

Type of flow (1)	Cause (2)	Elasticity (3)	Effects (%) (4)	Net effect on flow (%) (5)	Absolute addition to teacher supply (6)
New entrants					
(i) Graduates	$+10.00\%$ in *RSW*	$+1.8$	$+18.00$	$+13.56$	$+856$
	-22.21% in *K*	$+0.2$	-4.44		
(ii) Non-graduates	$+10.00\%$ in *RSW*	0	–	–	–
	-22.67% in *K*	0	–		
Leavers					
(i) Trained	$+10.00\%$ in *RSW*	-0.7	-7.00	-4.78	$+132$
graduates	-22.31% in *K*	-0.1	$+2.22$		
(ii) Untrained	$+10.00\%$ on *RSW*	0	–	–	–
graduates	-22.21% in *K*	0	–		
(iii) Non-graduates	10.00% in *RSW*	0	–	–	–
	-22.67% in *K*	0	–		
Total addition to net supply				$+8.85$	$+988$

Note: Estimated elasticities not significant at the 10 per cent level have been assumed to
be zero.

absolute addition to supply in column (6). Before going on to discuss these
results, we should draw attention to the incomplete nature of this illustrative
exercise. We have not estimated elasticities for re-entrants. In Tables 10.1
and 10.2, we are in effect assuming that these unknown elasticities are
zero and hence do not affect supply. Although this is probably not so, it may
be a reasonable approximation taking into account the minor contribution
of this flow to total supply of teachers.

The results of such a hypothetical flattening of the salary profile on the
supply of male teachers is positive with 857 extra teachers obtained
(about twelve per cent of the total net addition to the stock in 1972–73).[4]
The effect on the supply of female teachers is 988 teachers (about nine
per cent of the total net addition in that year). These results are not surprising; the policy has increased starting wages at the expense of future
earnings prospects, and we know that the effect of the starting level is in
general much stronger than that of the slope. Thus the increase in teachers
for almost all flows considered. However, it is interesting to look at these
results in more detail. In proportional terms, the policy has its largest
effect on those categories of teachers who take least account of changes in
career prospects. In the case of men, this explains the strong effect on
untrained graduate leavers, and to a certain extent on male non-graduate
new entrants. The other three flows, on the other hand, experience a much
smaller increase, especially that of non-graduate leavers for whom the
negative effect of the slope more than offsets the positive effect of the

starting level. In the case of women, the proportional effect is considerable for the two flows considered; in both cases the influence of the slope is very small relative to that of the level.

Tables 10.3 and 10.4 summarise the results of the second policy (steeper profiles). As expected from the relatively high sensitivity of all flows to starting salaries, steepening the profile produces an overall decrease in supply. For men, this decrease represents 6 per cent of the net addition to the stock, and for women, 8 per cent. The policy produces severe reductions in the level of those flows which are mainly affected by starting salaries, such as male non-graduate new entrants, male untrained graduate leavers and the female flows. As far as other flows are concerned, however, the steeper slope has an important counter-balancing effect; for male graduate entrants and male trained graduate leavers the detrimental influence of a lower starting point is almost exactly compensated for by the positive influence of a higher slope, while for male non-graduate leavers the slope effect outweighs the starting point effect, thereby reducing the number of leavers in this category by more than 100 teachers.

These results depend, of course, on the reliability of our estimates, but even if we take the magnitude of these estimates only in an indicative sense, it is clear that some general conclusions can be advanced. In teaching, both potential new entrants and leavers from the profession appear to react more strongly to changes in starting salaries than to changes in earnings potential.

TABLE 10.3 *Hypothetical effects on supply of male teachers of the 'steeper profile' policy (1973)*

Type of flow (1)	Cause (2)	Elasticity (3)	Effects (%) (4)	Net effect on flow (%) (5)	Absolute addition to teacher supply (6)
New entrants					
(i) Graduates	− 10.00% in *RSW*	2.2	− 22.00	− 0.04	− 3
	+ 21.96% in *K*	1.0	+ 21.96		
(ii) Non-graduates	− 10.00% in *RSW*	1.0	− 10.00	− 5.58	− 389
	+ 22.10% in *K*	0.2	+ 4.42		
Leavers					
(i) Trained graduates	− 10.00% in *RSW*	− 2.6	+ 26.00	− 0.35	+ 5
	+ 21.96% in *K*	− 1.2	− 26.35		
(ii) Untrained graduates	− 10.00% in *RSW*	− 1.4	+ 14.00	+ 14.00	− 137
	+ 21.96% in *K*	0	−		
(iii) Non-graduates	− 10.00% in *RSW*	− 1.6	+ 16.00	− 3.89	+ 108
	+ 22.10% in *K*	− 0.9	− 19.89		
Total addition to net supply				− 5.98	− 416

Note: Estimated elasticities not significant at the 10 per cent level have been assumed to be zero.

TABLE 10.4   *Hypothetical effects on supply of female teachers of the 'steeper profile' policy (1973)*

Type of flow (1)	Cause (2)	Elasticity (3)	Effects (%) (4)	Net effect on flow (%) (5)	Absolute addition to teacher supply (6)
New entrants					
(i) Graduates	− 10.00% in *RSW*	+1.8	−18.00	− 12.58	−794
	+ 27.12% in *K*	+0.2	+5.42		
(ii) Non-graduates	− 10.00% in *RSW*	0	–	–	–
	+ 27.69% in *K*	0	–		
Leavers					
(i) Trained graduates	− 10.00% in *RSW*	−0.7	+7.00	+4.29	−118
	+ 27.12% in *K*	−0.1	−2.71		
(ii) Untrained graduates	− 10.00% in *RSW*	0	–	–	–
	+ 27.12% in *K*	0	–		
(iii) Non-graduates	− 10.00% in *RSW*	0	–	–	–
	+ 27.69% in *K*	0	–		
Total addition to net supply				−8.17	−912

Note: Estimated elasticities not significant at the 10 per cent level have been assumed to be zero.

This is a plausible finding not only as far as entry decisions are concerned but also for leaving decisions. As seen in Chapter 6, by far the greatest numbers of leavers are found among those under 30, which would explain the high sensitivity of teachers to salaries in the early stages of their professional career. In these circumstances, it is not surprising that a policy postulating flatter profiles (an increase in salary for the younger majority) should be more successful in terms of total number than another aiming at steeper profiles. The fact remains, however, (and this is also clearly shown by our findings) that this type of policy will have a much stronger influence on some types of teacher than on others. Female teachers and male untrained graduate leavers are the two most sensitive groups to a wage policy that flattens the earnings profile. The effects of such a policy on experienced male trained graduates and male non-graduates, on the other hand, will be much weaker, or even negative.

10.1.2 *Optimal salary structures*

The above examples do not give a conclusive answer to questions about the 'best' salary profile. First, we have made the assumption that all teachers are equivalent as far as supply is concerned and only total numbers matter. In practice, however, teachers are valued differently by their employers (and they may actually have different productivities) depending on their training and/or their working experience. Second, we have ignored any constraints other than those set by the entry and leaving equations. In particular, we have ignored the fact that changes in the shape of the salary profile will entail changes in the salary bill and that this is limited by a given budget.

Appendix 10A sets out a framework of analysis which attempts to deal with these questions. There we investigate how our elasticity estimates can be used in order to arrive at some recommendation as to the best salary structure in relation to a given objective. If the objective is *to obtain as large a total stock of teachers as possible out of a given budget*, our knowledge about the supply responses to changes in the earnings profile enables us to establish the optimal salary structure (i.e. the optimal relationship between starting and average salaries).

This method deals explicitly with one of the issues mentioned above – the presence of a budget constraint – but, given the nature of our statistical results, it incorporates less satisfactorily the existence of heterogeneity in the stock of teachers. In the leavers analysis in Chapter 6 we have been unable to estimate different elasticities for teachers with different levels of experience, and this implies that we are in fact treating all teachers the same irrespective of the number of years they have been in the profession. In this respect, the only difference that we can incorporate is that between new entrants and leavers. Clearly this is not fully satisfactory because leavers comprise a large range of experience, but it may be more adequate than to consider *all* teachers as equally valuable. We have been more successful in determining different elasticities for teachers with different training, and this opens the possibility of studying the characteristics of optimal profiles that will maximise the supply of a given category of teacher or, if we are constrained to a unique salary structure, of investigating the effects on this common structure resulting from different valuations of each category of teacher. If the policy maker is prepared to make his valuation of each category explicit, then he would establish a salary profile that maximises not the total number of teachers, but a weighted average of the different categories, the weights representing his relative valuations.

In general the results obtained in Appendix 10A indicate that, as might be expected, the larger the supply response to the starting point, the lower will be the slope of the profile, and the larger the supply response to the slope, the steeper will be the optimal profile. The slope of the earnings profile is given by expression (10A.9) when no productivity considerations are made, and by expression (10A.11) when relative differences in productivity between new entrants and leavers are assumed. To evaluate each of these expressions we need to know not only the value of the supply elasticities, but also the optimal value of the entry and leavers flows, which in turn can only be found by solving a whole system of equations. Given the non-linearity of this system it is difficult to solve algebraically for any of the unknowns of the problem. An easier procedure is to evaluate (10A.9) and (10A.11) under the assumption that the actual flows are in the neighbourhood of their optimal level. This is clearly an approximation and may involve some errors, but it will provide us with an illustrative example of the properties of our solution. Furthermore, for those categories of teachers for which the estimated elasticities are reasonable, the approximation may be sufficiently close to allow the inference of some tentative conclusions. We will therefore restrict ourselves to the three categories of teacher for which the most reliable set of elasticities has been estimated – male trained graduates, female trained graduates and male non-graduates. Additionally, we will also consider the common salary structure for these three categories and we will compare it with the one that would result from aggregating over the whole profession.

Table 10.5 shows the optimal salary structures implied by our estimated elasticities; that is those average earnings as a percentage of the starting salary which, for a given budget, will maximise the stock of teachers. For purposes of comparison we show in the first column the actual structures for 1973. The second column shows the optimal structures when all teachers are considered equal irrespective of working experience, and the third when experienced teachers are valued twice as much as new entrants.

The figures in Table 10.5 reveal several interesting features. It is clear that if the policy maker were to maximise the number of teachers independently in *each* of the three categories considered, he would establish different salary structures. Since male trained graduates are the most responsive to future earnings, that profile would be the steepest and practically equal to the actual salary structure. The optimal profile for male non-graduates, on the other hand, would be lower than both the profile for male trained graduates and their own actual profile, but steeper than that for female graduates. The low response of female teachers to future earnings means that this last category would have a much flatter profile than the other two, and also much flatter than their actual profile. It is not surprising that we

TABLE 10.5   *Illustrative optimal salary structures (1973).* (Average salary of teachers aged 35–39 as a percentage of starting salary)

Criteria: maximise the stock of teachers subject to a budget constraint.

	Actual	Without productivity weight	With productivity weight
(a) Male trained graduates	203	193	194
(b) Female trained graduates	171	117	119
(c) Male non-graduates	199	153	168
(a) + (b) + (c)	195	149	159
All teachers	181	147	152

should have come to this conclusion. This is in fact analogous to the optimum of a discriminatory monopsonist, this time applied not to the level of wages, but to the shape of the salary profile.

The policy maker, however, may not act as a discriminatory monopsonist; in fact, there are legal and institutional constraints to this type of behaviour (sex equality laws and union bargaining practices). In such a case, what we would like to determine are the characteristics of the *common* profile that will maximise a certain measure of the stock of teachers. The fourth and fifth rows of Table 10.5 give us such profiles. In column two, the measure of the stock is simply the total sum of teachers, while in column three it is a weighted average in favour of experienced teachers. The figures show that the optimal aggregate profile is flatter than the actual profile. When a productivity weight is considered the optimal profile becomes steeper, but still remains flatter than the actual one. This is a consequence of the aggregate nature of our estimated elasticities. Especially for graduate teachers, the ratio between the slope and the level elasticities is practically the same for new entrants as for leavers. This explains the small increment in the steepness of the optimal profile for these two categories. On the other hand, the relative response of non-graduate leavers to the slope is substantially larger than that of non-graduate entrants, and this is reflected in the noticeable steeper optimal profile when productivity weights are applied.

The only weighting incorporated in the calculation of the aggregate optimal profiles is that associated with experience. Evidently, within the context of our estimates, there exist other criteria to weight the measure of the stock to be maximised, for example sex and training. We have not carried out this exercise, because we are not able to specify the relative weights that should be assigned to each category, but it is easy to see the conquences of different weighting schemes. If, for instance, a higher weight were placed on male trained graduates than on other categories, the aggregate optimal profile would become steeper, and the resulting proportion of male trained graduates in the stock would increase as compared with a situation in which no extra weight were considered.

In addition to the reservations pointed out above, the reader should bear in mind that these calculations have ignored re-entrants. We have in fact assumed that re-entrants are not responsive to changes in the earnings profile (or to earnings levels), but we suspect that this may not be true. We cannot claim to have arrived at an exact determination of the optimal salary structure in teaching, although we believe that, in a qualitative sense, our results are reasonably reliable. We do claim, however, to have developed a method of analysing this type of problem so that decisions about salary structures can be taken with an awareness not only of their financial implications but also of their implications for the size and composition of teacher supply.

10.2 Salary policies directed at the distribution of supply

In the previous section we considered policies to control the overall level of teacher supply. Our study has also produced results which have implications for the internal allocation of manpower. We have covered two different aspects of this internal allocation – the stability of the teaching force in individual schools, and the distribution of teachers between different schools and areas. Concerning the first, we investigate the use of the career structure as a policy instrument to control inter-school mobility. Secondly, we look at the effectiveness of specific school and area allowances. In addition we compare their effectiveness with that of an alternative more general salary policy, allowing sufficient flexibility in the salary system such that salary differentials are created in response to supply disequilibria.

10.2.1 *Inter-school mobility*

From the point of view of aggregate supply, inter-school mobility of teachers is irrelevant. From an educational point of view, however, the frequency with which a teacher changes his school may be very important. Some school mobility may be desirable in order to stimulate movement of new ideas and prevent schools from becoming too self-centred, but a very high level is probably educationally undesirable because it weakens pupil–teacher relationships. This is, to a large extent, an educational issue which we are not qualified to evaluate. However, we have identified in Chapter 7 some of the causes of inter-school mobility, and we are thus able to suggest some courses of action to control its magnitude.

For the secondary sector, the level of inter-school mobility is significantly related to the dispersion of promotion prospects among different types of school. This variable thus represents a clearly defined policy instrument which could be used to control the rate of inter-school mobility. An equalisation of promotion prospects between schools will result in a decrease in the rate of school mobility. The influence of this instrument, although significant, is not very large in magnitude (an elasticity lower than unity) and this suggests that policies aimed at controlling inter-school mobility should also take into consideration the differences between schools in terms of their non-pecuniary characteristics.

10.2.2. *Salary differentials*

Inasmuch as there will always exist localities which differ in their characteristics, some being more attractive than others, a uniform salary structure for the whole country will create disequilibria between supply and demand: those with good 'working conditions' will tend to be oversupplied and those with bad 'working conditions' will tend to experience shortages. Salary allowances can reproduce the differentials that a free market would have generated in order to equalise supply and demand. The same argument applies to characteristics concerning particular types of schools as opposed to geographical areas. The salary allowance for Social Priority Schools is an example of the former, while the London Allowance is an example of the latter.

Before going into the policy implications of our analysis of the London and the Social Priority allowance, it is convenient to consider the problem of area allowances in a more general perspective, and to evaluate in this context the actual methods followed to redistribute supply. In a market like that of school teachers, with a uniform salary structure for the whole country, disequilibria between supply and demand are almost certain to exist. In the more specific context of a shortage such as the one prevailing during the period of analysis, these disequilibria manifest themselves in the form of an uneven distribution of the stock of teachers. In a situation of surplus such as that which is developing in the mid 1970s, the position can be just as bad with oversupply and even unemployment in some areas coexisting for substantial periods with continuing shortages in others. In theory, a better distribution of the existing supply, or indeed a full equalisation of demand and supply for all the country, can be achieved by means of salary differentials between geographical areas. This is a policy which for historical reasons has had a very bad reception not only from the teachers' unions but also from educational authorities. The fact that only one such allowance exists (the London allowance) may be put forward as evidence of the widespread aversion to a generalised system of allowances. The main reason behind this is the reluctance to depart from the basic principle of equal pay for equal work. Instead, the government attempted to solve the shortage problem by means of the quota system and it has recently been suggested that the surplus problem might be attacked by means of a fixed 'establishment' of teachers for each local authority.[5]

It is difficult to justify the quota system on theoretical grounds. In general, and unless very special assumptions are made concerning the behaviour of teachers, this system will result in the loss of a part of the potential overall supply. Particularly during a period when the desired number of teachers was not even obtained in the most attractive areas, this result is clearly very inadequate since it aggravates the magnitude of the underlying shortage.

The quota system could only be justified in a situation where the policy maker regards the redistribution of supply (normally seen in terms of reducing the variation in pupil–teacher ratios) as of sufficient priority to outweigh the disadvantages of reduced overall supply, but not of sufficient priority to overcome objections to the existence of salary differentials. In the case of a surplus the setting up of an 'establishment' on the same basis for each local authority would result in some local authorities attracting more teachers than they were able or willing to employ, thus probably creating localised teacher unemployment, while others were still unable to fill their establishment with teachers of the type they were seeking.

A salary differential system, on the other hand, while succeeding in equalising pupil–teacher ratios, would not result in supply losses. This would be beneficial not only to the teaching profession inasmuch as more teachers could be obtained, but also to those teachers who were excluded under the quota system, since they could now obtain their desired job at the going salary. It is therefore important to look more closely at the reasons why a generalised system of area allowances has not been adopted. We must presume that both unions and educational authorities believe that the needed differentials would have to be so large and extensive as to be both morally and politically unacceptable. Can our analysis help in evaluating the magnitude of these differentials? In a somewhat indirect way, it can. The larger the response of teachers to internal differentials, the lower salary differentials will need to be to achieve a given redistribution of supply. We know from Chapter 7 that inter-regional movements of teachers are highly elastic to salary differentials. Although we cannot be precise as to the exact magnitude, we can conclude that given the responsiveness of internal movements to salary differentials, an even distribution of supply could be achieved without very large differentials.

We can summarise the above discussion in the following manner. First, if the responsiveness of internal movements to salary differentials is large, then the establishment of salary differentials would be the best method of redistributing supply, since they would not suffer from the defects of a quota system which may result in some loss of supply. Secondly, if salary differentials are regarded as unacceptable, this constraint implies two conflicting objectives: maximising supply and reducing the variation in pupil–teacher ratios. If the first is considered to be the highest priority, then the best course of action is to do nothing; if the second is the predominant objective, then a quota system would be the desirable policy. Presumably the government took this final view when they first introduced the quota system in the 1950s.

In the above we have discussed the problem of salary differentials in general terms. We now look at one form of differential which is being used in the teaching profession. Flat rate salary allowances such as the London allowance and the Social Priority allowance are relatively inflexible policy instruments. This is clearly shown in the analysis reported in Chapter 8, the main implications of which are discussed below.

From a superficial point of view it would seem that in 1971 the London allowance was working, London had the 'best' pupil–teacher ratio in the whole country. However, this aggregate measure is a poor representation of the actual state of supply in the area. When we disaggregate by age, an evident scarcity of experienced teachers appeared as the most significant characteristic of London. This can be explained by two well defined trends.

First, London attracted a much higher proportion of new entrants than any other region, and secondly, the outflow of teachers from the area, both through leavers from the profession and because of movements to other regions, was much higher and more heavily concentrated in the 20 to 30 age bracket than in the rest of the country. We have presumed that the causes of this large and young outflow were basically financial. As soon as young teachers are faced with increased financial responsibilities (i.e. marriage, search for adequate housing, children, etc.) the higher cost of living in London possibly made the London allowance (as it stood in 1971) insufficient for many of them.

In terms of our previous analysis, this means that the adverse conditions which make an area unattractive affect teachers differently according to their age and their position in the career structure. For London in particular, and probably for many other conurbations, these adverse conditions appear to affect teachers more towards their late twenties than at the beginning of their careers.

The Social Priority allowance is paid to all teachers in a particular group of schools whose pupils suffer from social deprivation in one form or another. These schools are usually undersupplied in much the same way as some geographic areas because of their relative unattractiveness to teachers.

The main conclusions from the study of this allowance are that the flat rate allowance may have increased total supply, but that this has been done at the expense of 'quality'. In particular, younger teachers have been attracted or retained by the allowance, resulting in some distortion of the age structure with relatively fewer teachers in the 30 to 50 bracket. This effect is similar to that associated with the London allowance.

What are the consequences of these findings for the level and shape of salary allowances? First, if an area or school type experiences a proportionally high outflow of teachers of a given age, then it is clear that the level of the allowance at that age is insufficient and should be revised. Furthermore, concerning the shape, our results suggest that an adequate allowance would have to increase substantially from a relatively low initial point to its highest level during the first few years of a teacher's service.[6]

It is revealing to look at the implications for fixed salary allowances of our findings on general earnings differentials in the profession (Chapter 9). We have discovered some interesting examples of salary differentials which have been produced in the teaching profession, not via fixed allowances, but via preferential promotion rates. In many cases these could be quite clearly associated with disequilibria between supply and demand. This tells us that the system is capable of spontaneously generating salary differentials, but the scale of these differentials is probably not sufficient. The question then is, if extra flexibility were exogenously introduced, would the system produce the needed differentials? If the answer were yes, then it is likely that such a method would be preferable to fixed allowances, since the educational planner would not have to be concerned with fixing differentials at the correct level.

An example of such an alternative policy was introduced for social priority schools in 1972, coexisting with the fixed allowance. This involves allowing local authorities to increase the number of senior posts in educational priority schools by up to 10 per cent, and is open ended in that the number of schools which can benefit is not limited in any way. The introduction of such a flexible salary instrument for redistributing supply is equivalent to leaving more room for market forces to operate, and thus creating *de facto* salary differentials for teachers in such schools. In the light of the poor results achieved by the School of Exceptional Difficulty allowance and the London allowance, the implication may well be that fixed rate allowances are not the best method of creating the necessary salary differentials to redistribute supply.

10.3 Concluding remarks

This chapter has considered some of the policy implications of our study. We believe that our analysis has led us to a better understanding of the workings of the labour market for teachers, which hopefully will be useful for policies to improve staffing and teacher quality in primary and secondary schools. It is evident, however, that our study is in effect only an attempt at demonstrating that this kind of analysis is of direct value to policy makers. Our study used statistical material from a period in which teacher 'shortage' was the main policy problem. We are entering a period is our contention that educational planners dealing with these new problems is our contention that educational planners deling with these new problems will make just as many mistakes as they did in the earlier situation if they ignore the effects of economic incentives on overall teacher supply and its distribution.

One obvious example of an opportunity missed in this context was the 1974 Houghton Committee whose deliberations were determined entirely by 'equity' criteria and an excellent chance was missed of establishing a salary structure capable of optimising teacher supply in the new situation which is developing. This is not a claim that the Houghton Award was necessarily too high, but, in making it, insufficient consideration was given to how salary scales could be used to improve the quality and distribution of teachers in a period in which overall supply is no longer a problem.

We would not want to claim that our study has solved all problems of teacher supply. Our policy analysis has been exclusively concerned with the use of salary instruments. This represents only one aspect of a more general supply policy, albeit a previously neglected one. A comprehensive model of supply should incorporate policies concerning the training of teachers to a larger extent than we have done here and also integrate it with a properly worked out demand model such as we have sketched in Chapters 2 and 9.

Decisions about teacher supply ought to be based on an appreciation of the fact that although it is a public sector activity with administered salary scales, there is a labour market for teachers. The system is a complex one and warrants careful monitoring. We believe that a *teacher supply research unit* should be established to keep under permanent review the relationships between teachers' salary policies, economic factors affecting the demand for teachers and teacher training and supply policies. At present these appear to be treated as separate issues and surprise is expressed when, for example, a shortage of teachers apparently suddenly becomes a surplus.

Such a body could provide data to both sides of the Burnham salary negotiating Committee and the Advisory Council on the Training and Supply of Teachers, it could monitor policy initiatives to investigate their effectiveness in achieving desired staffing objectives, and it might undertake applied research into the operation of the labour market along the lines suggested in the present study.

Epilogue

Some transatlantic comparisons[1]

M. J. BOWMAN
University of Chicago

Writing almost a century ago, John Bates Clark (1899) observed that the marginal productivity theory of wages 'would have to be applied in a special way to analysis of teacher pay', since the market provided no good direct measure of teachers' productivity. The marginal productivity rule enters into determination of wages as a measure of what a man (or woman) could earn in alternative employments. Clark assumed that those alternative earnings (opportunity costs of attracting a person into teaching) would roughly approximate his marginal productivity in the alternative employment. But even without making any such assumption, measurement by alternative options is the foundation for analysis of occupational choice or, in this case, of teacher supply. There is good reason for starting with a *supply* analysis based on responses of individuals, since the positive economics of the demand side of teacher markets tends to be elusive – especially where, as in England and Wales, there is a unitary salary scale over the entire nation. Much more attention has been given to positive economic analysis of teacher *demands* in the United States, where there are many separate, relatively autonomous employers ('firms'). Transatlantic similarities in analytical models, in observed behavior patterns, and in the nature of decision problems and of options on both the demand and supply sides of the market are all the more impressive, given initial institutional contrasts.

Several basic questions are common to this book and to work on salaries of teachers in the United States and Canada. (1) What determines teacher supplies and how responsive are potential teachers to changes in salary schedules? (2) What determines rates of teacher turnover or retention in the profession? (3) What are the patterns of mobility of teachers from one school or district to another, and what explains those patterns? As in the United Kingdom, there is concern in the United States about local differences in the competitive situation of educational authorities, but the relatively greater local autonomy in the United States gives work on this problem and on demand for teachers generally a greater economic (and political) interest. The recent spread of teacher unions in still-localized markets has spawned studies of the effects of this development paralleling research on other local wage determinants in public sectors that should have direct relevance to the United Kingdom as well. In attacking the question of effects of unions,

American economists have experimented with increasingly sophisticated models of determinants of teacher salaries in the absence of unionism and of effects of unions. Finally, there has been a sharp (and an earlier) turn in the United States from concern with teacher 'shortage' to consideration of problems and opportunities that have emerged with the shift to a situation of 'teacher surplus'.

No attempt will be made to sum up and evaluate the full range of the American literature on these subjects. Rather, I shall select for attention particular work that relates in direct ways to this book or to papers and discussions at the UK/US conference on teacher markets (held in Chicago in December 1976).[2] Discussion will be developed around the following main topics: (I) Teacher supplies, occupational choice, and life-earning paths; (II) Teacher mobility and inter-district competition; (III) The demand side of teacher markets; (IV) Effects of teacher unionization; and (V) Some implications of the shift from shortage to surplus. Discussion is confined to work on teachers in elementary and secondary schools.

I National supplies of teachers, occupational choice, and life-earning profiles in teaching

Any full explanation of teacher supplies, as of supplies to any other occupation, requires four things: (a) a market situation in which it is possible to identify supply as distinct from demand; (b) an analysis of the determinants of individual occupational decisions; (c) information about the distribution among the population of those traits that enter into (b); (d) realistic analysis would require that we take into account uncertainties and lags in or costs of information and job search. Obviously the data needed to meet all these specifications are never available, and if we had them they would swamp us. It is necessary to narrow the focus and simplify in order to move ahead.

(a) The analysis of teacher flows into and withdrawals from teaching in the United Kingdom was facilitated because the period covered was one of teacher shortage in the sense that anyone who was qualified and seeking work as a teacher under existing conditions and salary scales could get such a job. This situation is depicted graphically in Chapter 2. Implicitly, this is specified as a monopsonistic situation for the national teacher market in the United Kingdom, albeit a monopsonistic market in which salary levels are set by negotiation. A situation characterized unambiguously by teacher surplus would be a different story; I shall come to this later on.

(b) The analysis of occupational choice used in this book is rooted in human-capital theory. Three decision points are involved: at entry to colleges of education (most of whose graduates in fact became teachers); the decisions of men and women who had already completed investments of greater or lesser specificity in the formal education needed to qualify for teaching; and the decisions relating to continuation in or withdrawal from the profession after entering it. In the empirical work it was assumed implicitly that expansion of places in the Colleges of Education was the delayed effect rather than the cause of the increased numbers of young people qualified and willing to train as teachers – hence those data relating teacher wages to numbers entering colleges of education belong to the supply curve. Lags in response to wage increases are attributed in part at least to lags in the provision of places in those colleges. (This constraint on teacher supplies was stressed by Keith Norris (1970) with respect to the situation in England and Wales; he found for the mid 1960s a substantial excess of qualified applicants over places in the colleges of education.)

An important aspect of the use of human capital theory in this book is the emphasis on giving heed to anticipated paths of future earnings, not merely to starting salaries or to average salary levels in teaching as compared with other occupations. The introduction of slope as well as starting level of teacher salaries will seem familiar to policy makers who have been involved with the planning of teacher salary schedules even when they have not formally incorporated human-capital accounting into their analyses. Human-capital theory has been given explicit attention in some cases; among the first to do this were leaders in Quebec who were already using such analysis in setting up teacher salary schedules with arrangements for mid-career up-grading a decade ago. However, so far as I am aware, no one heretofore has entered wage level and slope as separate variables in an econometric analysis of *occupational* supply elasticities. This is an important contribution to the econometric analysis of occupational supplies, both for entry to an occupation and for retention in or withdrawal from it.[3]

Applications of human-capital theory to analysis of occupational choice are by no means new. Informally they date at least from Adam Smith. But in most cases the emphasis has been on investments in the acquisition of qualifications prior to entry into the occupation, rather than on subsequent acquisition of further 'human capital' or earning power. Raymond Walsh (1935) was probably the first to test out a human-capital theory of occupational choice that took into account investments in training for the occupation; his results were published in 1934. In 1937 Harold F. Clark published his *Life Earnings in Selected Occupations in the United States*. That work distinguished explicitly, in regard to occupational choice, among (i) average earnings (which reflect age composition of those employed in the occupation), (ii) the undiscounted mean for an individual lifetime (one measure of 'level' of earnings), and (iii) present values (at a 4 per cent discount rate). When set beside (controlling for) the undiscounted mean, Clark's present values become proxy measures of the implications of slope at a real discount rate of 4 per cent. In his chapter on teachers, Clark discussed the measurement problems of contrasts between rural and urban teachers, and of dealing with high turnover, and with transfers from rural to urban (or other) progressions through a teaching career. However, Clark wrote before the modern theory of investment in human beings had become an important part of the economics of human resources in general economic theory; his work is direct, essentially non-technical, and little known among economists. He was more interested in implications for vocational guidance than in the analysis of occupational supply elasticities that is so important in this book. Much better known among economists is the work on doctors and dentists by Friedman and Kuznets (1946); they took time costs of training explicitly into account in comparisons of present values (again at a 4 per cent discount rate) of life earnings of doctors with dentists. Friedman and Kuznets went on also to consider factors that might account for contrasts in present values – ability differentials, equalizing differences associated with non-pecuniary returns or amenities, monopolistic controls of entry to professional schools, and licensing. In the 1960s a number of more limited comparisons of rates of return to investments in training for high-level occupations (including college teaching) were published.

Meanwhile, Jacob Mincer (1974) and others have been analyzing earning profiles of broad categories of the population to distinguish investments in schooling and in post-schooling learning, but without regard to occupational choice. In fact the theoretical base of these analyses is in what Becker has called 'general' as against 'specific' training; what Mincer sorts out (if we accept his assumptions) is the post-school investments in the sorts of learning through experience and on-the-job training that increase the individual's productive capabilities and hence the saleability of his services *elsewhere* than in the firm or agency in which he received his post-school increments of human capital. This does not distinguish between occupation-*specific* training that is general in its applicability in other firms and training that yields returns only in the firm, however. With the partial exception of Zabalza's work on occupational choice with reference to teachers, I know of no work that has incorporated analysis of post-school investments into the analysis of occupational mobility or commitment using formal econometric models.

Even in the present book, relatively little is said about the fact that implicit in all analyses of occupational choice and of elasticities of supply with respect to withdrawal from an occupation (in this case teaching) are questions about the specificity of training and experience in their effects on later earnings in the chosen occupation as compared with others. Yet the question of occupational choice becomes important in a human-capital framework only to the extent to which qualifications are specialized to an occupation, so that returns to investments depend on entry to and continuation in that occupation. But as soon as we say this it becomes evident that in a human-capital perspective 'an occupation' is a sequentially linked career path. In the professions this could include engineer to production manager, lawyer to judge or senator, teacher to educational administrator. In the United Kingdom there seems to be a less clear demarcation between teacher and administrator than in the United States although even in the United States most educational administrators have been teachers.

The career-path view of occupations introduces further the question of how far entry into an occupation in itself entails further investment by the individual in that (whether by informal learning or in other ways) he (or she) acquires rising earning opportunities in that occupation but not elsewhere. Rigid linkage of tenure and pay to seniority virtually guarantees that there will be little inter-occupational movement once significant seniority advantages have been obtained, whatever the associations between real value of services rendered and seniority may be. But this is to say that the time paths of occupationally specific human capital, like firm-specific human capital, may depend either on increases in the capabilities of the individual or on more arbitrary institutional constraints that entail queueing for preferred jobs. In both the United Kingdom and the United States economic advancement in teaching as a career is unquestionably a mixture of these influences even in a period of relative teacher 'shortage'. But to sort out these elements requires types of data and analysis not available for this research. Despite extensive work in the United States, we still are not in a position to construct reliable educational production functions for analysis of how much difference teachers make in which sorts of educational 'outcomes'. We still are not much past the position described by John Bates Clark in 1899, of lacking direct measures of teachers' productivity.

(c) 'Human-investment' interpretations of decisions relating to occupational choice may be defined narrowly, to focus solely on pecuniary costs and returns (including forgone earnings) or 'human investments' may be defined more broadly to include non-pecuniary returns. In empirical applications some sort of pricing (direct or indirect) is involved. But individuals differ in the investments they make and in their occupational choices. The authors of this book set up a model in which those differences among individuals reflect differences of tastes. As Sherwin Rosen pointed out in discussing this work, aggregate supply in the market is in fact a reflection of a multivariate distribution on many characteristics, often with non-zero covariances. As he put it, the aggregate supply 'is swept out of a tail of this multivariate density function', not just of a density function of tastes. The problem on this point is to sort out the components of the density function that may be most relevant in the range in which supply elasticities are in fact observed. This problem is confounded further because of selectivity biases in using observed mean wages in two occupations where there is quality variation in both; as is pointed out by Rosen, 'the observed means come from truncated or censored distributions'.

(d) Occupational choice, including choice of educational paths leading to one rather than another occupation, is based on expectations about the future. Two observations claim attention here. First, among other things Rosen pointed out that the analysis did not distinguish between permanent and temporary shifts in starting salaries. This distinction, which plays an important part in determining the empirical findings in work by Richard Freeman on engineers (1971) and more recently on some other occupations (Freeman, 1976), may seem to be less important in work on teachers, whose salaries are less sensitive to economic fluctuations. There is a problem, nevertheless, in the fluctuations of relationships between teachers' pay and earnings in alternative occupations. Consideration of temporary and longer-term variations in relative earnings, and how people respond to those variations, raises questions for analysis of teachers' markets to which I shall return in connection with 'excess and shortage'.

Second, the specification of the form of the earnings function in empirical analysis affects relationships between measures of 'level' and 'slope'. Zabalza chose, for good enough reasons, to work with a formulation in terms of constant relative slope. But notice that any increase in starting wage holding relative slope constant must necessarily imply a rise in absolute slope. On the other hand increases in slope holding starting wage constant do not raise that wage; they do of course raise the level of salary later in the career. To double the relative slope with starting wage constant will raise earnings later on in the career by much less than those later earnings would be raised by doubling the starting wage while holding relative slope constant.[4] The relatively strong coefficients on starting wage and the comparatively weak ones on relative slope are in part (though only in part) a reflection of these facts.

In view of the high sensitivity to relative starting wages found in other studies of occupational choice taken together with the stipulations of Zabalza's model, it should come as no surprise that the elasticities he estimated on starting wages were twice or more those on proportionate slope. Empirically Zabalza found short-run entry supply elasticities on relative starting wages to be around 2 for male graduates, 1.8 for male non-graduates, and virtually zero for graduate and non-graduate females. In the equations for leavers from teaching these coefficients were very low for females, regardless of training. For males leaver supply elasticities on relative starting wage ranged from −2.6 for trained graduates to −1.4 for untrained graduates. The leaver coefficient on slope was virtually zero for the untrained male graduates; for the trained graduates and the non-graduates those coefficients were roughly half the elasticities on relative starting wages. In other words, the same relative elasticity patterns appear in the leaving as in the entry equations, but the elasticities are generally lower, as we should expect. What more do these results tell us about teacher supplies – or for that matter, demands – in a period of alleged teacher shortage?

First of all, they suggest that something could have been done about the shortage by raising salaries if a closing of the gap had been regarded as worth the cost. Here, however, we run into the problem of short-term relative to long-term elasticities and lags in supply adjustments, other considerations in decisions of educational authorities aside. (Behavior on the demand side is not part of this book, but others have undertaken just such an assessment.) In terms of occupational choice, the high sensitivity to starting wages is noteworthy nonetheless, and it is consistent with observations in studies for other professions in the United States (illustrated in Freeman 1971 and 1976). But what then about the high rates of teacher 'wastage', especially among young people? Remarking on the high wastage rates for young male non-graduate (as well as graduate) teachers and the rapid increase in wastage rates in the 1960s, Keith Norris (1970) suggested 'an implication that young people are either badly informed or that they base their decisions solely on starting salaries' (p. 133). Also, in his theoretical analysis Zabalza argued in connection with the leaving decision, or movements among jobs more generally, that such movements implied either initial imperfect information or changing market conditions. But do we in fact need any of those assumptions? The highest leaving rates and the lowest elasticities for both entry and departure were found among females and among male untrained graduates. This is exactly what we should expect if occupational mobility is related negatively to the degree of occupationally-specific traini̇re , positively to the relative attractiveness (financially and otherwise) of alternative sorts of employment. Some sorts of jobs can be good enough roads to others. Furthermore, if the shapes of earning profiles differ not only in level and relative slope but also in changes in relative slope, and if learning in one sphere is transferrable to another, career paths can very well involve changing 'occupations' as listed in official statistics. The specifications of a constant proportionate slope is a very unrealistic specification of an earning profile, whether in teaching or in other activities. Furthermore, the slope between starting age and age 35–39 (which is the base used by Zabalza) is definitely steeper than the slope at later years in most occupations, and over the span to age 39 that slope will be declining in relative even if not yet in absolute terms. There are no analyses in this book of effects of age or experience on determinants of leaving rates,[5] but we should not expect measures of either relative starting wages or proportionate slopes to around age 39 to have much effect on the decisions of teachers in their forties – quite aside from the fact (shown graphically in this book and evident much more generally) that leaving rates decline at older ages as the seniority benefits lost by an occupational shift become increasingly important. There is much to be learned from a more careful study of intra-generation occupational mobility or immobility, their causes and implications; movements in and out of teaching are a good place to begin.

Before leaving this broad topic a few words about the comments of Chicago discussants on the Turnbull–Williams analysis of teacher earnings functions are in order. Here, as elsewhere, some of the comments referred to methodological problems that pervade all studies in human-resource economics, as in many related fields – problems of bias because of truncated observations, misinterpretations because of omitted variables or errors in the variables, and so on. These observations were appreciated by the authors and generally there was no disagreement about the problems involved. The selectivity bias noted by Lazear in connection with the analysis of effects on earnings of supplemental training programs was an example, although in this case results are further confounded by bureaucratic rules that produce self-fulfilling prophesies. Elizabeth Landes observed a tendency, that disturbs me also, to treat as 'standardizing variables' some of the variables that deserve most attention in their own right. No doubt these are reactions we may expect from people who approach the work of a statistician from the orientations of human investment theory and the economics of female labor-force participation. Summing up, Landes cited first the major findings that (a) growth of earnings was greater among graduate teachers than among non-graduate teachers; (b) greater among secondary than primary teachers; and (c) greater for men than for married women. The earnings growth for women does not reflect the system of institutional allowances; it is paralleled by the situation in the United States. Landes observed also that 60 per cent of the difference between men and married women disappears when regressions are service-standardized, but a difference of 5 per cent persists, which must reflect the pattern of promotion. What lies back of this? Is the difference related to length of service in that we have here again a partially truncated distribution for women that distorts the comparison with men? Going further, Landes contrasts the small effects of discontinuity of service found by Turnbull and Williams when they used a dummy variable (1.7 per cent decrease in earnings for two or more years out of teaching) as compared with a finding by Mincer and Polachek of a 1.5 per cent decrease for each year out of the labor force for women in general. She cited further the finding of a 6 per cent sex difference among urban teachers in the United States after standardizing for years of service. Do British married female teachers spend less time out of the labor force than their United States counterparts, or is the depreciation of earnings for any given time out less in Britain? Finally, is the seeming earnings parity of single women with men teaching in the United Kingdom due to a truncated age distribution of single women? These are plenty of questions to challenge whoever goes on to look further into women in teaching and in the labor market more generally in Britain over the recent past and into the near future.

Most of the American studies relating to teacher attrition (withdrawal from teaching, whether to other employments or out of the labor force) deal with comparisons of teacher turnover in particular school districts. While attrition is separated from intra-occupational mobility wherever the data permit, there is only one attrition study to my knowledge in which use is made of salary structures, not just some sort of average salary indicator. This is a part of K. G. Pedersen's (1973) study of attrition and inter-district mobility of teachers in Michigan. (The data needed for a full analysis of the economic variables were available for the Detroit Metropolitan area only.) The attrition ratio in school-district i was the proportion of teachers in district i in 1965/66 who were not teaching in *any* school in the state of Michigan in 1966/67. Several variables relating to teacher education and school district characteristics were used in analyses done separately by sex, age (using age groups of under 30, 30–45, and over 45), and whether the teacher had a BA degree only or also a master's degree in teaching-roughly comparable to the British 'untrained graduates' and 'trained graduates' except that the American BAs who entered teaching commonly had some specific pedagogic training as part of their general college degree. There is no longer a sharp distinction between the graduate of a 'college of education' and of a general college that is still so important in the United Kingdom. In broad terms, the findings on leavers in this book about Britain and those in Pedersen's analysis of attrition in the Detroit Metropolitan area are similar:

(i) Attrition is higher among young teachers (both male and female) with limited teaching experience than among those longer in the profession;

(ii) As in the UK, attrition is higher when training is relatively general rather than specific to pedagogy;

(iii) Female attrition is less responsive to salary than is male attrition;

(iv) In the Detroit study use was made also of a present-value measure of expected future earnings back to the age of the decision maker (26 for the age group under 30, 38 for the middle age category, and 50 for those over 45). This present-value measure came through strongly in both zero-order and partial relationships with attrition for the older male teachers and in the partial coefficients for women in the age range 30–45.

Pedersen's analysis derives in a more direct way from human-capital accounting, and his equations do not automatically give us elasticity coefficients such as were estimated in this book.

II Teacher mobility

Analysis of teacher supplies in the aggregate at a national or even at a state or provincial level poses few problems of comparison between the United States and the United Kingdom except that the problem of identification of the supply schedule is much less in a national market with one uniform salary scale under unambiguous conditions of market disequilibrium and teacher 'shortage'. There is of course the advantage for the United States that cross-section data by districts are more easily used to explain the geographic allocation of teachers and their mobility from one place to another.

Clearly, limitations on observations inherent in the institutional characteristics of British teacher markets affect the extent of and the patterns of inter-school and inter-district mobility of teachers, and the scope for economic analysis of those patterns. However, as the analysis of earnings functions demonstrates, there is still room for some manoeuver within the Burnham system. The instrumental salary variable is in the promotion system, how promotions are used within schools, and how the Burnham system itself differentiates between secondary and primary schools and by size of school in the numbers of permitted higher-scale positions (allowances for special responsibilities and administrative posts). Also, these differences among schools along with the structure of the salary scale itself, have changed over time. Under these circumstances, the best indicator of differentials in earning prospects from one school or district to another are data on differences in promotion rates and on proportions of higher-scale positions.

Within teaching, advancement over and above the automatic seniority increments on the base scale in the United Kingdom may occur by promotion to new responsibilities within the same school or school district, or it may entail transfer into another school either with immediate promotion or with better internal promotion prospects. In the United States the same phenomena can be observed, but with the important difference that teachers may move to a different salary scale by transferring to another school district without necessarily being 'promoted' to a higher rank. Greenberg and McCall (1973) drew a distinction in their analysis of mobility in the San Diego teacher market that is of particular interest here. They used a human-capital model to deal with occupational choice and attrition, but suggested two special variants of the operation of 'internal labor markets' for analysis of teacher mobility. The 'manorial' type is a hierarchical structure, with entry at the bottom and advancement up through the system either within a particular place of employment or by movements across places of employment. This most nearly fits the United Kingdom structure. The other, 'guild' variant is a much more open, unstructured system once one has entered the occupation. Greenberg and McCall place the American teacher market between these two types. But the hierarchy is not necessarily just pecuniary; commonly new teachers start out in the most unpleasant and difficult schools, only working their way out of these as they acquire seniority.[6]

The processes by which teachers with various qualifications and degrees of seniority are allocated among schools and among districts can be important for the functioning of school systems, but may make very little difference in what the statistics of inter-area mobility would show us, 'schools of special difficulty' or 'priority schools' and their American counterparts aside. Regardless of the market structure, we would predict higher rates of economically-related mobility among young men than among young women to the extent that the former are more career-oriented, including the fact that they are less often the secondary earners in a family. Also, regardless of market structure we would expect more mobility among younger than among older teachers with equal commitment to the profession. (i) If individuals gain in teaching capabilities through experience they will have better bargaining power, and in addition more is known about them and they know more about themselves; a human-capital interpretation of mobility in an efficient competitive market would imply transfers among schools to better match the qualifications of the teacher with the demands (and ability to pay) of the school district. Given that there are costs of moving, there.is a premium on making early movements that will bring a longer period of higher earnings. Furthermore, if learning by experience follows a path that rises at a diminishing rate, we would expect a waning of any gain in bargaining power and even a decline due to skill obsolescence as teachers become older. (There is in fact some limited evidence that this is what happens, earning paths aside. Recognition of this fact may be reflected in earning profiles and the asymptotic limits on salary schedules.) (ii) But the same mobility path could be explained from a simple queuing theory in which people moved up to the limit of their qualifications (those qualifications remaining unchanged) as openings occurred at the level just ahead.

In the United States and Canada, as in the United Kingdom, the associations between age (and sometimes sex) and inter-school mobility consistently confirm the predictions of the human-capital and queuing models – of greater mobility among young teachers and a strong influence of economic variables on mobility decisions of male teachers. Women move more often without promotion or economic gain, men move more often than women where the change brings promotion or higher earnings. Again of special interest in relation to the analysis in this book is the work by George Pedersen.

Like the authors of this book, Pedersen (1973) specified characteristics of both areas of origin and areas of destination, including the composition of the teaching force, and he made use of all economic decision variables available to him. He had some good data, and he handled what he had in a somewhat different way – reflecting a more direct application of human-capital decision theory. In doing this, Pedersen was drawing very directly on Harvey's (1967) use of human-capital theory in an analysis of salary schedules in the various districts of Quebec prior to the institution of a uniform salary scale.

Pedersen examined mobility (and attrition) at specified ages for male and for female teachers with and without postgraduate teacher training – already mentioned above in connection with rates of attrition. Age specificity of the decisions aside, the most important contrast with the analysis in this book (given different institutional contexts) was in specification of the dependent variable itself and systematic use of attributes of both district of origin and of destination. Pedersen's 'velocity index of migration stream' was

$$VI_{ij} = \left(\frac{M_i}{P_i}\right)\left(\frac{M_{ij}}{M_i}\right) \div \frac{P_j}{P_t} = \frac{M_{ij}}{P_iP_j}P_t$$

where the first term (M_j/P_i) is the proportion of teachers migrating out of district i, the second term is the proportion of those leaving district i who went to district j, (M_{ij}/M_i). The denominator P_j/P_t is a correction factor that takes into account the size of district j relative to the total teacher establishment in the state of Michigan (or, for the metropolitan analysis, in the Detroit metropolitan area). In the all-Michigan analysis it was not possible to specify the relative level of education of migrant teachers. The economic variables available for the state analysis were average teacher salary in the district (of origin and of destination) and the equalized property valuation in each. The latter is in fact a reasonably good proxy variable for what a teacher might anticipate in long-term earning prospects, but it is also, of course, an indicator of the demand side of the market and perhaps of quality selectivity in teacher demands. Because of the way in which his regressions were set up, Pedersen could distinguish between the strength of economic (and other) variables as push factors, out of place of origin, and as pull factors, to destinations. Generally the push factors were the stronger, but with interesting exceptions.

The all-state regressions were run on six sub-populations, (by sex in the three age categories mentioned earlier). The proportion of total variance explained by the full regressions was small excepting for young females, who were moving in large numbers out of poor areas where school expenditures (and salaries) per pupil were low. This is in the main a migration of young women from rural areas (where teaching is a prime female occupation) into the cities. The data refer only to those who continued to teach, and should not be interpreted mainly as the offshoot of family migrations in pursuit of the husband's career. For males it was the pull factors that came through most strongly – high mean teacher salaries at the destinations for the young males and high expenditures per pupil at destination for older males.

The analysis of mobility *within* the metropolitan area was much better specified for teacher training and quality and for economic indicators. Furthermore, this sample excludes the flow of migrants from remote rural areas of the state. In this analysis the coefficients on most of the economic variables were perverse for the young females with bachelors' degrees only, but took on the expected signs at middle and older ages, coming through with high significance on present values in the migration of the oldest women. The findings for young males conformed much more tidily to economic expectations: movement into districts with high present values of expected salaries and high property valuations. In both the state and the metropolitan studies, the proportion of variance explained by economic factors declines with age, the proportion explained by other variables rises with age, especially among males. This, again, should not be surprising. Unfortunately a major problem of multicollinearity with the block of economic variables arises because of the lumping together of too many economic indicators; this does not distort the main results, but it interferes with more precise identification of effects of differences in salary levels and slopes in the metropolitan mobility analysis.

There can be no doubt that some of the puzzles with respect to young females in Pedersen's metropolitan sample reflected non-pecuniary advantages and disadvantages of teaching in one school or another. A chapter of this book treats effects of the London allowance and of allowances for schools of special difficulty. This could be regarded as a relatively small-scale version of a problem that has huge dimensions in the United States. And that problem is not primarily a matter of differences among districts in economic power; the difficulties are much more subtle and seemingly intractable in the short run, at least. Greenberg and McCall (1973) demonstrated for San Diego a problem that is pervasive: the inexperienced teachers start out in the problem schools and the slum areas. Some are knocked out of teaching through this experience, although controlling for other factors there does not seem to be a significantly higher attrition from such schools. There is definitely a tendency to progress from lower to higher SES[7] districts, in a non-pecuniary but nonetheless hierarchical structure with strong built-in elements of a queuing process. If this is the way things work in the United Kingdom also, we should hardly be surprised that the districts covered by the special allowances would have disproportionately young teachers, or that the main effects of that allowance would be to compensate starters in the teaching profession for a painful beginning of their careers.

At the UK/US conference on teacher markets Joseph Antos directed attention to the problem of trade-offs between earnings and job amenities and to the implications of such trade-offs for assessments of returns to human-capital investments for teaching. Drawing on work done previously with Sherwin Rosen, Antos used a simple hedonic pricing technique to estimate the contribution of 'job consumption' to the value of graduate education for high school teachers. He included estimates of the additional pecuniary and non-pecuniary benefits that accrue to teachers whose graduate education enables them to find employment as educational administrators. This latter question does not arise in the Burnham system, but disregard of promotions of teachers into administrative posts can seriously distort estimates of returns to education for teacher-administrators in the United States, along with comparisons of 'teacher mobility' here and there. (Studies not cited here show much higher inter-district mobility of administrators and into administration than for teaching per se.) The hedonic earnings function for teachers is represented by the relationship: $E = E(T, S)$ where E is earnings, T is a vector of teacher characteristics, and S is a vector of school characteristics. The model assumes operation of a competitive market for teachers.[8] Given an endowment (including prior training and experience) of teacher characteristics, the utility-maximizing teacher is assumed to select a school with the best available combination of school characteristics and salary. Under such assumptions, the premium paid to teachers in 'bad' schools would be just high enough to fill all positions in those schools. (In the empirical estimation Antos made the further assumption that educational administrators and teachers were interested in the same school characteristics, although they could set different values on these characteristics.) For teachers with some postgraduate work but without masters' degrees, Antos estimated negative non-pecuniary returns (compared to BAs), but with progressive gains in positive non-pecuniary returns at the middle and later ages. For PhDs and for teachers with specialist training the non-pecuniary returns were consistently and substantially negative. The variables listed by Antos for school characteristics included in the hedonic analysis include student mathematics scores, pupil/teacher ratios, racial composition, attendance and drop-out rates, advanced placement programs, remedial reading programs, and so on. While we are not shown the details of the hedonic function, the results suggest that highly trained teachers are assigned to problem schools and students, and that their monetary returns compensate for that fact – although there is no way of determining whether tastes in fact differ among the teachers in different training categories. Here, as in the mobility analysis, we in fact have demand-side factors operating in interaction with supplies.

No one can question the importance of the issues raised in Antos' paper or his earlier work with Rosen (Antos and Rosen 1975). Comments on this work by James Heckman centered on methodological and conceptual problems in the estimation of hedonic prices. In his words: 'The real problem, as I see it, is that hedonic accounting is only of interest if we know what exactly should be accounted for, at least in principle. Typically, we do not know what belongs in the earnings function. The problem is more than an omitted variable problem – it is an included variable problem as well.' Heckman's comments go further, to discuss the requirements for proper application of the hedonic approach with the use of instrumental variables and tests of the hedonic price estimates in subsequent analyses. Like Antos' work, these comments call for further explorations and suggest something of the direction that pursuit of this line of research might take. As things stand at present, for both England and the United States we are somewhere in limbo, it seems – whether we are concerned with occupational choice, or with personnel policy for the 'improvement' of teacher allocations, defining improvement in terms of some definition of the social interest.

III The demand side of teacher markets

Starting out with a situation and an analytical model most favourable to analysis of teacher supplies without too serious an identification problem, we have been moved steadily into questions and empirical estimates in which demand factors are inextricably involved. This book is on 'teacher supplies', but demand is there nonetheless, whether this is convenient for researchers or not.

Where there is just one uniform national salary scale with only very limited scope for manoeuver on the part of educational authorities, applications of econometrics to analysis of demand are limited and economic theory may seem to have relatively little to say. There are important economic questions to be asked, nonetheless – not so much about why particular decisions are taken as about what those decisions are and some of their economic implications. In attempting to track down possible work on this subject in the United Kingdom, we were so fortunate as to turn up an unpublished manuscript by Barry Thomas and David Deaton on labor shortages. They selected for examination three very different occupations: bus drivers, teachers, and draughtsmen. Emphasis in the analysis of the teachers' market is on its administrative features and the way they affected adjustments to shortage in the post-war years up to the early 1970s. (As in the present book, the analysis is confined to teachers in the maintained schools.) From the start, Thomas and Deaton point to the monopsonistic nature of the market for teachers, in which national wage negotiations set wages at a level that leaves LEAs with fewer teachers than they would like at the standard wage – that is, with 'shortages'. This, of course, is just what is depicted in the graphs of Chapter 2. Also, in Thomas and Deaton, as in Zabalza, Turnbull and Williams, the two-tier decision structure is emphasized. Responsibility for provision of education is with the LEAs, but they operate within a framework set at national level, much of their spending is mandatory, and they are subjected to considerable financial control from the center. Colleges of education are run locally, but their scale of facilities is set nationally. Two sorts of 'shortage' are distinguished – shortage relative to 'requirements' (defined in quantitative terms as a desired teacher/pupil ratio, which differs for different types of pupils), and shortage relative to the number of teachers wanted at the going salary rates. Shortage relative to demand will normally be less than shortage relative to 'requirements'; the latter was estimated to be close to 20 per cent in 1951, falling to around 7 or 8 per cent in 1970.[9] As in the present book, supply is taken as equal to teachers employed under the conditions of shortage, and available stock is then composed of previous stock (employed teachers) plus inflow of new entrants and re-entrants minus outflow. The empirical importance of the re-entry pool relative to the supply of new entrants is emphasized.

A simple specification of determinants of teacher supplies makes them a function of the state of the employment situation in the labour market in similar occupations, relative salaries, and hiring standards. The main question addressed by Thomas and Deaton is then what instruments were available or potentially available to reduce teacher shortage and which instruments were in fact used, to what extent. Of the many possibilities for 'positive adjustments', most were used in limited degree. Some, but very limited, use was made of changes in teacher pay, 'both of levels and structure'. The heaviest emphasis in positive adjustments was on (i) changes in the structure of hours of work and the expansion of part-time employment and (ii) the provision of extra training facilities. Heaviest of all was the use of a 'residual adjustment' of actual staffing standards.[10] Modifications in other standards and in provision of educational services were slight. The 'political opportunity cost' of alteration of established rules and practices is emphasized, with many illustrations. The time lags in supply adjustments associated with provision of new training facilities are discussed, along with the associations between rates of expenditure on those facilities and the percentage shortfall from teacher 'requirements'. Efforts to make teaching more attractive to returnees through the initiation of new part-time posts and changes in conditions of service that brought these more in line with full-time teaching were speeded-up in the middle 1960s, but there was apparently a lag in this response that cannot be explained by capital outlays and training time; if so this may contribute to the observed lags in 'supply' adjustments as estimated in Chapter 5 of the present volume. In any case, both the longer-term trend toward more part-time appointments and cyclical (shortage–excess) fluctuations around that trend could be important not only for teacher markets but for other markets in which women with higher education play a substantial part. The flexibility of part-timers as a reserve labor force in teaching has a reverse side, in the high risk of loss of jobs when education authorities come under financial pressure.

The analysis of use of pay adjustments in a period of teacher shortage is again characterized by consideration of lags in adjustments to changes in relative teacher shortage. The analytical model used is one that has become increasingly popular in econometric studies in recent years. It starts with the hypothesis that the rate of change in relative salaries will be a function of two variables: (i) the level of teacher shortage (measured as the gap between number of teachers and 'requirements' at the desired teacher–pupil norm), and (ii) the rate of change of teachers' union density (taken as a proxy measure of union 'pushfulness').[11] Despite intervening political and administrative factors, the results of this analysis were impressive. The rate of change in teacher salaries relative to earnings in related occupations was significantly affected by the degree of shortage.[12] Effects of union density were not significant but had the expected positive sign.

Thomas and Deaton deal with many other aspects of teacher shortage, including differences in shortage across fields of specialization and among local authorities. In part this analysis overlaps descriptive material in Chapter 3 of the present book, but for the most part the two studies are complementary. These brief comments cannot do their work justice. Particularly interesting, for example, is their exposition of reasons why wage adjustments may become a more costly strategy in dealing with shortage than used to be the case. Perhaps readers of this book will watch for their book.

Despite the fact that teachers in England and Wales can often gain economically by moving to a school that offers more positions of special responsibility, all of England is essentially one market for teachers and conforms closely to a monopsony model – albeit with a non-profit employer. By contrast, the greater autonomy of local educational authorities in the United States gives those authorities more freedom to differentiate their markets by manipulating salary scales. At the same time, teachers can move among and search out the options in different local markets, albeit at some cost for search and transfer. The American situation is thus better represented by a model of 'monopsonistic competition' than by monopsony, though again – as in Britain – we are dealing with non-profit enterprises. This mixed situation of demand competition and monopsonistic power in local markets for teachers is reflected in the research on demands for teachers in the United States. That work has been stimulated by two main concerns. The first is an old controversy that has become more intense – how great are the differences among different school districts in economic ability to provide educational services, and how disparate are their manifest desires to do so? These concerns have found recent expression in the courts and court cases have spurred further investigations. Second, as I remarked earlier, analysis of demand across school districts has been part of any study of effects of spreading unionization on markets for teachers.

A paper by Jackman, Foster, and Osborne on 'Central Control and the Local Demand for Teachers' straddled this gap between the British and American situations. That paper (which was included in the UK/US conference on teacher markets) aimed 'to assess the relative importance of central controls and local discretion in education' by analyzing the expenditures of local education authorities in England and Wales.[13] A first section outlined the administrative relationship among central government, local government, professional associations etc., in education. To me this was especially interesting (along with Chapter 3 of this volume) because of what seemed to be the implications with respect to the impact of economic factors on the emergence of new teachers' associations beside the old ones, and contrasts within the teaching (and educational administration) profession in positions taken on salary and related policies. Secondly, Jackman and his associates examined the extent of expenditure variation across local districts, comparing it with variation in the United States and with that in other services in England. The third section proceeded essentially in the style of many American studies to analyze factors that appear to account for expenditure variation among local education authorities.

A number of contrasts and parallels between the UK and the US situations emerge from a perusal of this paper. First, the authors contrast for England and Wales present constraints (both of the Burnham scales and the points system) with pre-Burnham local variations. As they remark, 'by fixing the salary for teachers, there is no mechanism to equate supply and demand of suitably qualified teachers, either in aggregate or in any particular local authority'. Attempts of local authorities to get around the problem of shortages through job up-grading and better conditions of work were countered (in the 1950s) by the introduction of a quota system (discussed in Chapter 3 of this book). There is also direct central control of capital expenditure. This is a much more rigid set of controls than is to be found in the United States, though American 'foundation programs' of state assistance to local districts resembles the need-based system of grants to local authorities in Britain. Even a system of 'power equalization' such as has been advocated by some people in the United States and as approximated in one or two states would entail less control than the system of educational finance in England and Wales. Under 'power equalization' local districts could vote higher taxes on themselves, but what they would actually get from those taxes would depend on their economic position. When a rich locality raised its school taxes, it would be allowed to keep only that part of the increase that would be realized by a similar increase in tax rate in the average school district; when a poor district increased its tax rate it would be allowed to draw from the state treasury an amount that would bring returns up to what they would have been with a similar rate increase in the average district. More extreme egalitarians go beyond 'power equalization' to argue that complete equality in expenditures per pupil should be enforced among districts within a state. However, that position is attacked from two sides: because it takes away a community's freedom to choose more and better schooling, and because the per pupil needs of some communities (especially in the slums and among minority language groups) are greater. There have been many American suggestions on working out new arrangements, but they all share two features. They imply greater centralization of control up to the level of the state (but not of the national government), and they leave wide discretion to the local educational authorities in how the budget will be allocated, including salary policies. Both federalism (state rather than national authority) and the degree of concern for local freedom of choice clearly signal the most important differences between the way in which markets for teachers have developed in Britain and in the United States (and in Canada), and related differences in suggested instruments for greater inter-district equalization.

But controls do not always work and freedom from central control does not necessarily bring diversity. There are two broad questions here. How much variability is there in total expenditures per pupil from one school district or local authority to another? And does relative freedom for decisions by local authorities result in substantial variation of local expenditures at any given budget or are conditions common to many districts such that within a state allocations of funds from given budgets are essentially uniform?

Jackman and his co-authors attacked the first of these two questions in two ways. First they took a look at effects (or lack of effects) of the quota system on the variance in local per pupil expenditures in England and Wales. There was reduction in variance across all authorities and among the county councils in the first half of the 1960s but no further reduction as the shortage of teachers became less severe – which is when, they reason, the quotas would presumably have had an effect. I suspect that by 1966 the variance was already so small that there was not much room for further up-grading of the quota-deficient areas relative to other areas. Constraints imposed by central government on staffing and salaries obviously contributed to this low variance, but the question still remains as to how far the variance could be explained in terms of district wealth and the 'price' of education to the district. Jackman *et al.* used a simple per pupil expenditure equation to test these relationships. Taking as independent variables block grants, household incomes, and 'relative price', they explained three fifths of the variance in expenditures among county councils but virtually none of the variance in expenditures among county boroughs.[14] Income and price elasticities of expenditures by the county councils were $+0.32$ and -0.35 respectively in contrast to much higher income elasticities (of unity or more) found in some recent American studies. Before taking these results at face value, it would be wise, however, to look further into the choice and specifications of variables. Especially open to doubt may be interpretations of the 'price variable' for the American studies and the extent of biases due to omission of variables in fact affecting prices – including, for the United States, differences between rural and urban districts in teacher salaries. ('Relative prices' for England and Wales was essentially a measure of the extent of 'matching grants' associated with local expenditures where an authority's rateable value is less than the standard rateable value.)

Studies of determinants of per pupil expenditures by school districts in the United States have been numerous, and I make no attempt to summarise them here. Certain studies seem especially pertinent, however, and I comment on points that seem especially interesting in relation to teachers. It has been shown, for example, that household income and assessed property valuation may have quite different effects on per pupil expenditures. One of the tidiest demonstrations of this fact was a study by Dale Fisher (1967) of the Chicago metropolitan area (outside of the city center). Areas with the highest property valuations had heavy industrial and commercial concentrations; raising tax rates was a way of obtaining funds with little burden on local families. In addition these were districts with relatively heavy expenditures on vocational programs in the secondary schools. Both the sizes of budgets and the ways they were used reflected differences in characteristics of the pupils and in the real 'price' of additional dollars for education from the perspective of local voters and school boards. A similar point was made by David Metcalf with reference to the price variable in the Jackman *et al.* equations for Britain.

A 1969 study by Robert Jewell (used by Alan Thomas in his critique of the paper by Jackman *et al.*) studied household demands for public elementary education in a suburb of Chicago. I summarize this study with special care because it is unique among analyses of demand. First, information concerning predicted effects of given increases or decreases in tax rates for elementary schools was obtained through interviews with the local school superintendent and checked with members of the Board of Education. These specifications referred to what would be added in staff, visual aids, special programs, changes in teacher/pupil ratios and so forth for given percentage increases in school taxes, what would be cut back with specified percentage cuts in those taxes. All additions or cuts referred to current expenditures and services. These were laid out on an interview form that showed also the current expenditures per pupil and the household's property tax implied by a given percentage increase or decrease in school tax. Respondents checked the tax rate they preferred under these conditions; the implied 'demand' for education expressed in terms of per pupil expenditures was then treated as the dependent variable. A number of household characteristics were tested as independent variables in a regression analysis of determinants of 'demand'. The most efficient explanatory model included the following variables:

(a) 'Price' to the household of public expenditures on schools. The measure of 'price' was the present property tax paid by the household, which depends directly on the assessed value of the household's real property within the school district.

(b) Household income.

(c) A household one-year benefit–cost measure, using an adjustment that took into account the number of children who would be enrolled in public elementary school in the coming year.

(d) Age of the head of the household.

(e) Father's level of schooling (years completed).

Variables (a) and (b) above gave a coefficient of determination of 0.490. Adding (c) raised this to 0.598 and adding (d) and (e) raised the coefficient of determination to 0.729, explaining almost three quarters of the variance; the 'price' variable was insignificant taken alone, but controlling for income it came through strongly and the coefficients on 'price' and income in an equation with those variables only proved to be insensitive to addition of the benefit–cost indicator; the coefficient on price was raised, that on income was unchanged with the addition of variables (d) and (e), for age of household head and the father's schooling.

The correlation between 'demand' and prior voting behavior on issues relating to elementary-school expenditures was only modest, though significant. This should not be surprising, since the school referenda had generally involved voting for or against investment in school buildings, which is not part of the scaling on current expenditures used in the analysis of household demand. As might have been predicted, in the votes equation the cost–benefit variable specified for 10 years replaced that specified for 1 year. Jewell's work is highly suggestive in implications for the processes of public choice – for the problem of diffusion (from school authorities to populace) of information about how resources are used and about the implications of changes in school taxes, and for the communication of preferences back to the public school authorities.

Several of the Rand studies on educational personnel relate to relationships between teachers' salaries and total per pupil district expenditures. The question in these cases is not so much what determines expenditures as what determines salary levels for given expenditures; do expenditures on teachers increase in proportion to increases in total expenditures? The first of these studies, by Arthur J. Alexander (1974) used data from 602 school districts in California. Shortly thereafter Barro and Carroll came out with a comparable study using data from Michigan; their paper at the UK/US conference on teacher markets derived primarily from this Michigan study.

Four major findings of the California study were confirmed for Michigan: (i) the elasticity of per pupil expenditure on teachers in relation to total per pupil expenditure was around 0.75; (ii) salary schedules were relatively insensitive to budget increases but closely related to wage rates in alternative occupations and to variations in the cost of living; (iii) there was extremely low variance in starting salaries for new teachers (with BA) in both Michigan and California although there was considerable variation in degree increments and modest variation in experience increments; (iv) teacher/pupil ratios were highly sensitive to total expenditure. In Michigan three fifths of added expenditures on teachers went to increase teacher/pupil ratios. This finding may be of particular interest in comparisons with the analysis by Thomas and Deaton of adjustments to teacher shortage in England and Wales – and also in relation to the salary-policy discussions in Chapter 10 of this Zabalza–Turnbull–Williams book. We may question interpretations of the finding from cross-section observations in Michigan that half of the increase in average salaries with higher total per pupil expenditures went into the hiring of more experienced and 'better' teachers, however. School districts that spend more at a given time have generally spent more in the past and they have more attraction for teachers; the higher experience levels of teachers in those districts are in part a fixed-salary cost that cannot be quickly reduced.

To translate cross-section observations into predictions of what would happen if budgets were increased is partly speculative; this problem has counterparts in many other sorts of studies. One difficulty in the present case goes back to the question: what determines the budget itself? What effect would an exogenous increase in budgets (say by injection of national funds – with no strings attached) have on budget allocation?[15] If we wanted to study determinants of salaries we might do better to use a recursive model – or, if the simultaneity problem of cause–effect relationships between salaries and budgets is critical (as John Akin argued in his comments on the Barro–Carroll paper) a reduced-form model.

One of the most frustrating problems in dealing with school expenditures (and with teacher-salary policy in particular) is of course to identify 'quality', including the even more subtle and complex question of what constitutes an optimal mix of the teaching force in terms of sex, seniority, training, and so on and the costs of those alternatives. A study by John D. Owen using data from 'the Coleman Report' (Owen 1972, 1974) used three 'quality' variables; he obtained the correlations below with state per capita income and with average salaries.

	State per capita income	Teacher salaries
Verbal ability	0.61	0.56
Experience	−0.47	−0.44
Highest degree	0.01	0.05

Results were similar for counties in Illinois. The negative coefficients on experience in the national analysis are unquestionably a reflection of associations between urbanization and growth or shrinkage of school populations and the proportions of newly hired teachers. The large positive experience differentials in salaries observed *within* school systems may say more about bureaucratic constraints than about teacher quality. For this reason, experience is better omitted in any 'quality' measure.[16]

IV   Effects of teacher unionization

The principal question that has been addressed by most economists who have attempted to identify effects of unionization in teacher markets has been, 'do unions raise teachers' salaries?' Much less attention has been given thus far to questions about how unions may affect differentials built into salary schedules or to other important aspects of the functioning of teacher markets. The paper on teacher unions (contributed to the UK–US conference) by Jay Chambers was no exception, and we can view it as part of a series of studies that have appeared in recent years in the United States.

To identify effects of unionization on teachers' pay it is of course necessary to estimate what salaries would be in the absence of union bargaining. Among the problems that arise in attempting such estimates are: (i) selectivity bias in the associations between unionization (however specified) and other attributes that affect salaries and are associated with unionization but that have been omitted from the analysis; (ii) possible depressive effects of unionization on the wages of non-union workers; (iii) spillover effects of unions that raise wages in non-union districts – often labelled the 'threat effect'. Identification of union effects is further confounded if or where teacher demands are monopsonistic, especially if degrees of monopsony and intensity of unionization are not orthogonal; this could be classified as a special variant of (i). The biases entailed in comparing unionized with non-unionized districts would tend to over-statement of union effects if (ii) is a problem, to understatement of those effects (as Jay Chambers argues) if in fact there are important positive spillover or threat effects of union wage bargaining on teacher salaries in adjacent non-union districts. For analysis of teacher markets, likelihood of substantial negative spill-over effects from unionized to non-unionized districts seems relatively small. However, this cannot be taken for granted; if union in urban districts bargain for higher wages at some trade-off for accepting lower teacher/pupil ratios (as they have done recently in New York City) the migration of rural teachers into the city would be discouraged and salaries in non-unionized rural school districts could be held back as a result. But attempts to identify effects of unionism in a sample of school districts that include both rural and urban, with unionism largely in the urban areas, runs into more serious difficulties than this on account of the problems of selectivity bias with poorly specified or omitted variables. Furthermore, several of the recent studies attempting to specify effects of unionization are flawed by the use of total expenditures per pupil or 'instructional costs' as an independent variable (along with unionization measures) in equations in which some measure of salary is taken as the dependent variable. Inclusion of per pupil expenditures among the independent variables removes from the coefficient on unionization any effects that may be realized through effects of union bargaining on total expenditures (i.e. on the total budget) of the district. This criticism applies to the first study by Kasper (1970), to that by Balfour (1974), to the study by Lipsky and Drotning (1976), and to the UK/US conference and other papers by Jay Chambers.[17] However, their results taking observations on a district by district basis have not differed greatly from findings in other studies. Effects of unions on salaries range below 5 per cent – with a few erratic and some more interesting exceptions.[18]

Three of the most interesting studies used more than one dependent variable. Robert J. Thornton (1971) assumed demand (N_d) to be a function of district size and of teacher/pupil ratio (taken as an index of quality). Supply (N_s) was a function of teacher salaries, a benchmark salary variable for wages in alternative occupations, and district size. The district is assumed unilaterally to set salaries at the intersection of N_s and N_d at the equilibrium wage W_s. Successful teacher negotiations would raise the wage above this equilibrium level. The greater the extent of that excess $D = W_u - W_s$, the greater will be the shortage (excess of demand over supply, $E = N_s - N_d$).[19] The sample was of school districts in cities of 100,000 or more population (which avoids the rural–urban problem mentioned above). The strongest salary predictor in every case was the benchmark (alternative) wage. Collective bargaining was estimated to raise the minimum wage for teachers with BA degrees by 3.7 per cent, their maximum wage by 5 per cent; the minimum for teachers with MA degrees was raised 2.3 per cent. An extremely high coefficient was obtained for the effects of unions on the maximum for the MA teachers, but this was a small sample and Thornton emphasized that this particular finding was undependable.

The study by Lipsky and Drotning (1976) was primarily a test of the initial effects of the Taylor law of 1967 in New York (excluding New York City). Collective bargaining began immediately after the Taylor law was passed, with 63 per cent of districts engaging in collective bargaining in 1968. In a well specified model (the inclusion of instructional costs aside) Lipsky and Drotning found no union impact in cross-section. A test for spillover effects separated out a group of relatively isolated districts, in which that effect could not have been expected. Comparing their wages with those in bargaining areas gave a strong union effect, but the upward bias in this finding is obvious. The strong effect of unions on salary change between 1967 and 1968 was clear enough, but the authors remind us here of Paul Douglas's observation that while initial effects of unionizing may seem large, later those effects fade. It would be surprising indeed if there were no jog in the salary time series at a point at which union bargaining suddenly became the way of doing things.

A highly sophisticated theoretical model of determination of teachers wages and of the role of unions was laid out in Frey (1975). Empirically, like most of us, he was forced to simplify and to use what were essentially reduced-form estimates. He worked with two dependent variables: the natural logarithm of base pay, and the natural logarithm of maximum pay. For his measure of alternative earnings he used nurses' pay. As others before him, Frey found that the strongest explanatory variable was the alternative wage; elasticities on the tax base and on medium family income were low. The impact of unionism differed with the labor market. It was positive when alternative wages were high, but negative when they were low. These results raise plenty of unanswered questions about the economic conditions that foster unionism and the political as well as the economic context of wage and related negotiations.

Effects of collective bargaining on teachers' salaries is examined in a valuable monograph by Gary Moore (1975) who commented also on prior work by Thornton and Frey and by Landon and Baird (discussed below). Moore's empirical work referred to school districts in the state of Nebraska in 1970–71 and in 1965–66. (The legal right to formally negotiate salaries had been established by legislation and in the courts in 1967 and 1969. Collective agreements occurred before 1967, but were necessarily less formal.) Moore followed Thornton in his specification of dependent variables. Independent variables included: school district ability to pay, A; willingness to pay, W (the general education mill fund levy of a district); total enrollments, E; school board monopsony power, M (from Landon and Baird, 1971); teacher monopoly power, N (professional negotiations).

For 1970–71 the coefficient on N (collective bargaining) was strongly positive, with higher t-values than any other variables. Nevertheless, it was generally in line with prior studies in that the estimated percentage effects were modest. They ranged from 2 per cent of the average BA minimum to 7 per cent of the average MA maximum. By contrast, the less formal collective bargaining of 1965–66 had very little effect, and was just barely significant at the 0.10 level in a 1-tailed test. The monopsony indicator (M) was not significant in the equations for average salaries in 1970–71 though it was significant at the 0.05 level in 1965–66.[20]

That teachers' wages may be held down by monopsonistic buying in the absence of unionism is a hypothesis that has been set forth by several economists, and it is implicit in some degree in all the cost-minimization models of school board decisions in which salaries constitute a policy instrument. In such circumstances, to raise the salary of newly-hired teachers in order to attract men and women of greater ability (at any given set of formal qualifications) it becomes necessary simultaneously to raise the pay of teachers already employed. This is the main characteristic of a monopsonistic situation in labor markets, and thus underlies much of the recent work on wage determination in the local public sector. But how elastic are teacher supplies to the decision making local educational authority? If teacher supplies were very inelastic to the district (not just to the nation as a whole), it would be possible to cut wages considerably without bringing about a 'shortage' (defining shortage as the gap between the numbers of teachers the district would be willing to hire at the lower wage and the numbers available at that wage). This phenomenon could be of some importance where the monopsonist had control of a labor market that was effectively isolated from competing buyers. If we regard the British teacher market as a single market, we might imagine that sort of power in the absence of collective action by teachers' associations. However, even aggregate elasticity of teacher supply is high. It is still more difficult to believe that monopsonistic power to press down on wages would be strong for local districts that compete with other districts for teachers' services, whether in England or in the United States. Any attempt to cut wages back when supplies to the locality are comparatively elastic would induce sharp cutbacks in available teachers, with substantial gaps between desired and actual teacher/pupil ratios. It has sometimes been argued, nevertheless, that differences across school districts in the extent of monopsonistic power distort estimates of the wage effects of unionization.

The principal exponents of this theme with reference to teachers are Landon and Baird, who have written about it in an independent study (1971) and in a critique of Thornton (1972). Taking as their monopsony indicator the number of school districts in a county, Landon and Baird (1971) ran equations with the logarithm of basic salary as the dependent variable. (These regressions on a national sample were run separately for districts with enrollments of 25 to 50 thousand, 50 to 100 thousand, and over 100 thousand.) They obtained significant results on the districts up to 100 thousand but not on the larger ones. Thornton (1975) repeated his equations with the Landon and Baird (1972) variable M, but found that the coefficients on M were insignificant and inclusion of M had no effect on the unionization or on any other coefficients. Thornton concludes that either monopsony was not as important a wage-discriminating factor among large-city districts as in smaller places or that the variable M was spurious. Within urban areas, at least, these results suggest that monopsony is not important (supplies are not inelastic) at the district level. In any case, the urban diffusion of collective bargaining is progressively wiping out intra-urban differentiation of teacher supplies except as these relate to amenities (positive or negative) of employment in one rather than another school or school district. Questions relating to market differentiation (monopsonistic situations) in rural areas remain.

Finally we come to the issue that was attacked in the UK/US conference paper by Chambers (as in his previous work on union bargaining and teacher pay). This is essentially an attempt to identify the positive spillover or 'threat' effects of union bargaining as such bargaining has been introduced or begun to diffuse in the United States. Initially, Chambers did his research on school districts in California, where bargaining has been spreading for some time (see Chambers, 1977). His most recent work has been done in Missouri, where teachers' unions are not legally recognized as bargaining agents but where collective negotiations of various degrees of formality proceed nonetheless. He distinguished unionization measures for the district and for the region of the state (the proportion of districts bargaining). The coefficient was virtually zero on the district measure in Missouri as in California; it was highly significant for the extent of bargaining in the region in which the district was located. This work has promise; it is to be hoped that Chambers will clean up his results by following through with suggestions by Nicholas Kiefer (his discussant) and others on the treatment of the district expenditure variables that bias his results, as those of some of his predecessors.

V From shortage to surplus

'Teacher shortage' in the elementary and secondary schools characterized most industrialized nations in the 1950s and 1960s as children of the post-war baby boom moved into elementary and then into secondary classes. Late in this period the effects of decelerating birthrates were partially neutralized in England and Wales as the school-leaving age rose for many youngsters. Meanwhile, there has also been a cycle of economic boom (or relative boom) and recession that has affected both demands for and supplies of teachers. As the authors of this book have emphasized, the empirical data they used refer to a period of shortage, but with a decreasing gap between 'desired' and actual teacher–pupil ratios and with teacher salaries declining relative to pay elsewhere. Essentially exogenous demographic and economic changes strongly conditioned the changes in teacher markets through the 1960s and the transition to 'surplus' in the 1970s. These changes have raised a number of questions relating to the operating of teacher markets and implications for salary policy and salary determination in both the United Kingdom and the United States.

Simplistic projections of teacher shortage and excess often ignore the fact that people make choices, they are not just objects in a pipe-line, and their decisions depend on how their options are changing. Commonly such projections, made on both sides of the Atlantic, are misleading. Better analyses of what has happened and is likely to happen have combined consideration of the exogenous demographic variables with evidence concerning occupational decisions at various stages in college and after entering the labor markets – including decisions to become teachers. This book has given relatively little attention to the underlying demographic variables, however. Attention has been concentrated on decisions rather than on demographic or broad economic changes, and decisions have been examined in a situation of shortage. Perhaps the implications, and the limitations, of the analysis developed here should be more carefully explored in the perspective of teacher surplus. I suggest that several directions of analysis should be pursued.

First, a better understanding of how events unfold, of future prospects, and of possible strategies of salary policy would be fostered by distinguishing more clearly between what might be done in a very short time perspective and what only in the longer term. Much of the discussion of salary policy by economists is still couched in an essentially static equilibrium-theoretic framework that ignores effects of today's actions on tomorrow's problems.

Second, we need to explore much more carefully the formation of expectations and how they are expressed in behavior under varying economic (and demographic) conditions. The unemployment variable used in this book as a proxy for anticipated relative search or waiting time might operate quite differently in another economic environment. So may incentives and constraints at later stages in the life cycle. We might well begin, for that matter, with the somewhat easier task of probing further into expectations and teacher supplies in the 1950s and 1960s.

Third, it is important to recognize that the notion of a teacher 'stock' used under the assumptions of shortage and inelastic demand for teachers may not serve well at all in a market in which many job seekers at the current wage are unsuccessful in their search. Treating 'stock' as synonymous with numbers in fact employed (as is done in this book and by other authors as well) can have an unfortunate result: it diverts attention from the potential supply of teachers (other than 'at the margin') and especially from the reserve supplies of re-entrants. This brings us to my fourth and fifth points.

Fourth, we have much to learn about what has in fact happened (and what are some of the possibilities) with respect to part-time employment in the schools. Part-time teachers may relieve temporary shortages and more part-time employment could ease the impact of lay-offs and unemployment of teachers when demographic relationships and tightening public budgets shrink the demand for teachers. This is not just a matter of the place of married women in the teaching force, though linkages with questions of female labour-force participation are involved.

Fifth, it is important to bear in mind that assessments of shortage or surplus may differ according to where one sits. Shortage is a worry to the buyer; it is a boon to the seller. Surplus, on the other hand, is a problem – sometimes a severe one – from the perspective of the seller, but surplus may be an opportunity for the buyer, the buyer in this case being the school board and parents.

Sixth and finally, several questions will surely grow in importance. How will collective bargaining affect the allocation of resources in the schools during the next decade or so? We may expect that teachers' associations will seek to protect job security in many ways that could work against real improvements in the schools.[21] Also, there is already a decided decline in the teacher attrition (and mobility) that was so bemoaned by some educational planners a few years ago. But whatever the gains from greater stability, diminished turnover in a period in which demand is stagnant can bring also rigidities and lack of manoeuverability compared with a time when there were plenty of jobs both in teaching and elsewhere. The problems ahead are difficult. It is not enough to sit back and say that 'economic forces are operating to reduce the numbers who are taking teacher. training, and thereby to diminish the problem of teacher surpluses in the future'.

References

Alexander, A. J. (1974), 'Teachers' Salaries, and School District Expenditures', Santa Monica, the Rand Corporation, California.

Antos, J. and Rosen, S. (1975), 'Discrimination in the Market for Public School Teachers', *Journal of Econometrics*, November.

Ashenfelter, O. (1971), 'The Effect of Unionization on Wages in the Public Sector: The Case of Fire Fighters', *Industrial and Labor Relations Review*, January pp. 191–202.

Baird, R. N. and Landon, J. H. (1972), 'Teacher Salaries and School Decentralization', *Education and Urban Society*, February, pp. 197–210.

Balfour, G. A. (1974), 'More Evidence that Unions do not Achieve High Salaries for Teachers', *J. Collective Negotiations* 3(4), Fall.

Barro, S. M. and Carroll, S. J. (1975), *Budget Allocation by School Districts: An Analysis of Spending for Teachers and Other Resources*, Santa Monica, the Rand Corporation.

Carroll, S. J., *Analysis of the Educational Personnel System*, Santa Monica, the Rand Corporation.

(1973), III. *The Demand for Educational Professionals.*

(1974), VIII. *The Market for Teachers.*

Carroll, S. J. and Ryder, K. F. Jr., *Analysis of Educational Personnel System*, Santa Monica, the Rand Corporation.

(1974), V. *The Supply of Elementary and Secondary Teachers.*

Chambers, J. G. (1977), 'The Impact of Collective Bargaining for Teachers on Resource Allocation in Public School Districts; The California Experience', *Journal of Urban Economics.*

Clark, H. F. (1937), *Life Earnings in Selected Occupations in the United States*, New York, Harpers.

Clark, J. B. (1899), 'Salaries of teachers', *Columbia University Quarterly* I(2), March, pp. 111–12.

Ehrenberg, R. (1973), 'The Demand for State and Government Employees', *American Economic Review*, 63, June, pp. 366–380.

Fisher, D. (1967), 'Local Determinants of per Pupil Expenditures in Suburban High-school Districts', unpublished PhD dissertation, University of Chicago.

Freeman, R. (1971) *The Market for College-Trained Manpower*, Harvard University Press.

(1976), *The Overeducated American*, New York, Academic Press Inc.

Frey, D. E. (1975), 'Wage Determination in Public Schools and the Effects of Unionization', in D. S. Hamermesh (ed.), *Labor in the Public and Non-profit Sectors*, Princeton University Press, pp. 183–219.

Friedman, M. and Kuznets, S. (1946), *Income from Independent Professional Practice, 1929–1936*, National Bureau of Economic Research, 72–73.

Greenberg, D. and McCall, J., *Analysis of the Educational Personnel System*, Santa Monica, The Rand Corporation.

(1973a), I. *Teacher Mobility in San Diego.*

(1973b), II. *A Theory of Labor Mobility with Applications to the Teacher Market.*

(1974), VII. *Teacher Mobility in Michigan.*

Hall, W. C. and Carroll, N. E. (1972), 'The Effect of Teachers' Organizations on Salaries and Class Size', *Industrial Labor Relations Review*, 26, pp. 834–41.

Harvey, V. (1967), 'Economic Aspects of Teachers' Salaries', unpublished PhD dissertation, University of Chicago.

Jewell, R. W., Jr. (1969), 'Household Demand for Public Schools', unpublished PhD dissertation, University of Chicago.

Kasper, H. (1970), 'The Effects of Collective Bargaining on Public School Teachers' Salaries', *Industrial and Labor Relations Review*, 24 (1), October, pp. 57–72.

Kershaw, J. A. and McKean, R. N. (1962), *Teacher Shortages and Salary Schedules*, New York, McGraw-Hill.

Kuh, C. (1976), 'Wage Determination for Teachers and the Demand for Educational Expenditures', Stanford University Department of Engineering and Economic Systems, mimeo, March.

Landon, J. H. and Baird, R. N. (1971), 'Monopsony in the Market for Public School Teachers', *American Economic Review*, 61, December, pp. 966–71.

(1972), 'The Effects of Collective Bargaining on Public School Teachers' Salaries; Comment', *Industrial and Labor Relations Review*, XXV, April, pp. 410–17.

Lipsky, D. B. and Drotning, J. E. (1976), 'The Influence of Collective Bargaining on Teachers' Salaries in New York State', in A. M. Cresswell and M. J. Murphy (eds.), *Education and Collective Bargaining*, Berkeley, California, McCutchan Publishing Co., pp. 425–51.

Mincer, J. (1974), *Schooling, Experience and Earnings*, New York, National Bureau of Economic Research/Columbia University Press.

Moore, G. A. (1975), *Some Salary Effects of Professional Negotiations in the Public Schools: The Nebraska Experience*, Lincoln, Nebraska, University of Nebraska Press.

Norris, K. (1970), 'The Economics of Teacher Supply: the English and Welsh Case', in Instituto Gulbenkian De Ciencia, Centro de Economia e Financas, *The Economics of Educational Costing*, Lisbon, pp. 125–40.

Owen, J. D. (1972), 'Toward a Public Employment Wage Theory: Some Econometric Analyses', *Industrial and Labor Relations Review*, 25 (2), January.

(1972), *School Inequality and the Welfare State*, Baltimore, Johns Hopkins University Press.

Padilla, A. H. (1975), 'The Market for Teachers in the Nation and the Southern Region', Southern Regional Education Board, Atlanta.

Pedersen, K. G. (1973), *The Itinerant Schoolmaster*, Midwest Administration Center, University of Chicago.

Schmener, R. W. (1973), 'The Determination of Municipal Employee Wages', *Review of Economics and Statistics*, 55, February, pp. 83–90.

Thomas, B. and Deaton, D. (1976), 'An Economic Analysis of Labor Shortage', typescript, University of Warwick, April.

Thornton, R. J. (1971), 'The Effect of Collective Negotiations on Teachers' Salaries', *Quarterly Review of Economics and Business*, 11(4), Winter.

(1975), 'Monopsony and Teachers' Salaries, Some Contrary Evidence; Comment', *Industrial and Labor Relations Review*, 28, Ch. 4, July.

Vaizey, J. (1976), *The Political Economy of Education*, Duckworth.

Walsh, J. R. (1935), 'The Capital Concept Applied to Man', *Quarterly Journal of Economics*, 49, February, pp. 255–85.

Zerfoss, E. and Shapiro, L. J. (1974), *The Supply and Demand of Teachers and Teaching*, The Nebraska Curriculum Development Center, University of Nebraska.

Data appendix[1]

In 1973 the Department of Education and Science made available to the London School of Economics copies of the data records of all full-time teachers in grant aided schools and establishments from 1963 to 1971. They were to form the data base for the research project upon which this book is based. Subsequently the DES also provided data for the year 1972. Most of the data used in the supply analysis reported in Chapters 5 and 6 was extracted from these records as was all the data for analysis reported in other parts of the book.

The content and format of the computerised data files are described in Section A.1. As explained in that section, computer resource limitations prevented us from fully utilising the complete data set. It was therefore necessary to produce new more manageable data files by using samples taken from the originals. Section A.2 describes the three different samples used in our analyses.

A.1 The DES 'TEACHERSMOVE' data files

The Department of Education and Science began computerising teacher records in 1963. A computerised census data file is built up by the DES from returns submitted by local authorities every year. These returns cover every teacher employed by local authorities or employed in establishments which are grant aided by local authorities (e.g. Colleges of Education and direct grant grammar schools) on 31 March.[2] Once the census file is complete a new file is created by comparing one year's census file with the previous year's and extracting certain information about each individual teacher on a two-year basis. These new files are known as 'TEACHERS-MOVE' files and are used to produce tables for 'Statistics of Education' (DES, annual – a) showing the movements and flows of teachers from one year to the next.

It was these 'TEACHERSMOVE' data files for the years 1962–63 to 1971–72 inclusive which the DES provided. They did, however, make the following modifications to the files before releasing them in order to preserve confidentiality. The unique reference number given to each teacher at the start of his career and the unique local authority and school reference numbers were all scrambled in order to prevent the identification of any individual teacher, school or local authority.

A list of the variables included on the 'TEACHERSMOVE' files is to be found in Table A.1. The 1971–72 file, for example, tells us for each individual teacher: age,.length of teaching service, type of school or establishment, region, qualifications, post held and salary for 31 March 1972. In addition it will tell us his type of school, region, qualifications and post held on 31 March 1971; and, by implication, it will tell us whether he is a new entrant (or re-entrant), whether he has left teaching during the year, whether he has been promoted, or whether he has moved school. Unfortunately one important item of information it will *not* tell us is his salary in 1971.

At the beginning of the research project we received nine 'TEACHERS-MOVE' files from the DES for the years 1962–63 to 1970–71 inclusive. Later on in the project we received a new version of the 1970–71 file[3] and a 1971–72 file.

TABLE A.1   *Variables included on the DES 'TEACHERSMOVE' files*

Variable number	Variable name	Explanation
1	DOB	Date of birth
2	AGE	Age in years as of 31 March year 2
3	REFNO	Seven digit unique reference number*
4	SEX	Male or female
5	S-SAL	Service for salary (i.e. incremental point)
6	UNIV	University attended (if applicable)
7	DEGYR	Year of obtaining degree (if applicable)
8	HONS	Good honours graduate or not (year 2)
9	CL-DEG	Class of degree (if applicable)
10	SUB1	First subject of degree (if applicable)
11	SUB2	Second subject of degree (if applicable)
12	SUB3	Third subject of degree (if applicable)
13	REDGP	Redfern group classification of degree subjects
14	REDSUB	Redfern subject classification of degree subjects
15	GRAD1	Graduate or not (year 1)
16	GRAD2	Graduate or not (year 2)
17	EQUIV1	Graduate equivalent or not (year 1)
18	EQUIV2	Graduate equivalent or not (year 2)
19	DOT-CD1	Post held in year 1
20	DOT-CD2	Post held in year 2
21	IN1	In service or not year 1
22	IN2	In service or not year 2
23	TRND1	Trained or not year 1
24	TRND2	Trained or not year 2

TABLE A.1   *Variables included on the DES 'TEACHERSMOVE' files (cont.)*

Variable number	Variable name	Explanation
25	T-NAT	Nature of training course
26	T-LEN	Length of training course
27	T-SUPP	Subject of training course
28	DOQ	Date of qualification
29	H-QUAL	Higher qualification if any (other than degrees)
30	QUALFN	Other qualifications if any
31	QUALD1	Qualified or not year 1
32	QUALD2	Qualified or not year 2
33	MARRY	Marital status of women
34	STAT1	Status of pensionable service year 1
35	STAT2	Status of pensionable service year 2
36	STATUS1	Legal teaching status year 1
37	STATUS2	Legal teaching status year 2
38	MOVE	Re-entrant to teaching or not
39	SALBAS	Basis for salary year 2
40	SALARY	Salary on 31 March or 1 April year 2**
41	ALLCES	Salary allowances
42	MIND	Moved school or not between year 1 and year 2
43	DENOM	Denomination of school (year 2)
44	S-SEX	Sex of pupils at school (year 2)
45	S-TYPE2	Detailed classification of school type year 2 (interpretation of those codes not provided by DES)
46	BM-GP	Burnham group of school (year 2)
47	SUPER	Superannuation category
48	BM-REP	Which Burnham report teacher comes under
49	MNPS1	In a maintained primary or secondary school or not (year 1)
50	MNPS2	In a maintained primary or secondary school or not (year 2)
51	SC-CD1	Type of school year 1
52	SC-CD2	Type of school year 2
53	LEA-SCHOOL	Combined local authority and individual school reference number*
54	S-TYPE1	Detailed classification of school type year 1 (interpretation of these codes not provided by DES)
55	REG1	Region year 1
56	REG2	Region year 2
57	DENT	Date of first entering qualified teaching

Source: DES Codebook: *B4*.
Notes:
*These variables were scrambled by the DES to preserve anonymity.
**31 March for the 1970–71 (OLD) and the 1971–72 'TEACHERSMOVE' files and 1 April for all the others.

A.2 The data samples

Each of the eleven 'TEACHERSMOVE' data files contained up to half a million teacher records and each file extended over four or five magnetic computer tapes. The computer required almost a complete night shift for each complete processing run on each file. As several computer runs are usually required for even the simplest of tasks, it was clear to us from the start that the University of London computer resources were not up to the task (or rather the share of these resources that we could call upon).

It was therefore decided to take samples from the complete files and base most of our analysis upon these samples. Initially a straightforward 1 per cent random sample was selected from each of the 'TEACHERS-MOVE' files and this sample then became the main data base for the project. Two further series of samples were taken for more specialised needs. A 5 per cent sample of graduate teachers and a clustered school-based sample. All three samples are described in some detail below.

The 1 per cent sample. As already explained, the seven digit teachers' reference number (variable 3) had been scrambled by the DES prior to release. However this had been done in such a way as to preserve a unique reference number for each teacher. It was decided to sample in such a way that the same teachers would be picked up by the sample on successive years' files (provided of course that they were still in service). The intention at that preliminary stage of the project was to link up the records of individual teachers over the full nine-year period, thus enabling cohort type analyses to be carried out. In the event this idea was not followed up in this study[4] since it was subsequently decided to concentrate on specifying supply functions for which purpose the original cross-sectional information was adequate.

The actual sampling procedure was to select every teacher on the original 'TEACHERSMOVE' files whose reference number ended in the digits '25'.[5] This gave a fairly accurate 1 per cent random sample because preliminary tests had shown that the final two digits were randomly spread across all possible values and not obviously related to any characteristic of the teachers (not true of the first two digits, for example, which were strongly related to age and length of service). Samples were originally taken from each of the nine 'TEACHERSMOVE' files from 1962–63 to 1970–71. Subsequently two further samples were extracted from the new version of the 1970–71 file and from the 1971–72 file.

The 5 per cent graduate sample. Although the sample size of the 1 per cent sample ($3\frac{1}{2}$ thousand) was adequate for studying the profession as a whole the number of graduates (800) was inadequate for the finer breakdowns of this group (e.g. by subject) which were required. A second series of samples of graduate teachers only was therefore extracted. Graduates comprise about one fifth of the teaching profession, a 5 per cent sample was therefore chosen so as to give a sample size approximately the same as that for the 1 per cent sample.

For consistency the sampling method used for the previous sample was retained and every graduate teacher whose reference number ended in one of the following five pairs of digits was selected: 14, 20, 28, 38, 43.[5] 5 per cent graduate samples were not extracted from the new version of the 1970–71 file nor from the 1971–72 file because these arrived at a much later stage in the project.

The SED clustered sample. This series of samples was designed to serve a different purpose than the previous two and for that reason a different sampling method was employed. The purpose was to study teachers in schools of exceptional difficulty (SED teachers) and compare them with teachers in other schools.[6] Because of the way school reference numbers had been scrambled, we were initially unable to identify SED teachers. The DES however agreed to provide us with a list of the scrambled version of the reference numbers of SED schools (about 500 schools). We were therefore able to extract all teachers in all SED schools from the 'TEACHERSMOVE' files (about 4,000 teachers). Because SED schools were not designated as such until 1968, we decided to confine our data extraction in this case to the seven files 1965–66 to 1971–72 inclusive (using the new version of 1970–71 only).

At the same time as this extraction of all SED teachers (not a sample) we extracted a 1 per cent random sample of non-SED primary school teachers[7] for comparison. The original 1 per cent sample was not suitable for this purpose because SED teachers were all clustered within particular schools. Furthermore, the same schools were involved from year to year and the same teachers only if they remained in an SED school. The comparison was therefore made with teachers in a random sample of non-SED schools again maintaining the same schools from year to year and not with a random sample of teachers which maintains the same teachers from year to year.

The non-SED sample had therefore to be based on school reference number and not on teacher reference number, as in the original samples. Preliminary analysis showed that neither the first nor the final digits of the 8-digit LEA/SCHOOL reference number were randomly distributed. The third, fourth and fifth digits were therefore chosen[8] and a 1 per cent sample was chosen by selecting every teacher in primary schools whose third, fourth and fifth digits were among the following ten: 283, 193, 439, 487, 731, 938, 475, 536, 909, 810.[9]

Appendix 4A

Subjective rates of discount implied by the model

4A.1 Rate of discount implied by the slope elasticity

Assuming that there is no unemployment in teaching, our model predicts that relative supply (RS_a) is a function of the return from entering teaching (R_a) relative to the expected return from entering some alternative occupation (ER_b). We can express this hypothesis as follows

$$RS_a = S(RR)$$

where RR stands for relative return and equals R_a/ER_b.

The effect on supply due to a change in the relative return should be the same regardless of the source of that change. For instance, the effect on supply of an increase in the relative return brought about by an increase in the starting point of the teaching profile, holding constant its proportional slope,[1] should be the same as the effect on supply of an increase in the relative return brought about by an increase in the proportional slope of the teaching profile, holding constant its starting point. In algebraic terms, we can express this as follows

$$\frac{d \log RS_a}{d \log RR(W_{ao})} = \frac{d \log RS_a}{d \log RR(\alpha)} \qquad (4A.1)$$

where $d \log RR(W_{ao})$ is the increase in the relative return due to an increase in the starting point of the profile, holding constant the slope, and $d \log RR(\alpha)$ is an equivalent increase in the relative return, but this time due to an increase in the *slope* of the profile, holding constant the starting point.

The left hand side of (4A.1) is simply η_1 because, as shown in section 4.4, a percentage change in the level of the profile will change the return to teaching – and therefore the relative return – by the same percentage (i.e. $d \log RR(W_{a0}) = d \log W_{a0}$).

To evaluate the right hand side of (4A.1) let us note, from the definition of the relative return, that

$$d \log RR(\alpha) = d \log R_a(\alpha) \qquad (4A.2)$$

For simplicity assume an infinite working horizon. This assumption is not critical to the argument developed here and it greatly simplifies the problem. Thus the return to teaching is

$$R_a = W_{a0} \sum_{t=0}^{\infty} \rho^t + \alpha W_{a0} \sum_{t=0}^{\infty} t\rho^t$$

or $$R_a = W_{a0}A + \alpha W_{a0}B \qquad (4A.3)$$

where $A = (1 + r)/r$ and $B = (1 + r)/r^2$

From (4A.3) it follows that

$$dR_a = W_{a0}Bd\alpha$$

which is equivalent to

$$\frac{dR_a}{R_a} = \frac{d\alpha}{\alpha} \frac{\alpha W_{a0}B}{R_a}$$

and can be approximated by

$$d \log R_a = d \log \alpha \frac{\alpha W_{a0}B}{R_a} \qquad (4A.4)$$

Using (4A.4), (4A.3), (4A.2) and (4A.1) we have

$$\eta_1 = \frac{d \log RS_a}{d \log \alpha} \frac{R_a}{\alpha W_{a0}B}$$

but $d \log RS_a/d \log \alpha = \eta_2$; therefore

$$\eta_1 = \eta_2 \frac{R_a}{\alpha W_{a0}B} \qquad (4A.5)$$

Then substituting (4A.3) into (4A.5) and rearranging, we obtain the expression for the subjective rate of discount

$$r = \alpha \left[\frac{\eta_1 - \eta_2}{\eta_2} \right]$$

4A.2 Rate of discount implied by the unemployment elasticity

A similar line of reasoning can be applied to the unemployment elasticity η_3. In this case we start by postulating that the effect on supply of an increase in the relative return due to an increase in the level of the teaching profile (η_1), should be the same as the effect on supply of an increase in the relative return due to an increase in the probability of being unemployed in an alternative occupation (i.e. due to an increase in U). We will then have

$$\eta_1 = \frac{d \log RS_a}{d \log RR(U)} \qquad (4A.6)$$

and, from the definition of relative return,

$$d \log RR(U) = -d \log ER_b(U) \tag{4A.7}$$

Again assuming an infinite working horizon, the expected return to choosing an alternative occupation is

$$ER_b = W_{b0} \sum_{t=t_b}^{\infty} \rho^t + \beta W_{b0} \sum_{t=t_b}^{\infty} t\rho^t$$

or

$$ER_b = W_{b0} \left[\frac{r + \beta(1 + rt_b)}{r^2(1 + r)^{t_b-1}} \right] \tag{4A.8}$$

Differentiating ER_b with respect to t_b, we have

$$dER_b = - \left[\frac{W_{b0}(1 + \beta t_b)}{(1 + r)^{t_b-1}} \right] dt_b$$

or equivalently

$$\frac{dER_b}{ER_b} = - \frac{1}{ER_b} \left[\frac{W_{b0}(1 + \beta t_b)}{(1 + r)^{t_b-1}} \right] dt_b$$

Then, substituting ER_b from (4A.8) and approximating dER_b/ER_b by $d \log ER_b$, we end up with

$$d \log ER_b = -H \, dt_b \tag{4A.9}$$

where $H = [r^2(1 + \beta t_b)]/[r(1 + \beta t_b) + \beta]$. For small β, H could be approximated by r, but we will continue the derivation without making this simplification. In Chapter 5 it is seen that this approximation gives results very close to those derived working with the full expression.

Before proceeding we need to establish how t_b (the time a person may expect to wait before obtaining a job in an alternative occupation) is related to the measure of unemployment used in the regression equation (4.11). To this end we assume that the probability of being unemployed at a given moment in time declines exponentially as time passes by.

$$U_t = e^{-gt} \tag{4A.10}$$

Then the expected duration of unemployment (that is, what t_b is meant to measure) will equal the sum over all periods of the probability of being unemployed in each of them. That is, the integral over t of the above function.

$$t_b = \int_0^{\infty} e^{-gt} \, dt = 1/g \tag{4A.11}$$

The rate of unemployment used in the estimation of (4.11) for graduate new entrants is the proportion of graduates seeking permanent employment on 31 December of the year of graduation. They have therefore been unemployed for about half a year. We then have from (4A.10) that

$$U = e^{-g(1/2)}$$

from where g can be obtained in terms of U

$$g = -2 \log U \tag{4A.12}$$

Substituting (4A.12) into (4A.11), we obtain

$$t_b = -1/(2 \log U)$$

which shows the relationship between the time a person may expect to find employment (i.e. the expected duration of unemployment, t_b) and the rate of (instantaneous) unemployment used in the regressions (U). Differentiating with respect to U we have

$$dt_b = \frac{1}{2(\log U)^2} \frac{dU}{U}$$

or

$$dt_b = \frac{1}{2(\log U)^2} d \log U \tag{4A.13}$$

Then, from (4A.13), (4A.9), (4A.7) and (4A.6) we arrive at the following equation

$$H = \left[\frac{\eta_3}{\eta_1} \right] 2 (\log U)^2$$

If we use the approximation mentioned above, H will reduce to r and the expression for the rate of discount will be

$$r = \left[\frac{\eta_3}{\eta_1} \right] 2 (\log U)^2 \tag{4A.14}$$

which is the one presented in the main text. If not, then r can be solved as the solution of the following quadratic equation

$$ar^2 - br - c = 0 \tag{4A.15}$$

where

$$a = \left[1 - \frac{\beta}{2 \log U} \right] (\tfrac{1}{2}) \eta_1$$

$$b = \left[1 - \frac{\beta}{2 \log U} \right] (\log U)^2 \eta_3$$

and

$$c = (\log U)^2 \beta \eta_3$$

In the numerical calculations presented in Chapter 5 we use both (4A.14) and (4A.15).

Appendix 5A[1]

The data for the new entrants regressions

5A.1 Teachers' salaries

Average salaries were obtained from the 5 per cent sample; details about elaboration and this sample are given in the data appendix (pp. 223–27). They correspond to average salaries paid from 1 April of the indicated year. Data for the years 1961 and 1962 were taken from Statistics of Education (DES, annual –a). Since they correspond to average salaries at 31 March and since from that date to 1 April there was an automatic service increment for most teachers (those below the maximum in their corresponding scale), we adjusted these data by adding an estimated increment of £22, to make them comparable to the subsequent data. From October 1959 to 1961 there was no negotiated increase in teaching salaries, and we assumed that the actual differences in the average salary are small enough to be ignored.

As the data for entrants refer to the number of teachers recruited *during* the year ending in March, and data for salaries refer to the average salary paid *from* the beginning of April, we cannot directly relate the two series. The relevant wage for entrants in, say, 1965 (recruited during the period 31 March 1964 – 31 March 1965) is the salary of year 1964 (paid from 1 April 1964).[2] Two exceptions to this rule are the years 1961 and 1967. In these years, because of pay freezes, the salaries recorded on 1 April do not reflect the level of earnings applicable during the whole of the following year. Because of this, the figures for these two years used in the regression exercise are estimated as an average of the salaries given in the Statistics for each of the two years.

5A.2 Alternative salaries

The data collected by the Scientific Institutes were used to estimate average salaries for subject groups 1 and 2. Because we only had data on one year for mathematicians, the average salary for group 1 was estimated as a weighted average of the series constructed from the data for physicists and chemists. For chemists we had the results of four surveys (1962, 1965, 1968 and 1971). The measure used for our analysis was median earnings for these four years; other years were estimated by linear interpolation, and those prior to 1962 by using the salary index of non-manual workers. For physicists we used the same method of calculation in the years 1968 and 1971. Unfortunately, the data from the 1960 and 1964 surveys were given in a different form, and we had to estimate average salaries for these two years by looking at the evolution of physicists salaries for members younger than 50. As before, data for other years were calculated by linear interpolation, and those prior to 1960 by means of the salary index of non-manual workers. The salaries for group 1 were finally calculated as a weighted average of these two series.

Average salaries for group 2 were calculated on the basis of the information given in the surveys of the Institute of Biology. Only two of them (1968 and 1971) gave information on the salaries of all members' categories; the 1961 and 1965 surveys only provide information on Fellows and Members. Given that we wanted a measure which includes all members, the average median earnings for 1961 and 1965 were estimated by adjusting the figures in accordance to the relative differences between Fellows and Members, and Licenciates shown in 1968 and 1971 surveys. The remaining years were calculated as in the previous case.

The survey of the Institute of Biology also provides information on median earnings of Female Fellows and Members. This permitted us to calculate an estimate of the relative differences between male and female earnings. For the three surveys on which this information is given (1961, 1965 and 1971) these differences were fairly constant at about 24 per cent. In working out the male and female series we therefore assumed that these differences had remained constant over the whole period. Finally, we also assumed that they were equally applicable to estimate the sex earnings differentials in the first group.

The salaries for groups 3, 4 and 5 were obtained as follows. For years 1970 and 1971 they were obtained as a weighted average of three categories: the occupational division 'managers', employees in local authorities (Administrative, Professional and Technical grades), and employees in the central government (executive, technical, and scientific grades). The data for these categories were taken from the *New Earnings Survey*, and were available for both male and female employees. To obtain the figures for the years prior to 1970, we used again the salary index for non-manual workers.

5A.3 Alternative earnings profile slope

The use of $AAW2$ and ASW to calculate K involves an approximation since these two variables come from different sources. For women, in particular, $AAW2$ is smaller than ASW, resulting in a negative value for K. This problem can be illustrated by means of Figure 5A.1. Starting salaries (W_b^0) are obtained from a sample of people whose earnings profile (1) lies above the earnings profile (2) from where average salaries ($\overline{W}_b$) are obtained. In the case of women, the second profile is so much lower than the first that the average salary figure obtained was less than the starting one. In the case of men, although the second profile was again lower than the first, the difference is not large enough to make the starting wage larger than the average wage. The figure below would represent the situation for women.

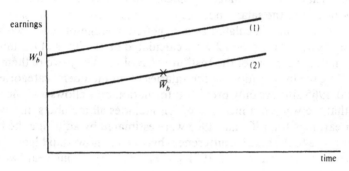

Figure 5A.1.

To solve this problem the following procedure was used. For a given year, we have information on the relationship between starting and average salaries obtained out of a single profile (DES, 1971b). What we did was to use the information for this year to adjust our data for the whole period under study. Let W_b^0 and $\overline{W}_b$ be the starting and average salaries obtained respectively from the profiles (1) and (2); we have information on these two variables for the whole period. Let $(W_b^0)'$ and $(\overline{W}_b)'$ be the starting and average salaries obtained from a third sample for the year 1966. Our first question is: what would the average wage of profile (1) be in 1966 if the relationship between starting and average wages was the same as the one given by the profile obtained from the third sample? Let us call this estimated average wage $\overline{W}^e$. Then it follows that

$$\frac{(W_b^0)'}{(\overline{W}_b)'} = \frac{W_{b(66)}^0}{\overline{W}_{(66)}^e}; \text{ or } \overline{W}_{(66)}^e = \frac{W_{b(66)}^0(\overline{W}_b)'}{(W_b^0)'}$$

The second question is: by which factor (c) do we have to multiply the actual average wage $\overline{W}_b$ to obtain the estimated average wage $\overline{W}^e$? This factor is given by

$$c = \frac{\overline{W}_{(66)}^e}{\overline{W}_{b(66)}}$$

Then, by assuming that the relationship between the estimated and the actual average wage is constant for the whole period, we obtain an adjusted alternative average wage by scaling up the series $\overline{W}_b$ by the factor c. If we call the adjusted variable $AAW2^*$, we have

$$AAW2^* = AAW2.c$$

Consequently, the slope variable used in the regressions will be defined as follows

$$K_t = \frac{TS_t}{AS_t} = \frac{(TBAW_{t-1} - TSW_{t-1})/TSW_{t-1}}{(AAW2^*_{t-1} - ASW_{t-1})/ASW_{t-1}}$$

In the calculation of c the information on the single earnings profile was taken from DES (1971b). $(\overline{W}_b)'$ and $(W^e_b)'$ refer to average and starting salaries (median earnings of those aged less than 25 years old) of people with qualification levels A and B (higher university degrees, first degrees and all other qualifications of the standard of a first degree). School teachers were excluded in calculating these salaries.

Tables 5A.1 and 5A.2 present the means and standard deviations of the variables used in the regression analysis for graduates and non-graduates.

TABLE 5A.1   *Means and standard deviations of the variables used in the regression analysis (graduate entrants)*

Variable	Mean	Standard deviation
Relative supply (RS)		
Male	0.1924	0.1041
Female	0.4024	0.1837
Relative average wage 1 (RAW1)		
Male	1.1698	0.0446
Female	2.1837	0.1483
Relative average wage 2 (RAW2)		
Male	0.8793	0.1020
Female	1.5375	0.5206
Relative starting wage (RSW)		
Male	0.9630	0.0500
Female	1.0183	0.0830
Teaching slope (TS)		
Male	1.0833	0.0390
Female	0.9038	0.0646
Alternative slope (AS)		
Male	1.2102	0.0795
Female	0.3849	0.0929
Relative slope differential (K)		
Male	0.8991	0.0695
Female	2.5169	0.7588
Rate of graduate unemployment (U)		
Male	4.4820	2.3216
Female	3.2353	1.8348

TABLE 5A.2   *Means and standard deviations of the variables used in the regression analysis (non-graduate entrants)*

Variables	Mean	Standard deviation
School leavers entering Colleges of Education (RESCE1)		
Male	0.1067	0.0113
Female	0.3112	0.0363
School leavers with 2 or more A levels entering Colleges of Education (RSCE2)		
Male	0.0714	0.0037
Female	0.2790	0.0154
Students completing initial training entering the profession (PE)		
Male	0.8728	0.0669
Female	0.9891	0.0670
School leavers entering the profession (RS)		
Male	0.0859	0.0055
Female	0.2579	0.0211
Relative average wage (RAW)		
Male	0.9608	0.0513
Female	1.6980	0.1268
Relative starting wage (RSW)		
Male	0.8047	0.0445
Female	0.8609	0.0441
Relative slope differential (K)		
Male	0.8206	0.1090
Female	1.8049	0.3699
General rate of unemployment (U)		
Male	3.0818	1.1017
Female	1.1364	0.2618

Appendix 5B
Details of the regressions for new entrants

This appendix contains details of the econometric exercise reported in Chapter 5 and presents some of the estimated equations. The full set of regressions is shown in an expanded version of this appendix, available upon request from the Centre for Labour Economics at the London School of Economics. In section 5B.1 we deal with graduate new entrants and in Section 5B.2 with the analysis for non-graduate new entrants.

5B.1 Graduate new entrants

The three variants (5.1) to (5.3) were estimated by Ordinary Least Squares and also by Weighted Least Squares methods to take into account the possibility of heteroscedastic errors arising from the cross-section components of our data. In Table 5B.1 we show, for male and female new entrants, the WLS estimates. For each equation the table shows the following statistics: number of observations (n), adjusted coefficient of determination ($\bar{R}^2$), and an F-statistic which tests for the validity of the restrictions imposed by the lag structures discussed in the text. The statistic measures the significance of the incremental value of the residual sum of squares resulting from the restriction, as compared with the residual sum of squares of the unrestricted equation. If F is significant, then the data rejects the restriction and the lag structure cannot be accepted. As can be seen in the table, the polinomial restrictions imposed are accepted in all cases.

We also tested for the validity of the restriction imposed on the slope coefficients in equation (5.3). The test showed that the incremental residual sum of squares due to the restriction was not significant, and therefore we selected equation (5.3) as the adequate specification. The calculated statistic for males was $F(1, 37) = 0.32$ and that for females was $F(1, 38) = 0.16$, while the critical value at the 5 per cent level was 4.08.

5B.2 Non-graduate new entrants regressions

We can analyse the flow of non-graduate new entrants according to the following framework. Let us denote the number of students with a given level of qualification leaving school in year t by SL_t, and the number of those

TABLE 5B.1 Weighted least squares estimates of the entry equation for male and female graduates. Dependent variable $\log(RS_{it})$

Independent variable	Males			Females		
	(5.1)	(5.2)	(5.3)	(5.1)	(5.2)	(5.3)
Intercept	-2.0546 (11.52)	-2.7212 (11.25)	-1.7701 (12.65)	-1.4168 (14.21)	-2.8452 (5.71)	-1.8726 (7.28)
D1	–	–	–	0.6708 (4.78)	0.5903 (6.17)	0.6786 (6.14)
D2	–	-0.4638 (5.30)	-0.4491 (4.94)	–	–	–
D4	0.6141 (5.57)	0.6010 (6.64)	0.6050 (6.69)	0.8439 (13.24)	0.9082 (14.54)	0.8593 (13.80)
D5	-0.5185 (4.59)	0.5366 (5.40)	-0.5385 (5.29)	–	–	–
RAW1L	2.4417 (4.53)	–	–	0.3408 (2.35)	–	–
RAW1L*D	-2.4772 (5.35)	–	–	–	–	–
RAW2L	–	3.8579 (3.57)	–	–	1.8005 (3.11)	–
RSWL	–	–	3.4505 (3.63)	–	–	2.8296 (3.39)
KL	–	–	1.6194 (2.43)	–	–	0.4295 (1.91)
UL	0.3960 (3.08)	0.3665 (3.18)	0.3322 (2.82)	-0.0344** (0.58)	0.1764 (2.14)	0.1926 (2.23)
n	45	45	45	45	45	45
R^2	0.7829	0.7957	0.7921	0.7103	0.7349	0.7541
F	$(3, 36) = 2.97$	$(3, 37) = 1.24$	$(3, 35) = 1.47$	$(1,39) = 0.01$	$(1,39) = 0.93$	$(2, 37) = 0.34$

Notes:
1. Figures in parentheses are absolute values of the t-statistics. Coefficients with one asterisk are *not* significant at the 5 per cent level, and with two at the 10 per cent level (one-tail test).
2. All independent variables (except the dummies for the intercept) are in logarithmic form.
3. The letter L after a variable denotes the lag structure specified in the text, and the F-statistic tests the validity of the restrictions imposed by that structure. The coefficient indicates the long-run elasticity of the corresponding variable.

entering Colleges of Education in year t by CE_t. Then, according to our occupational choice model, we hypothesise that the proportion of school leavers entering Colleges of Education will be a positive function of relative wages (W_t) and the rate of unemployment (U_t).[1]

$$\log \left[\frac{CE_t}{SL_{t-1}} \right] = \log a + b \log(W_t) + c \log(U_t). \tag{1}$$

Further we assume that only a fraction of those who enter Colleges of Education will finish their studies. If we denote the rate of drop-outs by δ, and the number of students completing courses of initial training in Colleges of Education in year t by CCE_t, we have that

$$CCE_t = (1 - \delta)CE_{t-3}^- \tag{2}$$

We also hypothesise that the proportion of those graduating who actually enter the teaching profession is a function of relative wages and job opportunities. If we call the number of non-graduate new entrants in year t, NGE; we have

$$\log \left[\frac{NGE_t}{CCE_{t-1}} \right] = \log d + e \log (W_t) + f \log (U_t) \tag{3}$$

or

$$\log (NGE_t) = \log d + \log (CCE_{t-1}) + e \log (W_t) + f \log (U_t) \tag{4}$$

Substituting (1) and (2) into (4), and assuming δ to be constant, we have

$$\log \left[\frac{NGE_t}{SL_{t-5}} \right] = m + e \log (W_t) + b \log (W_{t-4}) + f \log (U_t) + c \log (U_{t-4})$$

where $m = \log \left[da(1 - \delta) \right]$. $\tag{5}$

Although we will estimate the equation at each point of decision, expression (5) is the reduced supply equation in which we are interested. It states that the proportion of school leavers entering teaching is a function of relative wages and job opportunities, and that these variables exert their influence both at the point of entry into Colleges of Education and at the point of entry into the profession.

In the derivation of (5) we have assumed that at both points of entry, supply was affected by the current value of the independent variables, but this is not strictly necessary. If these variables enter with lags in (1) and (3), the final equation will also incorporate these partial lag structures.

Table 5B.2 presents the estimated equation (1) for male school leavers. The first two equations consider all entrants to Colleges of Education as a proportion of all 'qualified' school leavers. We denote this dependent variable by $RSCE1$. The last two equations consider only those entrants with

TABLE 5B.2   *Regression results for male school leavers entering colleges of education, 1963–73*

Independent variables	Dependent variables			
	log (*RSCE1*)	log (*RSCE1*)	log (*RSCE2*)	log (*RSCE2*)
Intercept	−2.5046	−1.7294	−2.8078	−2.4551
	(20.26)	(4.91)	(66.07)	(17.67)
$[(\frac{1}{3})RAW_{t-1} + (\frac{1}{3})RAW_{t-2}]$	1.8966*	–	1.0032	–
	(1.64)		(2.52)	
$[(\frac{1}{3})RSW_{t-1} + (\frac{1}{3})RSW_{t-2}]$	–	2.9954*	–	1.3560
		(1.82)		(2.09)
$[(\frac{1}{3})K_{t-1} + (\frac{1}{3})K_{t-2}]$	–	0.8562**	–	0.5465*
		(1.17)		(1.89)
U_t	0.2952	0.3036*	0.1836	0.2040
	(2.17)	(1.77)	(3.93)	(3.02)
n	11	11	11	11
$\bar{R}^2$	0.2160	0.2484	0.5941	0.4871
F	(2, 8) = 2.38**	(3, 7) = 2.10**	(2, 8) = 8.32	(3, 7) = 4.16*
DW	0.82^{++}	1.31^+	2.04	2.27

Notes:
1. All independent variables are in logarithmic form.
2. Figures in parentheses are absolute values of the *t*-statistic. Coefficients with one asterisk are *not* significant at the 5 per cent level, and with two at the 10 per cent level (one-tail test).
3. *DW* indicates the Durbin–Watson statistic. One cross indicates inconclusive results at the 5 per cent level for the test of first-order autocorrelated errors. Two crosses indicate evidence of autocorrelation.

2 or more 'A' levels as a proportion of the number of school leavers with that qualification level; we call this proportion *RSCE2*.

The best lag structure for both wages and profile slopes turned out to be an arithmetic average including two lagged values of the variable; for unemployment, current values were the most significant and no lags were included. Although all the signs appear as expected, the results for the first two equations are very weak; as measured by the *F*-statistic, neither of them is significant at the 5 per cent level. In the first equation we measured earnings only by relative average wages, and the estimated coefficient is only significant at the 10 per cent level; unemployment on the other hand appears well-determined. When the earnings profile is measured by starting point and slope, the performance of the equation remains weak and none of the coefficients is significant at the 5 per cent level. These results change substantially when instead of considering the whole flow of entrants we consider only those with 2 or more 'A' levels (last two equations). The equation with relative average wages is significant at the 5 per cent level, and that with relative starting wages and slope at the 10 per cent level. Excepting the slope variable, which is significant only at the 10 per cent level, all other coefficients are well determined and take the expected sign. Given the small number of observations on which they are based, we should not place much weight on these results. However, they suggest on the whole that the effect of wages and unemployment is very weak for the overall flow of entrants to Colleges of Education, but both have some significance in influencing entrants with 2 or more 'A' levels.

For female school leavers (Table 5B.3) unemployment appeared very insignificant in all specifications and was excluded from the regressions. Furthermore, only current values of wages were considered, since none of the lag structures tried was well determined. The pattern found for male school leavers repeats itself in this case; the overall flow is not responsive to earnings, with all coefficients very insignificant, while the flow of students with 2 or more 'A' levels appears to be sensitive to earnings, although with lower elasticities than in the case of male school leavers.

The estimation of the equation for entry to teaching after completing a College of Education course (equation 3) gave extremely poor results for female teachers; neither unemployment nor wages were significant at all in any of the several specifications tried. This suggests that female students completing courses of initial training enter the profession quite irrespective of wages and unemployment. In the case of men, however, the results indicate that although unemployment was not a relevant variable, earnings exerted some influence in the decision to enter the profession. After some experimentation, the lag structure selected was a weighted average of current and one-period lagged wages, with the higher weight $\frac{2}{3}$, placed on the

TABLE 5B.3 *Regression results of female school leavers entering colleges of education, 1963–73*

Independent variables	Dependent variables			
	log ($RSCE1$)	log ($RSCE1$)	log ($RSCE2$)	log ($RSCE2$)
Intercept	−1.1105	−1.2836	−1.5334	−1.3322
RAW_t	−0.1199**		0.4848	
	(0.23)		(2.63)	
RSW_t		−0.1336**		0.5597
		(0.15)		(2.24)
K_t		0.1571**		0.2430
		(0.72)		(3.89)
n	11	11	11	11
$\bar{R}^2$	−0.1046	−0.1332	0.3724	0.5720
F	(1, 9) = 0.05**	(2, 8) = 0.41**	(1, 9) = 6.93	(2, 8) = 7.68
DW	0.38^{++}	0.56^{++}	0.78^{++}	1.06^{+}

Notes: As for Table 5B.2.

current value. The two estimated equations, where all variables are in logarithmic form, are given below.[2]

$$PE_t = -0.0997 + 0.8954 \left[(\tfrac{2}{3})RAW_t + (\tfrac{1}{3})RAW_{t-1} \right]$$
$$\quad\quad\;\; (3.57) \quad\quad (2.07)$$

$$\underline{n} = 10$$
$$\overline{R}^2 = 0.2680$$
$$F(1, 8) = 4.30$$
$$DW = 1.23$$

$$PE_t = 0.3795 + 1.8365 \left[(\tfrac{2}{3})RSW_t + (\tfrac{1}{3})RSW_{t-1} \right] + 0.5525 \left[(\tfrac{2}{3})K_t + (\tfrac{1}{3})K_{t-1} \right]$$
$$\quad\;\; (2.86) \quad\;\; (3.71) \quad\quad\quad\quad\quad\quad\quad\quad\quad (3.04)$$

$$\underline{n} = 10$$
$$\overline{R}^2 = 0.6020$$
$$F(2, 7) = 7.81$$
$$DW = 2.01$$

The lag structure of the final supply equation was specified according to the estimated effects on the two points of entry. However, since the performance of the female structural equations was extremely poor at both points of entry, the estimation of the final reduced equation was not attempted for females. For male teachers the lag structures were as follows:

$$RAWL = \{(0.9/2.8) \left[(\tfrac{2}{3})RAW_t + (\tfrac{1}{3})RAW_{t-1} \right] + (1.9/2.8) \left[(\tfrac{1}{2})RAW_{t-5} \right.$$
$$\left. + (\tfrac{1}{2})RAW_{t-6} \right] \}$$

$$RSWL = \{(1.8/4.8) \left[(\tfrac{2}{3})RSW_t + (\tfrac{1}{3})RSW_{t-1} \right] + (3.0/4.8) \left[(\tfrac{1}{2})RSW_{t-5} \right.$$
$$\left. + (\tfrac{1}{2}) RSW_{t-6} \right] \}$$

$$KL = \{(0.5/1.4) \left[(\tfrac{2}{3})K_t + (\tfrac{1}{3})K_{t-1} \right] + (0.9/1.4) \left[(\tfrac{1}{2})K_{t-5} + (\tfrac{1}{2})K_{t-6} \right] \}$$

where all variables are in logarithmic form. As far as unemployment is concerned, the consideration of a four-period lag for men proved to be insignificant. So this variable was excluded from the final equation. Table 5B.4 shows the estimated final supply equations for male non-graduate entrants. The specification with starting point and slope of the earnings profile does much better than that with only average wages, showing a high and well-determined supply elasticity with respect to these two variables.[3]

TABLE 5B.4 *Regression results for the entry equation of male non-graduate teachers. Dependent variable $Log(RS_t)$*

Independent variable	1	2
Intercept	−2.4365	−1.3414
	(124.18)	(6.18)
$RAWL$	1.6246	
	(1.99)	—
$RSWL$		4.1776
	—	(5.03)
KL		1.2297
	—	(5.11)
n	10	10
$\overline{R}^2$	0.2482	0.7421
F	$(1, 8) = 3.97^*$	$(2, 7) = 13.95$
DW	0.91^{++}	2.26

Notes: As for Table 5B.2.

Appendix 6A
The data for the leavers regressions

Data for the variables L_{it} and S_{it} were obtained from *Statistics of Education* (DES, annual-a). Except for the age specific alternative wage, the sources for the data on salaries are the same as those specified in Appendix 5A.

The age specific measure of alternative average salaries was constructed on the basis of information given for the year 1966–67 in a survey of earnings of qualified manpower carried out by the Department of Education and Science, (DES, 1971b). The procedure followed can be summarised as follows. The survey gives age-specific information on salaries for a group of occupations (including teaching) and for three levels of qualifications (A, B, and C).[1] The problem with the data as given in this survey was that it included teachers in the sample. As these form a substantial proportion of the total (particularly for women and for non-graduates), the earnings profile for non-teachers had to be estimated. Given that the data for occupations was not disaggregated by qualification levels, we assumed that the total number of teachers in each age bracket was divided between levels A and B (together) and C in the same proportion as the total number of teachers in each age bracket of our one per cent sample was divided between graduate and non-graduate teachers. With this assumption we estimated from the survey data two age profiles for non-teachers – one for level A/B, and another for level C – for both men and women. Further we assumed that the shape of these profiles was constant over time and, on the basis of movements in average salaries for non-manual workers (*AAWI*), we calculated profiles for the whole period under study.

The data on unemployment was obtained from the Department of Employment Gazette, and it corresponds to the general rate of unemployment for Great Britain.

Table 6A.1 gives the means and standard deviations of all the variables used in the regressions.

TABLE 6A.1 *Means and standard variations of the variables used in the regression analysis (leavers equations)*

Variable	Mean	Standard deviation
Rate of leavers (RL)		
Male trained graduates	0.0343	0.0295
Male untrained graduates	0.0862	0.0774
Male non-graduates	0.0312	0.0244
Female trained graduates	0.0969	0.0683
Female untrained graduates	0.1496	0.1014
Female non-graduates	0.0891	0.0624
Relative average wage 1 (RAW1)		
Male graduates	1.1976	0.1203
Male non-graduates	0.9872	0.0580
Female graduates	2.2593	0.2363
Female non-graduates	1.9619	0.5632
Relative average wage 2 (RAW2)		
Male graduates	1.1586	0.0540
Male non-graduates	0.9662	0.0484
Female graduates	2.1487	0.1754
Female non-graduates	1.7173	0.1103
Relative starting wage (RSW)		
Male graduates	0.9727	0.0530
Male non-graduates	0.7978	0.0385
Female graduates	1.0483	0.0629
Female non-graduates	0.8596	0.0442
Teaching 'slope' (TS)		
Male graduates	1.0864	0.0418
Male non-graduates	1.0476	0.0839
Female graduates	0.8938	0.0843
Female non-graduates	0.8095	0.0786
Alternative 'slope' (AS)		
Male graduates	1.2564	0.0928
Male non-graduates	1.2564	0.0928
Female graduates	0.4414	0.0586
Female non-graduates	0.4414	0.0586
Relative 'slope' differential (K)		
Male graduates	0.8707	0.0861
Male non-graduates	0.8384	0.0922
Female graduates	2.0655	0.3731
Female non-graduates	1.8660	0.3114
General rate of unemployment (U)		
Male	3.0300	1.0950
Female	1.1400	0.2632

Appendix 6B

Details of the regressions for leavers

The method followed to arrive at our final estimates was the same as that used in Chapter 5. Table 6B.1 presents the weighted least squares estimates of equation (6.3) for all the categories of male and female teachers. An expanded version of this appendix with the full set of regressions is available on request from the Centre for Labour Economics, London School of Economics.

The F-test performed on the restriction imposed in equation (6.3) showed that in general the incremental residual sum of squares due to the restriction was not significant at the 5 per cent level. The calculated statistics for trained graduates were: male $F(1, 69) = 3.41$, and female $F(1, 68) = 0.20$, while the critical value is 4.0. For untrained graduates the statistics were: males $F(1, 69) = 0.50$, and females $F(1, 68) = 0.28$; both are insignificant at the 5 per cent level. Finally, for non-graduates the resulting values were $F(1, 69) = 3.69$ for males, and $F(1, 68) = 10.5$ for females. The female value is significant at the 5 per cent level.

TABLE 6B.1   *Weighted least squares estimates of equation (6.3) for male and female teachers. Dependent variable log (RL_{it})*

Independent variables	Male			Female		
	Trained	Untrained	Non-graduate	Trained	Untrained	Non-graduate
Intercept	−2.6138	−1.3985	−3.0747	−1.7417	−1.2935	−1.9719
	(39.35)	(27.21)	(28.25)	(26.22)	(11.76)	(41.98)
D2	−0.4258	−0.6761	−0.3472	0.3670	0.0385*	0.3426
	(6.64)	(13.99)	(3.76)	(7.95)	(0.94)	(12.96)
D3	−1.1223	−1.3141	−0.9308	−0.0417*	−0.4138	−0.1078
	(17.56)	(24.32)	(10.30)	(0.86)	(7.99)	(3.94)
D4	−1.5456	−1.5989	−1.3957	−0.7280	−0.8893	−0.7182
	(21.72)	(26.11)	(15.45)	(15.98)	(20.94)	(21.88)
D5	−1.6953	−1.6745	−1.6525	−1.1599	−1.1842	−1.1896
	(19.98)	(27.97)	(18.88)	(25.88)	(25.30)	(40.00)
D6	−1.8793	−1.9196	−1.7641	−1.4976	−1.6179	−1.5152
	(22.98)	(24.41)	(20.19)	(23.84)	(19.48)	(37.76)
D7	−2.0354	−2.0519	−1.7785	−1.5200	−1.6012	−1.5637
	(25.61)	(28.70)	(18.60)	(25.11)	(14.68)	(43.83)
D8	−1.5669	−2.0308	−1.3682	−0.9079	−1.8472	−1.2305
	(18.71)	(37.11)	(14.55)	(5.33)	(10.87)	(26.06)
RSW_t	−2.6378	−1.3971	−1.5834	−0.7567	−0.2005*	−0.0961*
	(7.87)	(4.39)	(6.61)	(3.65)	(0.81)	(0.54)
K_t	−1.1946	−0.2145*	−0.9392	−0.1451	0.1359*	0.0892*
	(6.56)	(1.24)	(8.79)	(2.07)	(1.05)	(1.12)
U_t	−	−	−	−0.1991	−0.0816*	−0.1001
				(3.25)	(0.84)	(2.03)
n	80	80	80	80	80	80
$\overline{R}^2$	0.9484	0.9570	0.9553	0.9019	0.8621	0.9872

Notes:
1. Figures in parentheses are absolute values of the t-statistic. Coefficients with one asterisk are not significant at the 5 per cent level (one-tail test).
2. All independent variables (except the dummies for the intercept) are in logarithm form.

Appendix 7A
The data for the mobility regressions

The data for the variable M_{ij} is taken from *Statistics of Education*, 1972, Volume 4 (DES, annual –a, Table 18). The stocks (T) were obtained from the 1 per cent sample, and their values are given in columns 1 and 2 of Table 7A.1. The dependent variable of the regressions was then obtained by dividing the number of movers by the corresponding sample stocks, multiplied by 100 (the sampling fraction).

The rate of expansion in the school population (RE) was taken from statistics on pupils found in *Statistics of Education*, Volume 1 for years 1970, 1971 and 1972 (DES, annual – a). The index was calculated by weighting each pupil in accordance with figures on desired pupil/teacher ratios contained in the Ninth Report of the National Advisory Council on the Training and Supply of Teachers (NACTST, 1965). It therefore gives an idea of the expansion of the region in terms of teacher requirements. The actual relative weights used were: for primary, 0.196; for secondary (non-sixth form pupils), 0.317; and for sixth form pupils, 0.487. After calculating the number of weighted pupils in each region for the years 1970, 1971 and

TABLE 7A.1 *Independent variables used in the inter-regional regressions*

	T (Male)	T (Female)	RE	A	P (Male)	P (Female)	P (Total)	$HP(\pounds s)$	W
	(1)	(2)	(3)	(4)	(5)	(6)	(7)	(8)	(9)
North	103	156	0.0216	0.320	0.204	0.167	0.181	6,293	0.996
Yorkshire and Humberside	172	204	0.0224	0.346	0.180	0.147	0.163	6,293	1.019
North West	185	295	0.0226	0.356	0.177	0.153	0.162	6,293	1.007
East Midlands	100	143	0.0292	0.395	0.220	0.154	0.181	6,948	1.006
West Midlands	159	196	0.0262	0.352	0.168	0.112	0.140	6,948	1.018
East Anglia	46	63	0.0394	0.302	0.022	0.032	0.028	10,332	1.010
Greater London	159	312	0.0170	0.435	0.245	0.178	0.201	11,992	1.085
South East	266	383	0.0370	0.349	0.176	0.156	0.164	12,014	1.000
South West	115	151	0.0325	0.286	0.103	0.125	0.116	8,674	0.983
Wales	93	126	0.0225	0.275	0.161	0.111	0.127	6,802	0.982

1972, the index was calculated in the following manner.

$$RE = \frac{1}{2}\left(\frac{P_{t-1} - P_{t-2}}{P_{t-2}} + \frac{P_t - P_{t-1}}{P_{t-1}}\right)$$

where P is the number of weighted pupils, and the subscript t refers to the year 1972. The values of this index are given in column 3 of Table 7A.1. The regional distances (D) were calculated by first roughly estimating a centre of gravity (with respect to population) for each region, and then by measuring the respective distances between these centres in miles. Given that the Greater London region is completely contained within the South East region, we assumed that the distance between these two regions and any other was the same; we also assumed that the distance between London and the South East was 35 miles. These estimates are shown in Table 7A.2.

The proportion of teachers younger than thirty (A) and the proportion of promoted teachers (P) were taken from the 1 per cent sample, and are given in columns 4 to 7 of Table 7A.1.

The housing costs variable was obtained from regional statistics of prices of existing houses in 1972 published by the Nationwide Building Society. Given the more simplified regional structure used in those statistics, we made the following adjustments: the value for North, Yorkshire and Humberside, and North West was obtained by averaging the two regions 'North Western' and 'North Eastern' used in the statistics of the Society; the values for East Midlands and West Midlands correspond to the region 'Midlands'; East Anglia corresponds to 'Eastern'; Greater London to 'London and South East'; South East to 'Southern'; South West to 'Western'; and Wales to 'Wales'. Column 8 of Table 7A.1 gives these values.

The standardised wage differentials are obtained from earnings functions for the year 1971, which are reported in Chapter 9. The value of this variable is shown in column 9 of Table 7A.1.

Finally, Table 7A.3 shows the means and standard deviations of the variables used in the regression analysis.

TABLE 7A.2 *Approximate distances between regions (miles)*

	1	2	3	4	5	6	7	8	9	10
North	–									
Yorkshire and Humberside	90	–								
North West	105	45	–							
East Midlands	140	50	70	–						
West Midlands	170	80	75	40	–					
East Anglia	190	120	155	90	115	–				
Greater London	240	155	175	110	105	75	–			
South East	240	155	175	110	105	75	35	–		
South West	275	190	180	145	70	180	120	85	–	
Wales	235	155	135	125	85	190	150	115	60	–

TABLE 7A.3   *Means and standard deviations of the variables used in the regression analysis*

Variable	Mean	Standard deviation
A. *Inter-school mobility variables*		
(i) *Rates of school mobility in primary*		
Male	0.1278	0.0305
Female	0.1136	0.0230
Total	0.1172	0.0243
(ii) *Rates of school mobility in secondary*		
Male	0.0967	0.0193
Female	0.1210	0.0245
Total	0.1071	0.0204
(iii) *Standard deviation of promotion prospects*		
Primary	0.0068	0.0035
Secondary	0.0424	0.0037
B. *Inter-regional mobility variables*		
(i) *Regional rate of mobility* (M_{ij}/T_i)		
Male	0.0027	0.0025
Female	0.0035	0.0032
Total	0.0032	0.0029
(ii) *Stock of teachers* (T)		
Male	139.80	58.88
Female	202.80	93.79
Total	342.60	150.30
(iii) *Rate of pupil expansion* (RE)	0.0270	0.0070
(iv) *Distance between regions* (D)	128.56	57.26
(v) *Age structure* (A)	0.3416	0.0467
(vi) *Promotion rates* (P)		
Male	0.1656	0.0601
Female	0.1340	0.0399
Total	0.1462	0.0467
(vii) *Housing prices* (HP)	8,258.90	2,240.95
(viii) *Standardised salary* (W)	1.0106	0.0277

Appendix 10A
Optimal salary structures

by A. ZABALZA AND R. LAYARD

The purpose of this appendix is to establish the characteristics of the salary structure that will maximise the long-run stock of teachers subject to a budget constraint. In the first section we solve this problem and arrive at a system of simultaneous equations which define the optimal salary structure. In the second section we show how productivity weights can be incorporated into the exercise, and in the third we indicate how these results can be generalised to more than one category of teacher. Finally, in the fourth section, we discuss the application of the results obtained to the teachers' market.

10A.1 The problem

We consider a two-period world. This simplifies the problem and brings out more clearly the essential characteristics of the solution. Teachers enter at the beginning of the first period. At the end of it, some of them leave the profession and others remain for a second period. Finally, those who have remained, retire at the end of the second period. Therefore, at any moment in time the stock of teachers in the profession (S) is

$$S = E + (E - L) \tag{10A.1}$$

where E and L are the flows of entrants and leavers respectively.

Teachers in their first period are paid W_0, and those in their second period $W_0(1 + \alpha)$, where $\alpha(\alpha > 0)$ is the rate of growth of earnings. The earnings profile is therefore defined by its level (W_0) and its proportional slope (α). The salary bill (B) will then be written as follows

$$B = EW_0 + (E - L)W_0(1 + \alpha) \tag{10A.2}$$

We assume that the flow of entrants at the beginning of the first period, and the proportion of entrants who leave at the end of this first period, are both responsive to the level and to the slope of the earnings profile.

$$E = e(W_0, \alpha) \qquad e_1 > 0 \text{ and } e_2 > 0 \tag{10A.3}$$

$$L/E = l(W_0, \alpha) \qquad l_1 < 0 \text{ and } l_2 < 0 \tag{10A.4}$$

The effects on these two flows of changes in the earnings profile can be measured by elasticities.

$$e_1 = \eta_1^e(E/W_0) \qquad e_2 = \eta_2^e(E/\alpha)$$
$$l_1 = \eta_1^l(L/EW_0) \qquad l_2 = \eta_2^l(L/E\alpha) \right\} \qquad (10A.5)$$

where η_1^e and η_2^e are the elasticities of the flow of new entrants with respect to the level and slope of the profile, and η_1^l and η_2^l are the equivalent elasticities for the proportion of leavers.

The problem consists in maximising (10A.1) with respect to W_0 and α, subject to the budget constraint (10A.2) and the functions (10A.3) and (10A.4). The Lagrangian is

$$\mathscr{L} = 2E - L - \lambda \left[EW_0 + (E - L) W_0(1 + \alpha) - B \right]$$

where λ is the Lagrangian multiplier. The first order conditions are

$$\frac{\partial \mathscr{L}}{\partial W_0} = 2e_1 - e_1 (L/E) - El_1 - \lambda \left[E(2 + \alpha) + W_0(2 + \alpha)e_1 - (1 + \alpha)L \right.$$
$$- W_0(1 + \alpha)(L/E)e_1 - W_0(1 + \alpha)El_1 \left. \right] = 0 \qquad (10A.6)$$

$$\frac{\partial \mathscr{L}}{\partial \alpha} = 2e_2 - e_2(L/E) - El_2 - \lambda \left[W_0(2 + \alpha)e_2 + W_0(E - L) - W_0(1 + \alpha) \right.$$
$$- W_0(1 + \alpha)(L/E)e_2 - W_0(1 + \alpha)El_2 \left. \right] = 0 \qquad (10A.7)$$

$$\frac{\partial \mathscr{L}}{\partial \lambda} = -EW_0 - (E - L) W_0(1 + \alpha) + B = 0 \qquad (10A.8)$$

After eliminating λ and substituting equations (10A.5) into (10A.6) and (10A.7) the expression for α is

$$\alpha = m_0 \left\{ \frac{[2E\eta_2^e - L(\eta_2^e + \eta_2^l)]}{[2E\eta_1^e - L(\eta_1^e + \eta_1^l)] - [2E\eta_2^e - L(\eta_2^e + \eta_2^l)] - m_1 c} \right\}$$
$$(10A.9)$$

where $m_0 = (2E - L)/(E - L)$, $m_1 = EL/(E - L)$ and $c = (\eta_1^e \eta_2^l - \eta_2^e \eta_1^l)$.

And from (10A.8) we have that

$$W_0 = B / \left[E(2 + \alpha) - L(1 + \alpha) \right] \qquad (10A.10)$$

Equations (10A.9) and (10A.10) together with the functions (10A.3) and (10A.4) form a simultaneous non-linear system of four equations in four unknowns (α, W_0, E and L). The system, therefore, completely defines the optimal profile and the optimal flows of entrants and leavers.

From (10A.9) we can conclude that if either the flow of entrants or the proportion of leavers (or both) are responsive to future earnings (i.e. if $\eta_2^e \neq 0$, or $\eta_2^l \neq 0$, or both), then the optimal profile will be upward sloping. Although no formal proof is provided, it will also be the case that the larger the slope elasticities are relative to the level elasticities, the steeper the optimal profile will be.

10A.2 Productivity increases over time

The previous exercise has considered all teachers as homogeneous despite their different levels of experience. It is plausible to assume that experienced teachers are more productive than those who have just entered the profession. We can incorporate this assumption by assuming that the productivity of workers in the second period relative to that of workers in the first period is equal to a factor π, where $\pi \geqq 1$.

The measure of output we would then want to maximise, subject to the same constraints as above, is

$$0 = E + (E - L)\pi$$

The expression for W_0 does not change. That for α will now be

$$\alpha = m_0$$

$$\left\{ \frac{[(1 + \pi)E\eta_2^e - \pi L(\eta_2^e + \eta_2^l)] - (\pi - 1)m_2 c}{[(1 + \pi)E\eta_1^e - \pi L(\eta_1^e + \eta_1^l)] - [(1 + \pi)E\eta_2^e - \pi L(\eta_2^e + \eta_2^l)] - m_1 c} \right\}$$

$$(10A.11)$$

where $m_2 = EL/(2E - L)$ and all other symbols have already been defined. In general, and provided that $\eta_1^e/\eta_2^e > \eta_1^l/\eta_2^l$, increases in π will make the slope of the optimal profiles steeper. If $\pi = 1$, then (10A.11) reduces to (10A.9).

10A.3 Aggregation over several categories of teachers

The above results can be generalised to situations in which there exist several categories of teacher with different supply elasticities. The problem now is to obtain a *common* earnings profile which will maximise the overall number of teachers subject to a budget constraint. Without loss of generality, let us assume that there exist two categories of teacher – male (m) and female (f) – so that

$$E = E^m + E^f$$
$$L = L^m + L^f$$

The maximand will now be

$$S = E^m + (E^m - L^m) + E^f + (E^f - L^f)$$

and the budget constraint

$$B = (E^m + E^f)W_0 + [(E^m - L^m) + (E^f - L^f)] W_0(1 + \alpha)$$

Assuming that the functions (10A.3) and (10A.4), and the respective elasticities, are defined for each of the above categories, the final expression for the level of the common profile would be the same as (10A.10) and that for the slope

$$\alpha = m_0 \left\{ \frac{(2EA_2 - LB_2)}{(2EA_1 - LB_1) - (2EA_2 - LB_2) - mC} \right\} \qquad (10A.12)$$

where

$$A_i = \frac{E^m}{E} \eta_i^{em} + \frac{E^f}{E} \eta_i^{ef} \qquad (i = 1, 2)$$

$$B_i = \frac{L^m}{L} (\eta_i^{em} + \eta_i^{lm}) + \frac{L^f}{L} (\eta_i^{ef} + \eta_i^{ef}) \qquad (i = 1, 2)$$

$$C = A_1 B_2 - A_2 B_1$$

and all other symbols have already been defined.

If we assume that experienced teachers are more productive than new entrants, the new slope expression will be

$$\alpha = m_0 \left\{ \frac{[(1 + \pi)EA_2 - \pi LB_2] - (\pi - 1) m_2 C}{[(1 + \pi)EA_1 - \pi LB_1] - [(1 + \pi)EA_2 - \pi LB_2] - mC} \right\} \qquad (10A.13)$$

where π has already been defined.

10A.4 The use of these formulae for the teachers' market

The results derived in the previous sections are based on a simple model of how the stock of teachers is determined, and therefore their application to actual data requires some discussion.

In the model used in this appendix we have collapsed the whole working horizon into two periods, with a wage W_0 in the first period and a wage $W_0(1 + \alpha)$ in the second. Given that our estimated elasticities have been based on a 'second period' wage equal to the average wage paid in the age bracket 35–39, the second period wage of the present model $[W_0(1 + \alpha)]$ will correspond to $\overline{W}$ of the empirical model. In other words, the α obtained by applying the estimated elasticities will not be the rate of growth of wages per 1 year, but the rate of growth per about 17 years (17 = 37–20). If instead of expressing the results in terms of α, we want to express them in terms of

$\overline{W}$ as a ratio of W_0, then since $\overline{W} = W_0(1 + \alpha)$ we will have

$$\overline{W}/W_0 = 1 + \alpha$$

A second issue, relating to the application of the above results to actual data, concerns the interpretation of the entrants and leavers flows. They enter the expressions for α in two ways, first as weights for the different elasticities, and second as elements of the multiplicative factor m_0. Concerning their role as weights, it is easy to see that they follow the same pattern as in the determination of the stock of teachers. Since in our model we have assumed that both periods have the same length, this is also reflected in the elasticity weights. In practice, however, the 'second period' is much longer than the first. Even considering things in average terms, we know that the average leaving age is much closer to the entry than to the retiring point, and therefore that in the above formulae the entry elasticities may be over-weighted relative to the leaving elasticities. Similarly, the particular form in which the entry and leaving flows enter the factor m_0 is a direct consequence of the two-period simplification used here. In a two-period world $(2E–L)/(E–L)$ is the ratio of the total stock of teachers over the stock of experienced teachers. The direct substitution of actual flows of entrants and leavers into that expression would therefore lead to an overestimate of this ratio.

One way of adjusting for these factors is to take these length differences explicitly into account. Suppose that the average age of entry is t_e, the average age of leaving is t_l and the average age of retirement is t_r. Then our two periods could be specified as follows[1]

1st period   2nd period

t_e t_l t_r

Call $t_l - t_e = a$ and $t_r - t_l = b$, then the steady state stock we will want to maximise is

$$S = aE + b(E - L)$$

subject to the budget constraint.

$$B = aEW_0 + b(E - L)W_0(1 + \alpha)$$

Under this new formulation the new expression for α would be

$$\alpha = m_0'$$

$$\left\{ \frac{[(a + b)E\eta_2^e - bL(\eta_2^e + \eta_2^l)]}{[(a + b)E\eta_1^e - bL(\eta_1^e + \eta_1^l)] - [(a + b)E\eta_2^e - bL(\eta_2^e + \eta_2^l)] - m_1' abc} \right\}$$

$$(10A.14)$$

where $m_0' = [(a + b)E - bL]/[(E - L)b]$, $m_1' = EL/[(E - L)b]$ and all other symbols have already been defined.

Expression (10A.14) corrects for the overweighting of the entry elasticities and shows that the factor m_0 is in effect the ratio of total over experienced teachers. Identical changes are found when this adjustment is applied to all the other exercises. In the numerical evaluations discussed in the text, we use the adjustments shown in (10A.14) and evaluate the factor m_0' with actual data on the stocks of total and experienced teachers.[2]

Notes

Notes to chapter 1

1 Assuming the existence of other sources of income, it could be the case that such a person may be willing to enter teaching at no pay whatsoever or even if he has to pay something. Many voluntary workers do just that. It does not affect the above argument, however.

2 The above argument has been couched in terms of flows of people entering the profession, but it applies equally to flows of people leaving the profession, as well as to the actual stock of people willing to teach.

3 We are, of course, ignoring the effects of inflation in such numerical examples.

4 The *present value* is the discounted value of a stream of expected earnings over a number of future years. The discounting rate varies between individuals but for accounting purposes is often taken as the current prevailing level of interest rates.

5 Doeringer and Piore (1971) and the growing literature on segmented labour markets constitute the only exception to the above statement. Their attention, however, has been the labour market as a whole rather than particular occupations. Also, their analysis places more emphasis on institutional factors, and less on economic factors, than ours.

6 See Bartholomew (1973) for an extensive analytical survey, and Turnbull (1974c) for an application of one such model to the teaching profession in England and Wales.

7 SED stands for 'schools of exceptional difficulty'.

Notes to chapter 2

1 Four-year courses leading to a degree are now increasingly common, but the above was essentially the situation during the period referred to by our analysis.

2 This is, numerically speaking, not strictly true because of discrepancies in the DES figures. See note to Table 2.2.

3 See, for example, Morris, Ryba and Drake (1973), and Thomas (1973a), concerning the UK, and Kershaw and McKean (1962) and Devine (1970), in relation to the USA.

4 It should be noted that in this case it is legitimate to speak of shortage, because although wages are flexible, there is still a factor in the market – the budget – which remains fixed and prevents demand and supply from adjusting to their equilibrium levels.

5 With suitable allowances for sparsely populated areas, and areas of high immigrant concentration.

6 The quota system was abandoned in 1975 since it was no longer required in the face of the emerging teacher surplus. A proposal made by one teachers' union

which certainly has the appeal of logical symmetry is that the quota should be replaced by an 'establishment' setting a minimum number of teachers that each LEA must employ (see House of Commons 1976, para. no. 787).

7 The above result is obtained applying average rates of increase over the whole period, while Figure 2.4 suggests that it may be more relevant to consider more recent rates of increase. A more sophisticated exercise, carried out in terms of net additions to the stock of teachers and incorporating the response of relative wages to the state of the market, showed that on past trends the system would reach its equilibrium point between 1977 and 1978. For details about this exercise, see Zabalza (1978b).

Notes to chapter 3

1 The four are: (i) Primary and Secondary Committee; (ii) Further Education Committee; (iii) Pelham Committee (Colleges of Education); (iv) Farm Institute Committee. They all negotiate salaries for teachers under their jurisdiction, but there are also several associated committees dealing with peripheral education employees (e.g. Soulbury Committee – education advisory staff).

2 The agreements, once accepted by the Secretary of State for Education and Science, then become statutory instruments under the Renumeration of Teachers Act 1965.

3 No published salary statistics are available between those dates.

4 Although the 1969 salary award was implemented from 1 April, any widening of differentials would not show up until later because of the delay in promoting teachers to fill the newly created posts.

5 From 1 May 1968 part-time qualified teachers are paid a fraction of their calculated full-time pay according to the hours they work.

6 Prior to the 1965 Report, Head Teachers were paid on the same system with an allowance for the post of Head.

7 'Service for salary' is not quite equivalent to teaching service; the difference lies in the award of increments for full-time training beyond the norm of 3 years. The most frequent example of this concerns trained graduates who are awarded one extra increment upon entering teaching, thus compensating for their fourth year spent in study on a teacher training course. They will consequently enter the basic scale at the same point as an untrained graduate who entered one year earlier. A second example concerns mature entrants to the profession who are awarded, at the discretion of the local education authority employing the teacher, between 1 and 3 increments for every three years spent in full-time employment beyond the age of 18.

8 Change from 1 unit by the 1969 Burnham Report.

9 Actually a range of scores is specified, allowing the local authority to allocate one score out of this range to each school. This range has subsequently been broadened and considerable variation has been reported in the allocation of a score to schools falling within the same range, both between authorities and within authorities.

10 Some head teachers deliberately hold 'points' in reserve at all times.

11 It is still possible for those on scale 1.

Notes to chapter 4

1 *In the literature on search, the specification of the uncertain environment is usually much more complex: each alternative involves a whole range of outcomes with an*

associated probability distribution. See, for instance, Mortensen (1970) and McCall (1970).

2 An alternative way in which the effect of employment opportunities could be modelled is discussed in Zabalza (1978c). The qualitative results reached are the same under both approaches.

3 The proof of this and the subsequent partial derivatives can be found in Zabalza (1976), Appendix 3A.

4 This curve is simply a section of the normal cumulative function.

5 *The results to be discussed here also apply for the more complicated model to be discussed in Section 4.2.*

6 The assumption of a normal distribution for the reservation wage makes the above result ambiguous since, as shown by Fisher (1969), the wage elasticity first increases and then decreases as we move along the distribution.

7 *Examples in which earnings prospects are only defined in terms of either average or starting salaries can be found in Altman (1969), Fisher (1969), Altman and Barro (1971) and Freeman (1975a) and (1975b).*

8 The proportional slope is equal to the absolute slope relative to the starting salary. That is, $\dfrac{1}{W_0}\left[\dfrac{W_t - W_0}{t}\right]$.

9 Given the complexity of expressions (4.7) and (4.8), these results have been obtained by numerical methods.

10 *A third circumstance could be people's taste for variety in jobs.*

11 For the derivation of equation (4.10) see Zabalza (1976), Chapter 3.

12 *These data correspond approximately to male graduate teachers, year 1971.*

13 *The expression used to calculate the discounted return of Figure 4.7 is*

$$R_a = W_{a0}\left[\frac{(1 + r)^{T-S+1} - 1}{r(1 + r)^{T-S}}\right] + \alpha W_{a0}\left[\frac{(1 + r)^{T-S+1}(1 + rS) - r(T + 1) - 1}{r^2(1 + r)^{T-S}}\right]$$

where S stands for years of service, and all the other symbols have the same meaning as previously. In the present exercise the proportional slope α will equal 0.0685 (i.e. $\alpha = 88/1283$).

14 *This will always be true for linear earnings profiles such as the ones considered here.*

15 *These effects are calculated for a rate of discount equal to 10 per cent. A higher rate of discount would leave unaffected the first effect (level effect), and would decrease the intercept (but not the final point) of the curve showing the effect of a change in the slope.*

16 We include in the concept of relative supply both the entry and leavers flows. We assume that the coefficients of the functions are positive (as in the entry equation), but the whole argument applies *pari-passu* with negative coefficients (as in the leaving equations).

17 Given that in the theoretical model we have assumed that occupational preferences are distributed according to some probability function, the logarithmic specification (4.11) can only be considered as an approximation to the functional form underlying our theoretical model. To check the accuracy of this approximation we also used in the empirical analysis a logit specification of the supply function and the results were practically identical to the ones obtained with equation (4.11).

18 From inspection of (4.8) it does not necessarily follow that the effects on supply of the two slopes should be of the same absolute magnitude. However, there are reasons to believe that this could be so. The effect of log (α) on log (c_{ss}) can be approximated by $-\alpha/[(m_a/n_a) + \alpha]$, and that of log (β) by $\beta/[(m_b/n_b) + \beta]$. But if r is small, $m_i/n_i \cong r$ for $(i = a, b)$ since $m_i = (T - t_i + 1)r^2 + rn_i$. Then the two effects reduce respectively to $-\alpha/(r + \alpha)$ and $\beta/(r + \beta)$, which are equal

in absolute value if, as is the case with our data, $\alpha \cong \beta$. In the empirical analysis, we will test for both possibilities: entering α and β unrestricted and restricting their effect to be equal in absolute value.

Notes to chapter 5

1 Evidently there is a third group formed by those trained and untrained graduates who did not enter the profession immediately after obtaining their degree or finishing the training course. As this group is small relative to the other two, we ignore it as far as the definition of the base is concerned.
2 For reasons discussed above, the denominator of this proportion is a weighted average of university graduates during two successive years, the weight (P) being the proportion of trained graduates over total graduates entering the profession. If we denote the absolute number of graduate new entrants as GE, and the absolute number of university gradates as UG, then the dependent variable can be expressed as follows

$$RS_{it} = \frac{GE_{it}}{P_{it}UG_{it-2} + (1 - P_{it})UG_{it-1}}$$

3 Institutes of Biology, Chemistry, Mathematics, and Physics.
4 See Appendix 5A for further detail on the sources and elaboration of these data.
5 See Appendix 5A (Section 5A.3) for the derivation of the slope of the alternative earnings profile.
6 Additionally to (5.3), we estimated an equation in which the coefficients of TS and AS were not constrained to be equal in absolute value, and we tested the validity of the restriction imposed in (5.3). Logit forms of all equations were also estimated. Another variant of the above specification was to define the unemployment variable as $(1 - U)$ rather than U; that is, as a proxy of the probability of employment. Since both modalities gave very similar results, only those from the above equations are reported here.
7 Since our main interest was to investigate differences in wage elasticities, we did not consider the possibility of dummies for the coefficient of the unemployment variable.
8 The approximation of the lag structure by a polynomial, as well as the subsequent restrictions, necessarily reduces the goodness of fit as compared with the unrestricted regression. The procedure was therefore accepted only after testing the validity of these restrictions. We deal with this question in Appendix 5B.
9 Details of the results of the various regressions that lead to the following conclusions are given in Appendix 5B. All these results are based on the double-log specification discussed in the previous chapter.
10 The only case in which this was not so was in the first specification of the female equation. Given the problems involved with the subject specific wage we need not place much weight on this particular result.
11 Originally the analysis was carried out by introducing dummy variables into the single equation. This method failed to detect any significant differences between subject groups but we felt that this was at least partly due to the constraint of a common intercept and unemployment elasticities.
12 The figures for school leavers used in this analysis do not include those students obtaining 'O' or 'A' levels in the further education sector.
13 The decline in 1973 and the even more substantial decline in the following years was the direct result of Government policy to reduce the number of places in Colleges of Education because of oversupply of teachers.

14 The exact specification of the model can be found in Appendix 5B.
15 The lag structures for men were $RAWL = 0.20 RAW_t + 0.10 RAW_{t-1} + 0.35$ $RAW_{t-5} + 0.35 RAW_{t-6}$; $RSWL = 0.25 RSW_t + 0.15 RSW_{t-1} + 0.30 RSW_{t-5} +$ $0.30 RSW_{t-6}$; and $KL = 0.25 K_t + 0.15 K_{t-1} + 0.30 K_{t-5} + 0.30 K_{t-6}$. For women $RAWL = RAW_{t-4}$; $RSWL = RSWL_{t-4}$ and $KL = KL_{t-4}$. Data on teacher wages were obtained from the CLE 1 per cent sample, and except for the subject specific wage, the alternative wages used were the same as for the graduate exercise.
16 The values of α for each category were: graduate males, 0.072; graduate females, 0.059; and non-graduate males, 0.062.
17 The factor log (U) was fixed at its mean value and equals -3.3129 for graduate males and -3.5077 for graduate females. The above rates of discount were also estimated using expression (4A.15) in Appendix 4A, with $\beta = 0.06$ for graduate males and $\beta = 0.02$ for graduate females. The results were very similar to those obtained with the approximation (4.14): 192 per cent for graduate males and 179 per cent for graduate females.
18 The rates of discount implied by the slope elasticity are largely consistent with results obtained by Rosen (1976) with data on earnings of male high school and college graduates. His figures were 7.25 and 8.75 respectively. Heckman (1976), on the other hand, obtained rates of discount for married males (also from earnings data) of the order of 18 to 20 per cent. None of these two studies report rates of discount for women. See also Friedman (1963) for related issues concerning the subjective rate of discount used by individuals.

Notes to chapter 6

1 The period 1 April to 31 March is used because the official DES central record of teachers uses this period.
2 Naturally other factors besides type of training will influence the leaving rate. In particular, certain types of teacher may be more committed to the profession than others.
3 For an explanation of data sources see Appendix 6A.
4 See Appendix 6A.
5 As with new entrants, a method of stepwise elimination was applied to equations including dummies for both intercept and wage variables. As before, we were unable to discover any significant difference of the wage effect between the several age brackets. The consideration of separate equations for age groups did not reveal any significant difference either. Also, as with new entrants, we estimated the logit version (see Chapter 4) of all the equations for this and all other categories of teachers. The results obtained were practically identical to the ones reported here. The results on the dummy variable for the different age groups closely reflected the relationship between age and leaving rates depicted by Figures 6.2 and 6.3, and will not therefore be discussed in this section.
6 Notice the close relationship between this finding and the 'added worker' hypothesis (see Mincer, 1966, for a summary of it). What we are observing here could be precisely that effect, but from the opposite point of view. According to that hypothesis, unemployment draws housewives into the labour force; here, unemployment discourages already working females from leaving the labour force, which amounts to something similar. An alternative interpretation could be that unemployment affects more female than male jobs. Given the little empirical support for the 'added worker hypothesis', this latter interpretation could be closer to reality than the former.

Notes to chapter 7

1 Partly in response to this adverse publicity, the DES commissioned a survey of school tunover (DES, 1974) in the school year 1972–73 finding a turnover rate of 21 per cent, which is reassuringly close to our figure for 1971–72.

2 We define a promotion as any ascending movement, over a one-year period, between seven different salary scales. To obtain these seven scales we recoded posts of head of department and graded posts into their equivalent under the post-1971 five-scale salary system; the extra two scales represent deputy heads and heads. This definition of promotions is slightly different from the one commonly accepted in the profession, but it gives approximately the same information. In particular, we underestimate the true rates of promotion in the deputy headship grades. For example, a teacher changing from a small school to a larger one, but remaining as a head or deputy head will not be recorded on our figures as having been promoted, even though he may obtain a considerable increase in salary. However, such promotions and other similar cases affect only a very small proportion of the total number of promotions during any one-year period.

3 The correlation between the percentage of promoted teachers and the *share* of internal promotions out of this percentage is as high as 0.87.

4 The London salary allowance and the Social Priority salary allowance are two exceptions to this rule. Such school based salary allowances are analysed in detail in the following chapter.

5 See Chapter 3.

6 This structure dates from 1971. Previously the salary system was composed of a basic salary scale and allowances for posts of responsibility. For the sake of simplicity, we discuss the calculation of the index in terms of the 1971–74 structure; the actual calculation, however, also took into account the old structure.

7 The definition of these size categories in terms of the 1971 Burnham group definitions is as follows:

	Primary		*Secondary*
Small:	groups 0 to 3	Small:	groups 0 to 6
Medium:	group 4	Medium:	groups 7 and 8
Large:	groups 5 and over	Large:	groups 9 and over

8 The regressions reported in Table 7.7 were also run using the coefficient of variation of promotion prospects instead of the standard deviation, and the results obtained were practically the same.

9 The data for this variable are taken directly from the standardised earnings function results reported in Chapter 9.

10 We define the level of promotions in a given region as the proportion of the stock in that region who were promoted during a one-year period.

11 See, Pay Board (1974), p. 18.

12 In 1971, 66 per cent of those teachers who moved region were younger than 30.

13 The process of selection consisted of a progressive elimination of insignificant variables, and in constraining some of the coefficients to be of equal absolute value and of opposite sign. This restriction was imposed on the P variable for men, and on the W and P variables for the total equation, and was decided on the basis of the similarity of the unconstrained estimates. In both cases, the validity of the constraints was tested by means of an F-statistic. For details about the procedure of selection and for intermediate results, see Zabalza (1976), Chapter 6.

14 If α is the regression coefficient, the standardised coefficient $\hat{\alpha}$ is obtained as

$\hat{\alpha} = \alpha(\sigma_x/\sigma_y)$, where σ_x is the standard deviation of the corresponding independent variable and σ_y is the standard deviation of the dependent variable.

15 For details of the results without London see Zabalza (1978a).

16 These coefficients represent the 'net' or 'ceteris paribus' effect, not the 'gross' effects which can be observed in simple tabulations.

17 There are differences in salary due to experience and qualification, but teachers in San Diego, unlike those in England and Wales, cannot receive a higher salary by changing school within the San Diego school system.

18 A description of the criteria to designate SED schools is given in Chapter 8.

19 The SED variable is included in the non-pecuniary category because this is what we are primarily interested in. However, a salary allowance of £75 was paid to those teachers, and in this sense it is also a pecuniary variable.

20 Figures from the 1 per cent sample indicate that it is only promotions into the head and deputy head grades which are biassed towards external appointments. About 25 per cent of promotions into scales 2 to 5 are external appointments, while as much as 54 per cent and 74 per cent of promotions into the deputy head and head grades respectively, are external.

Notes to chapter 8

1 It might be argued that the London allowance is only paid to compensate for the higher cost of living in the capital and not as a means of orientating teacher supply. However the fact remains that without the allowance, London would suffer from a severe teaching shortage, and that therefore it acts as an incentive to teachers to work in the Metropolitan area.

2 It is difficult to see how such an allowance structure could be actually implemented. If applied on top of an average salary scale, it would imply a whole set of different allowances (both in size and sign) according to the specific circumstances of each school grouping. Notwithstanding the difficulty of determining which grouping of schools should receive an allowance, the problems posed by the control and computation of each allowance would outweigh the possible benefits derived from the existence of a uniform basic salary scale.

3 An area only very slightly larger than Greater London and defined in the annual Burnham reports prior to 1974 (DES, annual – b).

4 Those areas are defined in post 1974 Burnham reports (DES, annual – b).

5 Including unqualified teachers and the full-time equivalent of part-time teachers.

6 This standardisation was carried out using the earnings function technique developed in Chapter 9.

7 In fact a very small proportion of teachers in the South East region also receive the allowance since they serve in the London Metropolitan Police Area (slightly greater in area than Greater London, and being the Burnham definition of the area to receive the allowance); the allowance was also subtracted from these teachers.

8 Now known as the 'Social Priority' allowance.

9 Not, it may be noted, as a result of any substantial research into the effectiveness of the allowance.

10 *Education*, 1 November 1974, No. 8, Vol. 144.

11 *Education*, 1 November 1974, No. 8, Vol. 144.

12 Table 8.9 indicates more graduates in SED schools but that more of these were untrained. However, after standardising for region, there are no more graduates in SED schools than in non-SED schools, but more of the SED graduates remain untrained.

13 A fact of course long recognised by the DES when they made married women returners 'off-quota'.
14 The results do indicate a positive and significant differential in favour of SED teachers in London both before and after the introduction of the allowance (2.4 per cent in 1972 net of allowance).
15 A major part of the recorded higher leaver rate in SED schools turned out to be due to unqualified teachers (see later).

Notes to chapter 9

1 There are also two good statistical reasons for using log salary as the dependent variable. It eliminates the problems of non-constant error variance and non-normality of the error term which occur when pure salary is the dependent variable.
2 For example, the coefficient δ_3 in equation (3) is equivalent to a $100 (1 - \delta_3')$ per cent differential in earnings between a graduate and a non-graduate, where δ_3' is the antilog of δ_3.
3 Even these 2-way terms do not exhaust the full total of all possible interactions. Three-way and multi-way cross-product terms could also be introduced representing more complex levels of interaction.
4 These two variables have a very high correlation of 0.899. This means that they should be considered as alternative measures of the same underlying variable rather than as independent complementary variables which can be entered into the equation together.
5 The length of service variable is actually defined as 'service for salary' *not* length of service. The main difference lies in the case of trained graduates who are awarded one extra year's 'service for salary' to compensate for their one year spent in training. Also there is often a difference for mature entrants who are usually awarded some service increments for their non-teaching work experience.
6 There are some exceptions to this, for example married women (see later).
7 In a separate exercise, a mathematical deterministic model (not a regression) to calculate each individual salary from length of service, qualification and post held 82 per cent were predicted to within 0.5 per cent of their actual salary, while many of the remainder could be explained by minor errors in the data (reference Turnbull, 1973).
8 Other studies, such as Williams *et al.* (1974) and Gorden *et al.* (1974) have included grade as an explanatory variable, but this was because they were attempting to explain variations within grades in labour markets where such things are possible (UK and US university teachers respectively).
9 This figure of 2 years is quite arbitrary, but it seemed to represent a reasonable compromise between getting enough observations (34 per cent of married women and 4 per cent men) and being a large enough gap to affect that teacher's subsequent career.
10 The result was still positive, though smaller when age was the standardising variable.
11 Average earnings were £1,560 in primary schools and £1,764 in secondary schools on 31 March 1971 (source: 1 per cent sample).
12 Given that the sector differential is wider for graduates than non-graduates, and that the sector differential is almost zero for all men, it seems likely that it is negative for non-graduate men teachers. Indeed, the published figures from which the profiles of Figures 9.2 and 9.3 are drawn, show this to be the case.

13 Graduate training was made compulsory for primary school teaching for those graduating after 1 January 1970, and in secondary teaching after 1 January 1974. However, mathematics and science graduates have been made a temporary exception from the latter requirement.

14 Our data do not enable us to identify the main subject of study for college trained non-graduate teachers. Neither can we identify the subject taught by teachers.

15 These are the 10 standard governmental planning regions of England and Wales.

16 And also from a small proportion of teachers in the South East who also received the London allowance by virtue of being located within the Metropolitan Police district.

17 This is not as obvious as it might appear at first sight. For example, *if* all teachers who were promoted during any given year had previously been earning less than the average (standardised for length of service etc.) *and* their subsequent increase in earnings brought them up to a point which was still below the average, *then* promoted teachers would be associated with *lower* earnings than unpromoted teachers. To say the least, such an event is extremely unlikely to occur. Promotions occur out of and into all salary scales and hence promotion in the immediately preceding year is associated with higher than average earnings.

18 We felt at one stage that these losses in earnings and perhaps the relatively low gain associated with non-graduates moving region could be due to movements out of the London region which involve the loss of the London allowance (approximately 8 per cent of salary). However, when the regressions were repeated excluding teachers in the London region, almost identical results were obtained.

19 In particular, as can be seen, the changeover to the new salary system benefited graduate teachers to a greater extent than non-graduate teachers.

20 The increase between 1963 and 1965 shown in Table 9.13 is not verified in the more reliable 5 per cent graduate sample, and hence we assume that it is an aberration of the sample.

21 The new, much increased, two-tier London allowances negotiated in 1974 were about 15 per cent of average earnings; this represents a continuation of the above trend and a considerable advance for the earnings differential of London teachers. A third tier allowance has also been established (smaller than the London allowance) covering much of the South East region; this will raise the relative earnings of the South East teacher, which Table 9.16 shows to have been declining during the period 1963 to 1972.

22 In 1971, 5.2 per cent of Welsh school leavers entered a college of education compared with 3.1 per cent in England. Also 7.0 per cent entered a university compared with 6.1 per cent for England. Furthermore, in the same year, 24 per cent of Welsh university graduates entered teacher training compared with 14 per cent in England. (Source: *Statistics of Education, 1971*, DES (annual – a) and *First Employment of University Graduates*, University Grants Committee (1972).)

Notes to chapter 10

1 For an illustration of how supply elasticities can be used in conjunction with non-controllable variables for purposes of planning supply over time, see Zabalza (1977).

2 It should be noticed that in order to adjust for age variations over the period

of study, the average salary used to estimate elasticities was that corresponding to the 35–39 age bracket. For reasons of consistency, all calculations reported in this chapter are also based on this adjusted measure of the average salary.

3 The slope variable considered here (K) is defined in Chapter 5.

4 This, and all other effects considered in this chapter are first period effects. From lag structure estimated in Chapter 5, we know that there will also exist effects on the flow of new entrants in subsequent years, although of a much lower magnitude.

5 See for example, p. 233, Evidence para. 787 of House of Commons (1976).

6 The new 'social priority' allowance introduced in 1975 does indeed follow this pattern, with two steps.

Notes to Epilogue

1 I am heavily indebted to C. Arnold Anderson, who played a major role in surveying the literature on which much of this Epilogue is based, and who contributed substantially as a friendly critic on an earlier draft of this discussion. This work and the UK/US conference on teacher markets was financed by courtesy of the Ford Foundation.

2 Nine papers were presented at the conference. Four were devoted to parts of this book; discussants were Sherwin Rosen (University of Rochester), David Metcalf (University of Kent), B. Jovanovic (University of Columbia), Robert T. Michael (Stanford University), E. A. Hanushek (Yale University), Elizabeth Landes (University of Chicago), and Edward P. Lazear (University of Chicago). A fifth UK paper was 'Central Control and the Local Demand for Teachers' by R. A. Jackman, C. D. Foster and M. Osborne, discussed by J. Alan Thomas of the University of Chicago. The US papers were:
    1. S. M. Barro and S. J. Carroll (Rand Corporation), 'Teachers' Salaries and School District Expenditures' (discussed by John S. Akin, University of North Carolina at Chapel Hill).
    2. Joseph R. Antos (US Department of Labor) 'The Impact of Human Capital on Working Conditions and Upward Mobility of High School Teachers' (discussed by Charlotte Kuh, Harvard University and J. J. Heckman, University of Chicago).
    3. Jay G. Chambers (University of Rochester), 'Effects of Union Bargaining on Teachers' Earnings; A Report on Research in California and Missouri' (discussed by N. M. Kiefer and M. W. Reder, both of the University of Chicago).
    4. W. L. Hansen, H. Newburger, D. Stapleton, F. Schroeder, B. A. Weisbrod, and D. Youngday (all of the University of Wisconsin, Madison), 'The Market for Academic Economists; An Econometric Model'. Discussants were Robert E. Lucas, University of Chicago, and S. J. Nickell, London School of Economics. This very interesting paper is not mentioned further in this Epilogue because it refers to higher education and would take us too far away from the subject of the present book.

3 Harvey (1967) analyzed salary schedules in the various school districts of Quebec using a full-fledged human capital model to assess incentive effects on supplies by training, and George Pedersen (1973) used a salary level and a slope variable in his study of teacher attrition and of teacher mobility.

4 Treatment of slope and the lack of specification of salary prospects and supply (or attrition) responses by age raises some problems in connection with policy applications discussed in Chapter 10. For example, at older ages (higher exper-

ience levels) up to approximately age 35, the implications of slope for decision-relevant salary *level* can be important in the perspective of a potential leaver. But let us consider for the moment a model in which we treat the entry elasticities of supply as though entry to teaching implied a full-time commitment to teaching, and consider the treatment of salary policy in Chapter 10 in that light. We then encounter several problems. The slope coefficient is measured on the years 22–39; if we take age 39 to be at the midppint in a life as a teacher (implying retirement at age 57) there is no increase of slope holding budget constant that could possibly yield a higher present value than a horizontal earning profile (unless people have *negative* discount rates); the only pay-off to choosing the steeper slope must come from extra earnings anticipated for the years after age 57. Furthermore, it is highly unrealistic to suppose that real earnings would continue to increase beyond age 39 at the rates at which they may increase before that age – and equally unrealistic to assume that potential teachers would assume a linear proportionate slope. The policy implications of the findings in this study may be more important for decisions relating to the desired composition of the teaching force than to its aggregate size so far as analysis of slope versus level of wages is concerned. The observations on flat rate allowances and their deficiencies are much more incisive in my judgement than the more generalized analyses of level versus slope under given budget constraints.

5 Age is of course taken into account in specification of the earning profile, but that is not by any means the same thing.

6 Incidentally, some writers have interpreted the directions of mobility from unattractive to attractive schools as a reflection of initial ignorance of new teachers about the options, followed by correction of initial error with further 'job search'. That interpretation has little validity for those urban teacher markets of which I have any knowledge – which is not to say, however, that high calibre beginning teachers cannot break the queue. Much could and should be done to investigate further just how far queuing for careers may replace other ways of allocating teachers with the spread of unionization of teachers and the negotiation of tenure and promotion priorities under conditions of teacher surplus.

7 SES stands for socioeconomic states.

8 This is an oversimplification. As Antos has pointed out, 'although the interpretation of the regression coefficients as hedonic prices is more understandable if the market is perfectly competitive, the presence of market imperfections does not invalidate the approach'.

9 'Requirements' themselves change with changing conditions, however, which modifies estimates of gaps between the desired and the actual – whether in England or in the United States.

10 Padilla (1975) shows just such a process for the United States, where pupil/teacher ratios in both elementary and secondary schools declined as teacher shortages became less of a problem.

11 This draws on previous work by J. A. Thomas.

12 Whether incomes policy had any effect on teacher salaries in the United Kingdom over the decade of the 1960s is not clear; teachers' relative pay declined in those years, but it must be remembered that over this period the 'teacher shortage' was diminishing.

13 The analysis and results of the study are discussed more fully in C. D. Foster, R. A. Jackman and M. Perlman, 'Local Government Finance', forthcoming.

14 Turnbull pointed out that the income variable in the equation for county

268   *Notes to pp. 211–227*

boroughs was poorly specified (they used SEG, which is SES in American usage), whereas that for the county councils was much better.

15 In a 1973 study using national data Carroll found substantial differences in expenditure patterns of school districts in different regions. In that study he distinguished between 'discretionary' and total budgets. As we might expect, the percentage of discretionary budgets spent on professional staff other than teachers was higher the larger the 'discretionary budget' whereas proportions of discretionary budgets spent on regular teachers was less than their percentage of total budgets.

16 Neither this book nor the conference papers dealt with determinants of achievement or performance of pupils. This is an important topic, and one on which there has been a rapid accumulation of research studies. It does not seem appropriate to pursue this topic here, however.

17 In his dissertation, however, Chambers experimented with total expenditures as a dependent variable.

18 For summaries of estimates of union effects in various studies, see Lipsky and Drotning (1976), pp. 448–9, and Frey (1975), p. 198, and the excellent discussion by Moore (1975). Charlotte Kuh (1976) got extremely erratic results according to the year sample, using a model that resembles Frey's but with more elaborate empirical explorations. Chambers got negligible coefficients with district indicators of unionization, but pulled his estimates up to 15 per cent effects when the unionization was the extent of bargaining in the *region* in which the district was located.

19 Thornton's indicator for E was per cent of full-time classroom teachers with less than standard teaching certificates.

20 The variable M was significant at the 0.05 level for the BA minimum in 1970–71, but not otherwise.

21 Richard Murnane has been working on this matter recently. Unfortunately, his findings are not yet available.

Notes to data appendix

1 This appendix describes the data base and the sample extracted for this study. An expanded version of this appendix, containing a discussion of sampling errors and comparison of the samples with published statistics is available on request from the Centre for Labour Economics, London School of Economics.

2 Establishments included on the data files are: maintained primary and secondary schools, special schools, direct grant grammar schools, further education colleges (including polytechnics) and colleges of education. Our research study has, however, only been concerned with teachers in maintained primary and secondary schools which comprise over 80 per cent of the total on the data files.

3 The old version of the 1970–71 file gave salaries for 31 March 1971. On 1 April 1971 a new salary and career structure was introduced in the teaching profession (see Chapter 3). The new version of the 1970–71 file gave salaries for 1 April 1971 and consequently incorporated those changes.

4 Philip Turnbull has produced linked data files from this 1 per cent random sample as part of his thesis on 'The careers of teachers' at London School of Economics.

5 Selected from random number tables from the 100 possible digits from '00' to '99'. Hence the '1 per cent' and '5 per cent'.

6 This analysis is reported in Chapter 8.

7 Practically all SED teachers were in primary schools.

8 Three digits were chosen instead of two in order to reduce the chances of a freak biassed sample.
9 Chosen from random number tables from the '1,000' possible 3-digit numbers in the range '000' to '999'.

Notes to appendix 4A

1 And any other variable in the supply function. This will be the assumption for all the exogenous changes considered in this appendix.

Notes to appendix 5A

1 An expanded version of this appendix, setting out some of the data used in the new entrants regressions, is available upon request from the Centre for Labour Economics at the London School of Economics.
2 It is for this reason that teachers' salaries enter with one lag in the relative wage expressions. Alternative salaries also enter with one lag because they are given for October of each year.

Notes to appendix 5B

1 To simplify the exposition we ignore here the specification in which the earnings profile is measured by two variables.
2 Due to the extension of teacher training courses from two to three years, the number of non-graduate entrants into teaching is abnormally low in 1963. This year has therefore been excluded in the estimation of these equations; this leaves ten observations corresponding to the period 1964–73.
3 Logit results were again practically identical. $RAW = 1.63$, $RSWL = 4.19$ and $KL = 1.23$.

Notes to appendix 6A

1 Level A corresponds to higher degrees, level B to first degrees and all other qualifications of the standard of a first degree. Level C corresponds to qualifications below first degree level (including a teacher certificate).

Notes to appendix 10A

1 This assumes that the average age of leaving is independent of the earnings profile.
2 For the categories of teachers that have been considered in the calculations, the adjustment factors a and b are: for male trained graduates, 6.9 and 30.5; for female trained graduates, 5.7 and 32.5; for male non-graduates, 7.6 and 28.2; for these three categories as a whole, 6.6 and 30.4; and for the whole profession, 5.4 and 31.2.

Bibliography

Part A
General Bibliography

Ahamad, B. (1970), 'A Post-Mortem on Teacher Supply Forecasts', *Higher Education Review*, Vol. 2, No. 3, Summer.

Alexander, W. (1971), *The 1971 Burnham Primary and Secondary Report: A Commentary*, Councils and Education Press.

(1973), 'The Future of Burnham', *Education*, Vol. 141, No. 17, 27 April.

Almon, S. (1965), 'The Distributed Lag Between Capital Appropriations and Expenditures', *Econometrica*, Vol. 33, January.

Altman, S. H. (1969), 'Earnings, Unemployment, and the Supply of Enlisted Volunteers', *Journal of Human Resources*, Winter.

Altman, S. H. and Barro, R. J. (1971), 'Officer Supply – The Impact of Pay, the Draft, and the Vietnam War', *American Economic Review*, September.

Armitage, P. (1970), 'Notes: Postscript on Teacher Supply', *Higher Education Review*, Vol. 3, No. 1, Autumn.

Bartholomew, D. J. (1973), *Stochastic Models for Social Processes* (2nd edition), London, John Wiley.

Beals, R. E., Levy, M. B. and Moses, L. N. (1967), 'Rationality and Migration in Ghana', *Review of Economics and Statistics*, Vol. 49, September.

Becker, G. S. (1964), *Human Capital. A Theoretical and Empirical Analysis with Special Reference to Education*, New York, National Bureau of Economic Research.

Berkson, J. (1944), 'Approaches of the Logistic Function to Bio-Essay', *Journal of the American Statistical Association*, Vol. 39, September.

Blaug, M. (1970), *An Introduction to the Economics of Education*, London, Allen Lane.

(1976), 'The Empirical Status of Human Capital Theory: A Survey', *Journal of Economic Literature*, September.

Bowman, M. J. (1963), 'Educational Shortage and Excess', *Canadian Journal of Economics and Political Science*, November.

Britton, E. (1972), Salaries Claim 1972/72, The Case of the Teachers Panel for Presentation to the Arbitral Body 26 April 1972, London, NUT, mimeo.

Central Statistical Office (1973), *Annual Abstract of Statistics, 1973*, London, HMSO.

Coates, R. D. (1972), *Teachers' Unions and Interest Group Politics*, Cambridge University Press.

Coleman, J. S. (1966), *Equality of Educational Opportunity*, Washington, DC, US Government Printing Office.

Department of Employment (monthly), *Department of Employment Gazette*, London, HMSO.

272   Bibliography

(annual), *New Earnings Survey*, London, HMSO.

Devine, E. J. (1970), *Analysis of Manpower Shortages in Local Government*, New York, Praeger.

Doeringer, P. B. and Piore, M. J. (1971), *Internal Labor Markets and Manpower Analysis*, Massachusetts, Lexington.

Drapper, N. R. and Smith, H. (1967), *Applied Regression Analysis*, New York, Wiley.

Education (1972), 'Burnham Negotiations', *Journal of the Association of Education Committees, Education Digest*, 15 September. London, Councils and Education Press Ltd.

(1973), 'Teachers Unions', *Journal of the Association of Education Committees, Education Digest*, 15 June. London, Councils and Education Press Ltd.

(1974a), *Journal of the Association of Education Committees*, 11 January, Vol. 143, No. 2. London, Councils and Education Press Ltd.

(1974b), *Journal of the Association of Education Committees*, 1 and 8 November, Vol. 144, Nos. 8 and 9. London, Councils and Education Press Ltd.

Fisher, A. C. (1969), 'The Cost of the Draft and the Cost of Ending the Draft', *American Economic Review*, Vol. 59, June.

(1970), 'The Cost of Ending the Draft: Reply', *American Economic Review*, Vol. 60, December.

Freeman, R. (1971), *The Market for College-Trained Manpower*, Cambridge, Mass., Harvard University Press.

(1975a), 'Supply and Salary Adjustments to the Changing Science Manpower Market: Physics, 1948–1973', *American Economic Review*, Vol. 65, March.

(1975b), 'Overinvestment in College Training', *Journal of Human Resources*, Vol. 10, Summer.

Friedman, M. (1963), 'Windfalls, the Horizon and Related Concepts in the Permanent Income Hypothesis' in C. Christ (ed.), *Measurement in Economics*, Stanford, University Press.

Gorden, N. M., Morton, T. E. and Braden, I. C. (1974), 'Faculty Salaries: Is there Discrimination by Sex, Race and Discipline?, *American Economic Review*, Vol. 64, June.

Greenberg, D. and McCall, J. (1974), 'Teacher Mobility and Allocation', *Journal of Human Resources*, Vol. 9, Fall.

Greenwood, M. J. (1971), 'An Analysis of the Determinants of Internal Labor Mobility in India', *Annals of Regional Science*, Vol. 5, June.

Halsey, A. H. (ed.) (1972), *Educational Priority. Volume 1 – EPA Problems and Policies*, London, HMSO.

Heckman, J. J. (1976), 'A Life-Cycle Model of Earnings, Learning and Consumption', *Journal of Political Economy*, vol. 84, August.

Hilsum, S. and Start, K. B. (1974), *Promotion and Careers in Teaching*, London, NFER.

Houghton, Lord (Chairman) (1974), *Report of the Committee of Inquiry into the Pay of Non-University Teachers*, London, HMSO.

House of Commons (1976), *Tenth Report of the Expenditure Committee, 1975/6*, London, HMSO.

Inner London Education Authority (ILEA) (1972a), 'The Effect of the £75 Allowance on the Turnover of Teachers in those ILEA Schools Receiving it', Research and Statistics Group, mimeo RS 516/72.

(1972b), 'The Special Needs Scheme: Interviews with Heads and Assistant Teachers', Research and Statistics Group, mimeo RS 531/72.

Institute of Biology (1961, 1965, 1968, 1971), *Remuneration Surveys*, London.

Institute of Chemistry (1962, 1965, 1968, 1971), *Remuneration Surveys*, London.

Institute of Mathematics (1971), 'Remuneration Survey, 1971', *Bulletin*, Vol. 7, September.

Institute of Physics (1960, 1964, 1968, 1971), *Remuneration Surveys*, London.

Jack, A. B. (1970), 'A Short Run Model of Inter-Regional Migration', *Manchester School*, Vol. 38, March.

James, Lord (Chairman) (1972), *Teacher Education and Training. Report of a Committee of Enquiry*, London, HMSO.

Johnston, J. (1972), *Econometric Methods* (2nd edition), New York, McGraw-Hill.

Kershaw, J. A. and McKean, R. N. (1962), *Teacher Shortages and Salary Schedules*, New York, McGraw-Hill.

Klinov-Malul, R. (1974), 'Is it Worthwhile to get a First?', *Economic Journal*, Vol. 84, March.

Leeds University Careers and Appointments Service (1961–71), *Annual Reports*, Leeds University.

Levin, H. M. (1968), *Recruiting Teachers for Large City Schools*, Washington, Brookings Institution.

Levy, M. B. and Wadycki, W. J. (1974), 'Education and the Decision to Migrate: An Econometric Analysis of Migration in Venezuela', *Econometrica*, Vol. 42, March.

Manzer, R. A. (1970), *Teachers and Politics*, Manchester, Manchester University Press.

McCall, J. J. (1970), 'Economics of Information and Job Search', *Quarterly Journal of Economics*, Vol. 84, February.

McNair, Sir Arnold (Chairman) (1944), *Teachers and Youth Leaders: Report of the Committee Appointed by the President of the Board of Education to Consider the Supply, Recruitment and Training of Teachers and Youth Leaders*, London, HMSO.

Metcalf, D. and Bibby, J. (1972), 'Salaries of Recruits to University Teaching in Britain', *Higher Education* Vol. 1, Autumn.

Mincer, J. (1966), 'Labor Force Participation and Unemployment: A Review of Recent Evidence' in *Prosperity and Unemployment*, R. A. and M. S. Gordon (eds.), New York, John Wiley.

(1974), *Schooling, Experience and Earnings*, New York, National Bureau of Economic Research/Columbia University Press.

Morris, N., Ryba, R. and Drake, K. (1973), *How Many Teachers?*, London, NUT.

Mortensen, D. T. (1970), 'Job Search, the Duration of the Unemployment, and the Phillips Curve', *American Economic Review*, Vol. 60, December.

National Advisory Council on the Training and Supply of Teachers (NACTST) (1962), *Seventh Report: The Demand for and the Supply of Teachers, 1960–1980*, London, HMSO.

(1965), *Ninth Report: The Demand for and the Supply of Teachers, 1963–1986*, London, HMSO.

National Union of Teachers (NUT) (1970), *Teachers' Salaries*, Campaign Brief 7, London, NUT.

(1971), 'The Origin and Work of the Burnham Committee', unpublished mimeo.

(1973), *Burnham in the Seventies, A Discussion Document for Members of the National Union of Teachers*, London, NUT.

NUT, Miscellaneous publicity documents from 1961 to 1973 kindly supplied by F. Jarvis of the NUT Publicity Department.

Office of Population Censuses and Surveys (OPCS) (1973), *Census 1971: Economic Activity Tables, Part 1 (100% Sample)*, London, HMSO.

274   *Bibliography*

Ollerenshaw, K. and Flude, C. (1974), *Returning to Teaching*, University of Lancaster,
Pay Board (1974), *London Weighting*, Advisory Report No. 4, London, HMSO.
Pederson, K. G. (1973), *The Itinerant Schoolmaster. A Socio-Economic Analysis of Teacher Turnover*, Midwest Administration Centre, University of Chicago.
Reynolds, L. G. (1951), *The Structure of Labor Markets*, New York, Harper.
Robbins, Lord (Chairman) (1963), *Higher Education: Report of the Committee Appointed by the Prime Minister, 1961–1963*, Annex AA to Appendix 1, London, HMSO.
Rosen, S. (1976), 'A Theory of Life Earnings', *Journal of Political Economy*, vol. 84, August.
Rottenberg, S. (1956), 'On Choice in Labour Markets', *Industrial Labour Relations Review*, Vol. 9, October.
Royal Society (1969), *The Shortage of Mathematics and Science Teachers in Schools*, London, The Royal Society.
Sahota, G. S. (1968), 'An Economic Analysis of Internal Migration in Brazil', *Journal of Political Economy*, Vol. 76, March/April.
Schultz, T. W. (1963), *The Economic Value of Education*, New York, Columbia University Press.
Sjaastad, L. (1962), 'The Costs and Returns of Human Migration', *Journal of Political Economy*, Vol. 70, Supplement, October.
Smith, A. (1776), *The Wealth of Nations*, A. Skinner (ed.), 1970, London, Penguin.
Swann, M. (Chairman) (1968), *Committee on Manpower Resources for Science and Technology*, London, HMSO, Cmnd 3760.
Taylor, W. (1969), *Society and the Education of Teachers*, London, Faber.
Theil, H. (1971), *Principles of Econometrics*, New York, Wiley and Sons.
Thomas, R. B. (1973a), 'On the Definition of Shortages in Administered Labour Markets', *Manchester School*, June.
  (1973b), 'Post-War Movements in Teachers' Salaries', *Industrial Relations Journal*, Autumn.
  (1975), 'The Supply of Graduates to School Teaching', *British Journal of Industrial Relations*, Vol. 13, March.
Tropp, A. (1957), *The School Teachers*, London, Heinemann.
Turnbull, P. and Williams, G. (1974), 'Sex Differentials in Teachers Pay', *Journal of the Royal Statistical Society*, Series A, Vol. 137, No. 2.
  (1975), 'Qualification Differentials in Teachers Pay', *British Journal of Industrial Relations*, Vol. 13, July.
University Grants Committee (1972). *First Employment of University Graduates, 1970–71*, London, HMSO.
Webb, B. (1915), *English Teachers and their Professional Organisation*, Special Supplement to *New Statesman*, Part 1, 25 September 1915, Vol. 5, No. 129; Part 2, 2 October 1915, Vol. 5, No. 130.
Weeden, R. (1973), *Labour Migration*, NIESR Regional Papers II, Cambridge University Press.
Weiss, Y. (1971), 'Investment in Graduate Education', *American Economic Review*, Vol. 61, December.
  (1972), 'The Risk Element in Occupational and Educational Choices', *Journal of Political Economy*, Vol. 80, November/December.
Westoby, A., Webster, D. and Williams, G. (1976), *Social Scientists at Work*, Society for Research into Higher Education, University of Surrey.
Williams, G. (1973), 'Graduates and the Labour Market', *Three Banks Review*, September.

(1974), 'Closing the Gap in Teachers Pay', *Education*, 3 May.

Williams, G., Blackstone, T. and Metcalf, D. (1974), *The Academic Labour Market*, Amsterdam, Elsevier.

Zabalza, A. (1976), 'Occupational Choice and Labour Market Adjustments. The Case of Teachers in England and Wales', unpublished PhD Thesis, London School of Economics.

(1977), 'An Optimal Wage Policy Rule for the Labour Market of Teachers in England and Wales', *Operational Research Quarterly*, Vol. 28, No. 1, ii.

(1978a), 'Internal Labour Mobility in the Teaching Profession', *Economic Journal*, vol. 88, June.

(1978b), 'From Shortage to Surplus. The Case of School Teachers', *Applied Economics*, vol. 10. December.

Ziderman, A. and Morris, V. (1971). 'The Economic Returns on Investment in Higher Education in England and Wales', *Economic Trends*, No. 211, May.

Part B
Publications of the Department of Education and Science

(Note: All of the following are published by HMSO in London on behalf of the Department of Education and Science.)

DES (annual – a), *Statistics of Education*, Volume 1: *Schools* Volume 2: *School Leavers CSE GCE;* and Volume 4: *Teachers.*

(annual – b), *Scales of Salaries for Teachers in Primary and Secondary Schools in England and Wales, (Burnham Reports).*

(annual – c), *Employment and the Distribution of Teachers: the teachers' quota.* (Published from 1964 to 1971 as a circular to Local Authorities; Circulars 1/64 to 1/71.)

(1964, 1968, 1969, 1973–1975), *Reports on Education*: 'The Teachers' Quota', No. 8 February 1964 and No. 42 January 1968; 'The Supply of Teachers', No. 51 December 1968 and No. 78 July 1973; 'Teacher Turnover', No. 79 May 1974; 'Teachers for the 1980; Statistical Projections and Calculations', No. 82 March 1975.

(1965a, 1967a, 1971a, 1972a), *Report of the Arbitral Body on the Salaries of Teachers in Primary and Secondary Schools, England and Wales.*

(1967b), *Children and their Primary Schools: A Report of the Central Advisory Council of Education* (Chairman: Lady Plowden).

(1971b), *Statistics of Education, Special Series No. 3. Survey of Earnings of Qualified Manpower in England and Wales, 1966–67.*

(1972b), *Education: A Framework for Expansion*, Cmnd 5174.

Part C
Internal CLE papers

(Available on request from the Centre for Labour Economics, London School of Economics, Houghton Street, London, WC2A 2AE.)

Armitage, P. and Williams, G. (1973), 'Student Numbers and Resource Allocation in Higher Education', MOD/RM/35.

Psacharopoulos, G. (1973), 'A Survey of Earnings Functions', *RS*/22.

Turnbull, P. (1973), 'The Salary Calculation Program', TE/PP/4.

(1974a), 'Institutional Background to the Teaching Profession', TE/PP/11.

(1974b), 'Personal Characteristics and the Earnings of Teachers: An Earnings Function Approach', TE/RM/7.

(1974c), 'A Stochastic Model of the Career System for School Teachers', TE/PP/12.

(1975a), 'Regression Results to TE/RM/7', TE/PP/14.

(1975b), 'The First Eight Years – A Cohort Analysis of Teachers Entering Service Between 1.4.62 and 31.3.63', TE/PP/18.

(1975c), 'A Case Study: The School of Exceptional Difficulty Allowance', TE/RM/10.

Zabalza, A. (1978c), 'The Determinants of Teacher Supply', CLE Discussion Paper No. 20.

Zabalza, A. and Turnbull, P. (1974), 'A Case Study: Regional Differences with Special Reference to London', TE/RM/5.

Index